71/94

 St. Louis Community College

Forest Park
Florissant Valley
Meramec

Instructional Resources
St. Louis, Missouri

GAYLORD

DECEPTIVE ADVERTISING
Behavioral Study of a Legal Concept

DECEPTIVE ADVERTISING

Behavioral Study of a Legal Concept

Jef I. Richards
University of Texas at Austin

LEA

LAWRENCE ERLBAUM ASSOCIATES, PUBLISHERS

1990   Hillsdale, New Jersey   Hove and London

Lawrence Erlbaum Associates, Inc., Publishers
365 Broadway
Hillsdale, New Jersey 07642

Library of Congress Cataloging-in-Publication Data

Richard, Jef I.
    Deceptive advertising : behavioral study of a legal concept / Jef
  I. Richards.
      p. cm.—(Communication)
    Includes bibliographical references and index.
    ISBN 0-8058-0649-0
    1. Advertising laws—United States. 2. Advertising, Fraudulent—
  United States—Psychological aspects. I. Title. II. Series:
  Communication (Hillsdale, N.J.)
    [DNLM: 1. Advertising—standards—United States. 2. Advertising—
  United States—legislation. 3. Behavior. 4. Crime. 5. Lying.
  HF 5827.8 R516d]
  KF1614.R53   1990
  343.73′082—dc19
  [347.30382]
  DNLM/DLC
  for Library of Congress   89-16777
                                                                          CIP

Printed in the United States of America
10 9 8 7 6 5 4 3 2

Contents

Preface

The elemental concept behind this book was born in 1980. Then a law student, I was asked by one of my former undergraduate professors, Dick Zakia (Rochester Institute of Technology), about the laws regulating deceptive pictures in advertisements. Thinking I could run to the law library and find an article on the topic, to quickly satisfy his curiosity, I promised to look into it. It seemed inconceivable, but there was *nothing* written on this topic. Even the Federal Trade Commission (FTC) had paid it little heed. This lack of attention to so important an issue piqued my own curiosity, so I asked Dick, a psychologist and photographic scientist, to help me research the topic.

With Dick's guidance, I began exploring the advertising and psychology literatures, again certain that volumes must have been written about the effects, on consumers, of pictures in advertising. After exhaustive research I was once again astonished to find *nothing* written in book or journal, despite the copious use of visual communication techniques in advertising.

The culmination of this project, nearly a year later, was my first law journal article, with Dick as my co-author. Our primary conclusions were that pictures could and should be given more attention by federal regulators, and that there was a need to integrate into the regulatory process more extensive use of psychological theory and methods to study the deceptiveness of pictures. One tool we then suggested, from exploring this area, was Osgood's semantic differential . . . an idea that finally bears some fruit in this book.

While the article was under review, I sent a copy to Dee Pridgen, at the FTC. Dee, having just co-authored an article with Ivan Preston, sent our paper to him for his comment. Ivan had worked as a consultant for the Commission staff, and had written extensively about the behavioral effects of deceptive advertising. This began a fruitful relationship with Ivan.

After 3 years of practicing law, in 1984, I enrolled in the Mass Communication doctoral program at the University of Wisconsin—Madison, with Ivan as my advisor. My purpose was to further develop my knowledge of the advertising process and to begin integrating communication theory, psychological research methods, and law. Ivan's interests were similar to mine, and he quickly took me under his wing. In very short order, we found ourselves working together on several research projects.

With Ivan's direction, the influence of Gerald Thain, Esther Thorson, and Bob Drechsel, in particular, my vision of advertising and its regulation coalesced. Although my intentions have changed little over the past 9 years (i.e., to encourage more extensive and higher quality research into the deceptive potential of certain advertising appeals), these members of the faculty at the University of Wisconsin were instrumental in helping me to focus my ideas. This book represents the net result of those 9 years of study and thought.

Throughout the book I criticize earlier efforts by researchers working in this area. The inherent danger in such criticism is that it might discourage them, or others, from additional exploration of this domain. My criticisms, however, are not intended to suggest their works are fatally flawed, or that they contribute nothing to our knowledge. Quite the contrary, those works are invaluable. The criticisms are offered merely to illustrate some areas where I believe additional improvements can be achieved. My hope is that this book will serve as a platform for expanded behavioral research into how consumers are deceived by advertising claims, and what cognitive processes are involved in that deception.

A Note About Citation Form

I have chosen a legal footnote form of citation, for reasons of personal preference. Footnotes permit the author to provide much more information than a bibliographic approach, without obstructing the flow of the main body of text. The footnotes included here conform generally to the *Uniform System of Citations* (published by Harvard Law Review) used in the legal profession.

References within the footnotes (e.g., 16 GA. L. REV. 77) provide a volume number (e.g., 16), followed by an abbreviation of the journal in which the article or other material appears (e.g., the Georgia Law Review), which is then followed by the page number (e.g., 77). Below is a list of some of the abbreviations used throughout this book:

Word	Abbreviation
Academy	Acad.
Advertising	Adv.
Affairs	Aff.
American	Amer.
Annual	Ann.
Behavior(al)	Behav.
Business	Bus.
Consumer	Cons.
Experimental	Exper.
Journal	J.
Law	L.
Marketing	Mktg.
Policy	Pol.
Proceedings	Proc.
Psycholog(y/ical)	Psychol.
Public	Pub.
Review	Rev.
University	U.

Most other abbreviations found herein are the names of schools, where a law journal or review is published.

Acknowledgments

In writing this book, I certainly owe a debt of thanks to many people. Certainly the first is my mentor and friend, Ivan Preston. Ivan has been instrumental in forming my "world view" of advertising regulation. Although we do not always view issues in precisely the same way, through his instruction (and persuasion) I have come to appreciate new and different ways of looking at these issues.

I likewise owe much to others at the University of Wisconsin. In particular, to Gerald Thain, who elevated my legal sophistication regarding advertising regulation. He served as a litmus, against which I tested my legal theories, and as a catalyst to keep me asking questions. Esther Thorson piqued my inquisitive nature and creativity, while proving that it is indeed possible to be both a productive researcher and an incredibly good teacher. The taxonomy in chapter 4 is directly attributable to Esther's prodding. Bob Drechsel helped me to maintain sanity while surrounded by insanity. He taught me it is possible to do serious research without taking it too seriously.

I would also like to thank Charles Salmon and John Murry, at the University of Wisconsin, for cheerfully "volunteering" to be a part of my doctoral committee on a last-minute basis. And, I thank George John and Mike Houston, now at the University of Minnesota, for their earlier participation on that committee.

Finally, Dick Zakia, at the Rochester Institute of Technology, is solely responsible for my initial interest in advertising law. My debt to Dick, and to his wife, Lois, is immense.

J. I. Richards

CHAPTER 1

Introduction

Unfortunately, it is not adequate, for either the advertiser or the regulator, merely to know that deception is wrong. What is needed is, first, a common understanding of deception that focuses on the consumer. Then, accepted ways of detecting deception must be devised.[1]

—David M. Gardner

Behavioral scientists' research about advertising deceptiveness is in its infancy. Consumer researchers have done very little research into deceptiveness, and what they have done typically is either predicated on an erroneous understanding of the law, or provides less psychological insight into how consumers are deceived than could be offered if they used their capabilities to the fullest extent. If and when they do the latter, they have the potential to make significant improvements in the way the law deals with deceptiveness.

Consequently, there is a need for a more thorough conception by behavioral researchers of how deceptiveness is viewed under the law and of how deception occurs in consumers' minds, along with a concomitant need for a more uniform method for testing the deceptiveness of questionable claims. The purpose of this book, therefore, is to (a) provide consumer researchers a more complete understanding of deception and its regulation, (b) present an expanded information-processing theory of deceptiveness that meets the needs of both the Federal Trade Commis-

---

[1]Gardner, *Deception in Advertising: A Conceptual Approach*, 39 J. MKTG. 40 (January 1975).

sion (FTC) and the researchers, and (c) derive a more sensitive and appropriate method for measuring deceptiveness.

The criticism by Gardner that opened this chapter appeared in print more than a decade ago, when empirical research into deceptive advertising was still relatively new in the behavioral literature. The remark identified the need for a sounder theoretical and methodological research foundation that draws upon the law but that centers on consumer psychology. Although his statement might have led scholars to a systematic study of deceptiveness, little progress has been made toward this firmer foundation. Rather than adhere to this sage advice, deceptiveness research since that time follows no pattern or progression.

A more sophisticated exploration of deception demands a base on which to build that discussion. From the small body of literature concerned with cognitive theory and research methods regarding deceptiveness it is clear that three major components of this foundation need further development: (a) a proper *understanding* by consumer scientists of the legal parameters of deception, (b) a broader *theoretical* model of how ad misrepresentations affect the consumer, going beyond the FTC's implicit model to identify the cognitive processes involved, and (c) an empirical *method* specifically tailored to test for deceptiveness of claims. I address all three of these issues, the first in chapters 2, 3, and 4; the second in chapter 5; and the third in chapters 6 and 7. These points are briefly discussed in the following three sections.

LEGAL AND BEHAVIORAL CONCEPTS

The second and third chapters, following this introduction, describe the *legal* situs of deceptive advertising. First the legal perspective of deception as a legal concept is considered, then the legal view of deceptiveness as a behavioral concept is addressed. This serves two purposes. One, it establishes the norm by which suspected deceptions are pursued in today's regulatory environment. Two, it helps consumer researchers conceptualize the relationship of law and behavior in deceptiveness. The intent is to inform scientists about the law of deception. If the goal of those researchers is to impact public policy, the legal realities must be considered in their research designs, and care must be taken to avoid legally irrelevant issues. Then, in the fourth chapter the behavioral researchers' views of deceptiveness are discussed, contrasting this to the legal view and considering its juxtaposition in a broader social view of deception.

Deception is a multidisciplinary construct, circumscribed by the law but descriptive of consumer behavior. Literature on this topic, consequently, arises in both the legal and the behavioral journals. But, lawyers and scientists speak different languages.[2] Lawyers, for example, discuss the *competence*,[3] *materiality*,[4] and *relevance*[5] of evidence offered to prove a fact, whereas scientists may refer to the *validity*[6] or *reliability*[7] of that same evidence. Each of these terms has a very specific technical meaning within that field, but they are not meanings shared with the other discipline. These differences are more than simple semantics or definitions; they reflect fundamental differences in how practitioners of these two professions view *evidence*. So, too, does the term *deception* connote different meanings within these two specialties. The natural consequence is that behavioral scientists who engage in a dialogue about deception may, without intending to do so, describe a form of *deception* not recognized by law, or, perhaps worse, they may avoid the topic for fear of misstating the legal construct. A behavioral researcher concerned with deceptive ads must comprehend which factors are most important not just to consumer receipt of the ad message, but also to the proof of deceptiveness in a regulatory arena.[8] The factors important under the law are but a small subset of the factors likely to play a role in a broader scheme concerned with social equity.

These three chapters should all contribute to a better understanding

---

[2]*See* discussion of this problem in Preston, *Researchers at the Federal Trade Commission—Peril and Promise*, 1980 CURRENT ISSUES & RES IN ADV. 1. Pollay, in criticizing the Commission for failing to make more extensive use of psychological research bearing upon the deceptiveness of claims, remarks, "Some evidence and convincing arguments suggest that lawyers and psychologists operate with distinct, and perhaps irreconcilable, orientations and methods." Pollay, *Deceptive Advertising and Consumer Behavior: A Case for Legislative and Judicial Reform*, 17 KAN. L. REV. 625, 637 (1969).

[3]Competency deals with the qualifications and fitness of a witness to give testimony in a court. *See* E. W. Cleary McCORMICK'S HORNBOOK ON EVIDENCE 2D 139 (1972).

[4]Materiality is the importance of certain evidence to proof of a particular fact in the case. *Id.* at 434.

[5]Relevancy concerns the requirement that evidence must logically tend to prove a material fact. *Id.* at 434.

[6]Validity is the extent to which differences in scores on a measurement reflect true differences among individuals, groups, or situations. *See* G.A. CHURCHILL, MARKETING RESEARCH: METHODOLOGICAL FOUNDATIONS 2D 75 (1979).

[7]Reliability involves the similarity of results provided by separate but comparable measures of the same trait. *Id.* at 259.

[8]Preston made a similar point, declaring, "It is the researchers who must bend their viewpoint to accommodate the other viewpoint, because the game is always played on the lawyers' turf." Preston, *The Difference Between Deceptiveness and Deception, and Why it Should Matter to Lawyers, Researchers, and Advertisers*, 1982 PROC. OF THE AMER. ACAD. OF ADV. 81. In another paper Preston suggested, "When he is adequately familiar with the lawyer's method as well as his own . . . the researcher can proceed toward a true *interaction* of behavioral science with law, with innovative results." Preston, *A Comment on "Defining Misleading Advertising" and "Deception in Advertising,"* 40 J. MKTG. 54 (1976).

of deceptiveness by consumer scientists, completing the first leg of the foundation for future deceptiveness research. Once deceptiveness is adequately understood, it is possible to construct a legally valid information-processing theory of how consumers are deceived.

A THEORETICAL APPROACH

The second step to erecting this foundation is to draw upon the relationships described in chapters 2–4 to compose a cognitive theory, more extensive than any previously developed in the deception literature, of how representations in an ad may affect deceptive impressions in consumers' minds. Although both the FTC and the researchers seem to have rudimentary theories, no theory yet describes the major steps of information processing that cause deceptive beliefs. This might be sufficient for FTC practices, but it is unsatisfactory to cultivate quality behavioral research into deceptiveness. The aim of the FTC is to *identify* deceptive claims, whereas the behavioral scientist wants also to know *why* certain claims deceive. Chapter 5 presents a more complete theory, explaining where errors may arise in processing ad claims, with the intent of showing behavioral scientists how they might improve their own contributions to the legal process.

Research has focused on FTC trends and use of evidence, but the closest it has come to theory is use of numerous sociopsychological theories to highlight what researchers consider weaknesses in the FTC approach.[9] Each one isolates only a small piece of the overall process. To argue the FTC should consider incomplete comparisons,[10] evaluative claims,[11] or pictures[12] as potentially misleading is fine, but in a sense premature. Those propositions were developed without benefit of a general theory of how deceptive messages are processed in consumers'

---

[9]This phenomenon might be said to permeate consumer behavior research. In his Presidential Address before the Association of Consumer Research, Olson accused, "[W]e have become skilled at *borrowing* theories from other disciplines and *applying* them to our problems . . . Our discipline applies borrowed theory, but does relatively little to develop theory." Olson, *Presidential Address-1981: Toward a Science of Consumer Behavior*, 9 ADVANCES CONS. RES. v., vi. (1981). I make no claim, however, that the theory I present here is without its roots in other disciplines, for clearly that would be untrue. What it does, however, is take one step toward a specialized theory, about the entire process of deceptiveness, rather than to focus on a single element of that process.

[10]Shimp, *Do Incomplete Comparisons Mislead?*, 18 J. ADV. RES. 22 (1978).

[11]Shimp and Preston, *Deceptive and Nondeceptive Consequences of Evaluative Advertising*, 45 J. MKTG. 22 (1981).

[12]Richards and Zakia, *Pictures: An Advertiser's Expressway Through FTC Regulation*, 16 GA. L. REV. 77 (1981).

minds. In other words, they were discussed out of context. Although these suggestions may help refine a theory, they should not precede it.[13]

This observation-before-theory approach is inductive. To discover *why* certain claims deceive, fulfilling the scientist's goal, demands a *deductive* approach. Deduction permits *prediction* of whole classes of claim types that may be deceptive. Behavioral researchers' greatest contributions to regulation might be these predictions. Consequently, a theory of the deception process needs to be developed.

Very few researchers have tried to develop a behavioral theory of deception. Some important errors are present in the few existing theories and none of them accounts for all known sources of variance in processing deceptive ad claims. Chapter 5 considers each model, and their deficiencies, and advances an improved theoretical model. This theory presents a more useful alternative for behavioral scientists than its predecessors.

As an outgrowth of this theory, a behavioral *definition* of deceptiveness is also constructed. A plethora of definitions have been expounded by researchers, but they express discordant views of deceptiveness. Chapter 5, therefore, offers a definitional expression of the theory presented there. This should help alleviate some confusion by researchers, while presenting a concise conception that is legally and behaviorally valid. For this foundation to be complete, there remains only the question of *how* to research deceptiveness, which the next section addresses.

A TOOL FOR RESEARCH AND EVIDENCE

The final piece to this research foundation is an appropriate method for testing deceptiveness. Although several methods are presently used, those measures are typically designed to assess ad efficacy rather than deceptiveness and are merely adapted to test deceptiveness. Chapter 6 presents a method of more specific application. Although it may not be appropriate to detect deceptiveness in *every* fact situation, it should be suited to most.

There are nearly as many methods used to measure deceptiveness as

---

[13]This need for theory *before* research (deductive reasoning) is a basic premise of scientific inquiry. Empirical studies are used to test hypotheses, which are deduced from theory. F. N. KERLINGER, FOUNDATIONS OF BEHAVIORAL RESEARCH 2D 16–26 (1973). Cohen noted, "There is . . . no genuine progress in scientific insight through the Baconian method of accumulating empirical data without hypotheses or anticipation of nature. Without some guiding idea we do not know what facts to gather . . . we cannot determine what is relevant and what is irrelevant." M. COHEN, A PREFACE TO LOGIC 148 (1956).

there are studies and cases concerned with deception. The FTC uses numerous methods, and academic researchers apply different methods each time they explore some new aspect of deception.

This is not inherently bad, but it presents two problems. First, each method has a different sensitivity to the construct assessed, and involves different influential or confounding variables. Because of these differences we cannot, with great certainty, decide whether discovered deceptiveness in one case but not another is attributable to different ads or different methods of testing. A standardized procedure would control for this needless source of variance.

Second, if the method is properly constructed it should be useful not only for scholarly research purposes, but also for proving deceptiveness in FTC proceedings. Each new method presented in an FTC hearing faces formidable barriers to acceptance as a technique probative of deceptiveness. Each method must be proved empirically valid and reliable, and each creates its own line of precedent.[14] A litigant introducing a new method encounters substantial uncertainty, especially because the FTC lends no guidance for how to adequately test deceptiveness.[15] A method optimized to detect deceptiveness could serve as a presumptively acceptable technique that could be used with relative assurance of acceptance by the Commission.

The method presented in chapter 6 addresses weaknesses of these commonly used methods. This technique is purposely structured for use in both FTC hearings and academic studies. Rather than follow the conventional FTC practice of using survey methods, it takes a controlled experimental approach, permitting greater causal inference. It is structured with an eye toward being practical for use in FTC cases, as well as being statistically robust. A process is also presented for consistent case-to-case derivation of questions to use in the measurement instruments. minimizing unnecessary variance in the process when used as legal evidence.

Finally, in chapter 7, this proposed method is used to test claims formerly determined deceptive by the FTC, comparing results from this method to actual FTC decisions made with conventional methods. This method is the final piece to the triad presented here, making this proposed theoretical and methodological foundation for future deceptiveness research complete.

---

[14]Preston, *Extrinsic Evidence in Federal Trade Commission Deceptiveness Cases*, 1987 COLUM. BUS. L. REV. 633 (1987).

[15]Richards and Preston, *Quantitative Research: A Dispute Resolution Process for FTC Advertising Regulation*, 40 OKLA. L. REV. 593 (1987).

SUMMARY

The body of literature addressing the legal parameters of regulating deceptive advertising[16] or other aspects of ad regulation[17] is rich, and can be found elsewhere. By far the lion's share of that literature, however, takes a strictly legal perspective of ad regulation. The present approach, by contrast, takes primarily a behavioral perspective, addressing the law only insofar as necessary to ensure legal validity of the behavioral discussion. I state this qualification for two reasons. First, because it is beyond the scope of this book to recant the full breadth of legal thought regarding advertising regulation, it may be advisable for readers to pursue a deeper understanding through reference to other literature. Second, because the focus of what follows is a behavioral view of deceptiveness, and because of similarities in legal approaches under other laws of deceptive advertising, much of the material that follows can be easily adapted to the regulatory acts of the various states, to civil actions under the Lanham Act,[18] and even to the laws existing in other nations.

The material that follows presents a foundation for future behavioral research into deception, to assist behavioral scientists to optimize their contributions to the regulatory process. It is a foundation composed of three discrete parts: (a) an understanding of the variables involved in deception, and the roles they play in regulation; (b) a full-blown theoretical model of consumer information processing involved in deception, and (c) an improved method of testing for deception.

This foundation is an attempt to elevate the sophistication of behavioral research about deception. Through better understanding, direc-

---

[16]Richards and Zakia, *supra* note 12; Thain, *Consumer Protection: Advertising—The FTC Response*, 27 BUS. LAW. 891 (1972); Kramer, *Marconian Problems, Gutenbergian Remedies: Evaluating the Multiple-Sensory Experience Ad on the Double-Spaced, Typewritten Page*, 30 FED. COM. L. J. 35 (1977); Pridgen and Preston, *Enhancing the Flow of Information in the Marketplace: From Caveat Emptor to Virginia Pharmacy and Beyond at the Federal Trade Commission*, 14 GA. L. REV. 635 (1980); Millstein, *The Federal Trade Commission and False Advertising*, 64 COLUM. L. REV. 439 (1964); Pitofsky, *Beyond Nader: Consumer Protection and the Regulation of Advertising*, 90 HARV. L. REV. 661 (1977); Ford and Calfee, *Recent Developments in FTC Policy on Deception*, 50(3) J. MKTG. 82 (1986).

[17]Richards, *Clearing The Air About Cigarettes: Will Advertisers' Rights Go Up In Smoke?*, 19 PAC. L. J. 1 (1987); Thain, *Suffer the Hucksters to Come Unto the Little Children? Possible Restrictions of Television Advertising to Children Under Section 5 of the Federal Trade Commission Act*, 56 B.U.L. REV. 651 (1976); Note, *Fairness and Unfairness in Television Product Advertising*, 76 MICH. L. REV. 498 (1978); Laczniak and Caywood, *The Case For and Against Televised Political Advertising: Implications for Research and Public Policy*, 6 J. PUB. POL. & MKTG. 16 (1987); Wyckham, *Self-Regulation of Sex-Role Stereotyping in Advertising: The Canadian Experience*, 6 J. PUB. POL. & MKTG. 76 (1987).

[18]15 U.S.C. § 1125(a).

tion, and means for deceptiveness research, behavioral scientists should be able to make greater contributions to the regulatory process. The next chapter begins this building process by describing the "legal" view of deception as a legal concept, slowly turning to the "behavioral" view in succeeding chapters.

CHAPTER 2

The Law's View of Deception as a Legal Concept

This is the first of three topics that demonstrate the varying views of deception taken by lawyers and behavioral researchers. First examined in this chapter is the law's view of deception as a legal concept. A side issue of that topic is some erroneous views by behavioral researchers of deception as a legal concept. Next examined is the law's view of deception as a behavioral concept, in chapter 3, and finally, the behavioral researcher's view of deception as a behavioral concept, in chapter 4.

LEGISLATIVE HISTORY

The FTC is charged with responsibility to regulate "unfair or deceptive acts or practices in or affecting commerce."[1] As regards the application of that directive to advertising deception, the Commission is given little statutory guidance. This stems, at least in part, from the Commission's original legislative mandate: to inhibit restraints against trade and protect business from the unfair trade practices of their competitors.[2] It was an outgrowth of the Sherman Act, an antitrust law prohibiting contracts, combinations, and conspiracies in restraints of trade[3] and monopolization

---

[1]15 U.S.C. §45 (1982).

[2]Rublee, *The Original Plan and Early History of the Federal Trade Commission*, 11 ACAD. POL. SCI. PROC. 666, 667 (1926).

[3]*Supra* note 1, at § 1.

or attempts to monopolize.[4] It was an agency with a mission not specifically aimed at the regulation of advertising, so its enabling legislation offered no specifics about what constituted regulable advertising claims.

The powers and reach of the Commission at its advent were much narrower than they are today. Section 5 of its enabling act ("the Act," herein), in 1914, provided only that "unfair methods of competition in commerce are hereby declared unlawful."[5] Before the commissioners really got their feet wet upholding this law they were already interpreting it to cover misleading advertising, confronting two advertising cases almost immediately.[6] The Commission at that time justified a broad interpretation of its powers, to cover consumer harms as well as direct trade injuries, declaring, "[w]henever such confusion and deception [to the consuming public] occurs there also results a damage to the trade and manufacturers. . . ."[7]

That construction was upheld by the Seventh Circuit Court of Appeals just 3 years later.[8] This court made a finding of law in favor of the FTC's interpretation, and made a declaration with wording that echoed through the agency and the courts into the 1980s:

> The commissioners, representing the government as parens patriae, are to exercise their common sense, as informed by their knowledge of the general idea of unfair trade at common law, and stop all those trade practices that have a *capacity or tendency* to injure competitors directly *or through deception of purchasers*, quite irrespective of whether the specific practices in question have yet been denounced in common-law cases.[9]

Soon thereafter, however, the Supreme Court pruned back this power somewhat, announcing that, to the contrary, the "specific practices" challenged as unfair methods of competition by the FTC must formerly have been condemned at common law, antedating the FTC Act.[10]

The Court had some trouble, in the years that followed, deciding the breadth of FTC powers,[11] but in 1931 it erected a fence around those powers that restricted the Commission to clear antitrust and antimonopoly and related unfair trade practices, *not extending to protection of consum-*

---

[4]*Id.*, at § 2.
[5]Federal Trade Commission Act of 1914, Pub. L. No. 203, 38 Stat. 717 (1914).
[6]Clarence N. Yagle, 1 F.T.C. 13 (1916); A. Theo. Abbott & Co., 1 F.T.C. 16 (1916).
[7]Yagle, *supra* note 6, at 15.
[8]Sears, Roebuck & Co. v. FTC, 258 F. 307 (7th Cir. 1919).
[9]*Id.*, at 311 (italics added).
[10]FTC v. Gratz, 253 U.S. 421 (1920).
[11]FTC v. Winsted Hosiery Co., 258 U.S. 483 (1922).

ers.[12] This move all but eliminated deceptive advertising from the scope of FTC action.

In 1938 Congress stepped in to untie the hands of the regulators, passing the Wheeler–Lea Amendment to the 1914 Act.[13] This amendment extended Section 5 of the Act to read, "Unfair methods of competition in commerce, and unfair or *deceptive* acts or practices in commerce, are hereby declared unlawful."[14] This provided the Commission with the legislative blessing to deal with consumer deception, eliminating the need to justify agency actions through reference to unfair competition.[15]

Except for modifying "in commerce" to read "in or affecting commerce," in 1975,[16] Section 5 and its statutory guidance for advertising regulation continue to be limited to that one sentence. The only additional direction provided in the Act is the designation in Section 12 of *false advertising* as being a violation with respect to certain products, including food, drugs, devices, and cosmetics,[17] and the definition of that term as an advertisement that is "misleading in a material respect."[18] In practice, the FTC has come to incorporate the latter phrase into its

---

[12]FTC v. Raladam Co., 283 U.S. 643 (1931).

[13]Act of March 21, 1938, Pub. L. No. 447, § 3, 52 Stat. 111 (amending 15 U.S.C. § 45 (1934)).

[14]*Id.* (italics added).

[15]In Scientific Mfg. Co. v. FTC, 124 F.2d 640 (3rd Cir. 1941), the Third Circuit Court of Appeals reflected, "[t]he Commission could thenceforth prevent unfair or deceptive acts or practices in commerce which injuriously affected the public interests alone. . . ." *Id.* at 643-44. For a more thorough review of these historical developments, *see* Millstein, *The Federal Trade Commission and False Advertising*, 64 COLUM. L. REV. 439 (1964).

[16]Magnuson-Moss Warranty—FTC Improvement Act of 1975, Jan 4, 1975, Pub. L. N. 93-637, 88 Stat. 2193.

[17]H.R. REP. No. 1613, 7th Cong., 1st Sess. 4 (1937), at 5 (codified at 15 U.S.C. § 55(a)(1) (1982)).

[18]Act of March 21, 1938, ch. 49, § 4, 52 Stat. 116 (1938) (amending 15 U.S.C. § 45 (1934)) (emphasis added). That section does provide a few more specifics:

> The term 'false advertisement' means an advertisement, other than labeling, which is misleading in a material respect; and in determining whether any advertisement is misleading, there shall be taken into account (among other things) not only representations made or suggested by statement, word, design, device, sound, or any combination thereof, but also the extent to which the advertisement fails to reveal facts material in light of such representations or material with respect to consequences which may result from the use of the commodity to which the advertisement relates under the conditions prescribed in said advertisement, or under such conditions as are customary or usual. No advertisement of a drug shall be deemed to be false if it is disseminated only to members of the medical profession, contains no false representation of a material fact, and includes, or is accompanied in each instance by truthful disclosure of, the formula showing quantitatively each ingredient of such drug.

understanding of deceptiveness in the case of all advertising.[19] No other statutory definitions or explanations exist to aid the FTC or the courts in the regulation of advertising misrepresentations.[20]

INTERPRETING THE ACT

Both the FTC and the courts have added flesh to this skeletal prohibition. Much of the interpretation has been reflective of the Commission's mission or goal, of which the Third Circuit Court of Appeals in *Regina Corp. v. FTC*[21] said, "The purpose of the Federal Trade Commission Act is to protect the public, not to punish the wrongdoer . . . and it is in the public interest *to stop any deception at its incipiency*."[22] FTC action, therefore, is prophylactic, not punitive.

Resulting from this preventative purpose, the Commission repeatedly declares *intent* of the advertiser is irrelevant to a determination of deception.[23] After all, the purpose of the FTC is to protect the consumers and competitors, not to punish advertisers for a bad intent.

Also resulting from the preventative purpose is the finding that "actual

---

[19]*See, e.g.,* FTC v. Colgate-Palmolive Co., 380 U.S. 374, 386 (1965); Moretrench Corp. v. FTC, 127 F.2d 792, 795 (2d Cir. 1942). The Commission's recent policy statement even notes that "materiality" applies to Section 12, but then proceeds to discuss it as if it applies to all "deceptive acts or practices." *Policy Statement on Deception,* in the form of a letter from Chairman James C. Miller III to Congressman John D. Dingell, October 14, 1983 (appended to Cliffdale, 103 F.T.C. 110, 174 (1984)).

[20]There are, however, many product-specific prohibitions and definitions that have been provided by legislation, which may aid the FTC in some instances. *See, e.g.,* Textile Fiber Products Identification Act, 72 Stat. 1717 (1958), 15 U.S.C. § 70; Fur Products Labeling Act, 65 Stat. 175 (1951), 15 U.S.C. § 69; Wool Products Labeling Act of 1939, 54 Stat. 1128 (1940), 15 U.S.C. § 68.

[21]322 F.2d 765 (3rd Cir. 1963).

[22]*Id.* at 768 (emphasis added). *See, also,* Gimbel Bros. v. FTC, 116 F.2d 578, 579 (2d Cir. 1941); Progress Tailoring Co. v. FTC, 153 F.2d 103, 105 (7th Cir. 1946).

[23]FTC v. Sterling Drug, Inc., 317 F.2d 669, 674 (2d Cir. 1963); Goodman v. FTC, 244 F.2d 584, 592 (9th Cir. 1957); Chrysler Corp. v. FTC, 561 F.2d 357, 363 (D.C. Cir. 1977); Koch v. FTC, 206 F.2d 311, 317 (6th Cir. 1953); Gimbel Bros., Inc. v. FTC, 116 F.2d 578, 579 (2d Cir. 1941); L. & C. Mayers Co. v. FTC, 97 F.2d 365, 367 (2d Cir. 1938). *See also,* Thompson Medical Co., Inc., 104 F.T.C. 648, 788 (1984), at n. 6, *aff'd,* Thompson Medical Co. v. FTC, 791 F.2d 189 (D.C. Cir. 1986). However, this is something of an overstatement. As the decision in *Thompson Medical* clearly reveals, intent or "deliberateness" can be an aggravating circumstance for consideration by the Commission. More accurately, intent is not *necessary* for a finding of deception, but the existence of intent may be a factor considered in the Commission's determination.

deception" is unnecessary in FTC cases.[24] If actual, completed, deception need not be shown in an FTC case, there must be a surrogate indicator of this actual deception to prove a claim "deceptive" within the meaning of the Act. I adopt Preston's[25] term, *deceptiveness*, to refer to this surrogate indicator of "deception" throughout this book. The court in *FTC v. Sterling Drug, Inc.,*[26] using words from the Supreme Court of 1919, recites:

> In order to best implement the prophylactic purpose of the statute, it has been consistently held that advertising falls within its proscription not only when there is proof of actual deception but also when the representations made have a *capacity or tendency to deceive*. . .[27]

So, from 1919 until 1984 the FTC proscription circumscribed representations with a mere "capacity or tendency" to deceive. Deceptiveness was the capacity or tendency of a claim to result in deception, and it was this *deceptiveness, not deception*, that was required for the Commission to act against an advertisement. This is seen as an important distinction when the researchers' viewpoint is discussed.

Deceptiveness is interpreted to constitute a violation even when it does not apply to all consumers. Traditionally, there has been a violation if the deceptiveness occurred for some "substantial number," which may be a small percentage such as 20% as long as the FTC feels the public interest calls for protecting such a proportion.[28]

Although deceptiveness in a small percentage of consumers is sufficient to invoke regulatory action, should the FTC act when that small percentage only represents a particularly ignorant segment of the population? Such a "Mortimer Snerd" standard was, in fact, established by the Supreme Court in 1937, when it declared, "There is no duty resting upon a citizen to suspect the honesty of those with whom he transacts business. Laws are made to protect the trusting as well as the suspicious."[29]

---

[24]*See, e.g.,* Feil v. FTC, 285 F.2d 879, 896 (9th Cir. 1960); Jacob Siegel Co. v. FTC, 150 F.2d 751, 755 (3rd Cir. 1944); Cliffdale, *supra* note 19, at 165, Note, *Developments in the Law: Deceptive Advertising,* 80 HARV. L. REV. 1005 (1967), acknowledges, "[T]he Commission need not show that there has been actual deception." *Id.* at 1040.

[25]Preston, *The Difference Between Deceptiveness and Deception, and Why It Should Matter to Lawyers, Researchers, and Advertisers,* 1982 PROC. OF THE AMER. ACAD. OF ADV. 81 (1982).

[26]*Supra* note 23.

[27]*Id.* at 674 (emphasis added). *See, also,* Arrow Metal Products Corp. v. FTC, 249 F.2d 83, 85 (3rd Cir. 1959); Jacob Siegel Co. v. FTC, *supra* note 24, at 755; Beneficial Corp. v. FTC, 542 F.2d 611 (3rd Cir. 1976).

[28]Preston and Richards, *Consumer Miscomprehension as a Challenge to FTC Prosecutions of Deceptive Advertising,* 19 J. MARSHALL L. REV. 605, 609 (1986).

[29]FTC v. Standard Education Society, 302 U.S. 112, 116 (1937).

Consumers, reasoned the Court, should not be forced to question every assertion made by an advertiser in order to safely transact business in the marketplace. This was interpreted perhaps even more forgivingly in a frequently quoted remark from the Seventh Circuit in *Aronberg v. FTC*:[30]

> The law is not made for experts but to protect the public—that vast multitude which includes the ignorant, the unthinking and the credulous, who, in making purchases do not stop to analyze but too often are governed by appearances and general impressions.[31]

Through these descriptions of the FTC's function, the Court effectively abolished the pre-FTC notion of *caveat emptor*, or "let the buyer beware."[32] The Commission, however, in the early 1960s backed off that Mortimer Snerd position remarking, "[a]n advertiser cannot be charged with liability in respect of every conceivable misconception, however outlandish, to which his representations might be subject among the foolish or feeble-minded."[33]

However, even in the late 1970s, in *Beneficial Corp. v. FTC*,[34] the Third Circuit appeared somewhat to embrace the Mortimer Snerd standard. The petitioner, here, was charged with unfair and deceptive trade practices for having advertised that it was providing an "Instant Tax Refund" to customers, without explicitly indicating that this was nothing more than a conventional loan based on the customer's credit worthiness. The court in this case expressed the following:

> The testimony of some consumers . . . was that . . . they failed to understand that Beneficial was offering only its normal loan service with normal finance charges. . . . *These consumers may well have been singularly dense*. They were,

---

[30]132 F.2d 165 (7th Cir. 1942).

[31]*Id.* at 167.

[32]The Supreme Court in FTC v. Standard Education Society, *supra* note 29, and repeated by the Second Circuit in FTC v. Sterling Drug, Inc., *supra* note 23, declared:

> The central purpose of the provisions of the Federal Trade Commission Act under discussion is in effect to abolish the rule of *caveat emptor* which traditionally defined rights and responsibilities in the world of commerce. That rule can no longer be relied upon as a means of rewarding fraud and deception. . . .

Id. at 674. For further discussion of the principle of *caveat emptor, see* I.L. PRESTON, THE GREAT AMERICAN BLOW-UP: PUFFERY IN ADVERTISING AND SELLING, Chap. 4 (1975).

[33]Heinz W. Kirchner, 63 F.T.C. 1282, 1290 (1963), *aff'd*, 337 F.2d 751 (9th Cir. 1964). *See also*, International Harvester Co., 104 F.T.C. 949, 1056-57 (1984).

[34]*Supra* note 27.

nevertheless, a part of the audience to which the advertisements were directed.[35]

The court held that even these "unthinking" consumers were deserving of FTC protection.

More recently, the new majority on the Commission under the thumb of a Reagan appointee, Chairman James C. Miller III, stepped even farther back toward *caveat emptor*. This Commission announced that only those consumers "acting reasonably under the circumstances" were deserving of governmental intervention.[36] This new standard appears to parallel the "reasonableness" standard of negligence in tort law.[37] If consumers are negligent in their buying behavior, it seems, the FTC will refuse to intervene.

It appears, therefore, that the extent of deceptiveness in the population necessary for FTC intervention (i.e., the percentage of consumers affected) must now be greater than in earlier cases. Deceptiveness, therefore, must occur in some proportion of consumers "acting reasonably under the circumstances" before the regulators will act.

Through a careful tactical manipulation of terms the Commission also subtly altered the standard for what constitutes deceptiveness, while trying to give the impression that nothing had changed.[38] It substituted "likely" for "capacity or tendency," while inaccurately remarking that the standard had always been "capacity *and* tendency."[39] By replacing "or" with "and," citing a single recent case as its precedent, the Commission essentially changed history and modified the standard from a mere *possibility* to a *probability* that the challenged claim will deceive consumers.[40] This new definition appears, then, to require a higher standard of proof than the older one before an ad can be regulated (i.e., it provides less protection to consumers than did its predecessor). This probability, of course, applies only to the population to whom the ad is addressed, not to the public-at-large or to all who may have seen the ad.[41]

All of these principles help to define the FTC's statutory authority

---

[35]*Id.* at 618 (emphasis added). *See, also*, Standard Oil of California v. FTC, 577 F.2d 653 (9th Cir. 1978).

[36]Cliffdale, *supra* note 19, at 165.

[37]RESTATEMENT OF LAW 2D, §§ 282-83 Torts (1965).

[38]Cliffdale, *supra* note 19.

[39]*Id.*

[40]There are actually a few cases using "and," but the vast preponderance of cases over the past seven decades use "or."

[41]Thompson Medical Co. Inc., *supra* note 23, at 789 n. 7; Herzfeld v. FTC, 140 F.2d 207 (2d Cir. 1944); Aronberg v. FTC, 132 F.2d 165, 167, *rehearing denied*, (7th Cir. 1943); Benrus Watch Co. v. FTC, 352 F.2d 313 (8th Cir. 1965), *cert. denied* 384 U.S. 939 (1966); Murray Space Shoe Corp. v. FTC, 304 F.2d 270 (2d Cir. 1962).

over deceptive advertising. These principles should aid researcher understanding of what is and what is not considered deceptive from the legal perspective.

MATERIALITY

As mentioned earlier, the FTC is required to ensure that a claim is both "deceptive or unfair" and "misleading in a material respect."[42] Although the statutory provision for materiality explicitly applies only to food, drugs, devices, and cosmetics, this requirement has consistently been applied to actions regarding deceptive advertising of other products and services.[43]

This element has remained relatively unchanged over the years. In 1943 the Tenth Circuit Court of Appeals remarked, "It is sufficient to find that the natural and probable result of the challenged practices is to cause one to do that which he would not otherwise do."[44] It is not enough, therefore, that a consumer receives a message that misrepresents the product, that message must be important to the consumer's purchase decision. This is in substantial agreement with the 1984 *Cliffdale* decision, stating, "[A] material representation, omission, act or practice involves information that is important to consumers, and, hence, likely to affect their choice of, or conduct regarding, a product."[45] The commission under James Miller, unlike its redefinition of deceptiveness discussed earlier, appears to have made little substantive change in the materiality standard.[46]

---

[42]*See*, American Home Products, 98 F.T.C. 136, 368 (1981), *aff'd*, 695 F.2d 681 (3rd Cir. 1982).

[43]*See, e.g.*, FTC v. Colgate-Palmolive Co. 380 U.S. 374, 386 (1965); Moretrench Corp. v. FTC, 127 F.2d 792, 795 (2d Cir. 1942). *See discussion* in Moore, *Deceptive Trade Practices and the Federal Trade Commission*, 28 TENN. L. REV. 493, 502 (1960).

[44]Bockenstette v. FTC, 134 F.2d 369, 371 (10th Cir. 1943).

[45]Cliffdale, *supra* note 19, at 165.

[46]Commissioner Bailey argued that there has indeed been a change. She posited that the materiality standard, as formulated by Chairman Miller in the Commission's 1983 Policy Statement, "has the potential to be the wolf in sheep's clothing." *Policy Statement on Deception, supra* note 19, at 195 (P. Bailey, dissenting). This view results from the fact that, although the policy statement and its definition of materiality clearly state that it is the "likelihood" which is salient, the policy statement later confuses the issue by remarking, "[I]njury and materiality are different names for the same concept." *Id.* at 183. However, because that remark is clearly inconsistent with the "likelihood" component of the definition that appears one page earlier in the same statement, *id.* at 182, and because Commission decisions since that statement have not borne out Commissioner Bailey's fears, I hold to the position that there has been no substantive change in the materiality standard.

DECEPTIVENESS + MATERIALITY ≠ REGULATION

The FTC is unable to pursue all regulable claims, given its limited resources. Those resources must be carefully marshalled. As Eckhardt stated in 1970:

> The Federal Trade Commission currently receives about 9,000 complaints a year. It is able to investigate only one out of eight or nine of those, and of the small fraction investigated, only one in ten results in a cease and desist order. To achieve this record the Federal Trade Commission has a staff of 1,200, including 500 lawyers. It operates on a $14 million annual budget.[47]

Precisely how those resources are marshalled is something of an unknown. Political visibility certainly must play a role in the Commission's decision whether or not to act, but it is unlikely that an agency would publicly admit that influence.[48] Nonetheless, the influence of publicity surrounding the report by "Nader's Raiders" in the late 1960s is well known to have influenced the aggressiveness of FTC regulation.[49] The effects of that report, as well as the influence of public outcries regarding specific products (e.g., cigarette advertising) are well documented by regulatory insiders.[50]

It is equally obvious that amount of potential physical or economic injury resulting from a deceptive claim will be a factor.[51] Chairman Miller, in 1983, stated as policy, "[W]hen consumers can easily evaluate the product or service, it is inexpensive, and it is frequently purchased, the Commission will examine the practice closely before issuing a complaint

---

[47]Eckhardt, *Consumer Class Actions*, 45 NOTRE DAME LAW. 663, 670 (1970).

[48]Cohen, *The Federal Trade Commission and the Regulation of Advertising in the Consumer Interest*, 33 J. MKTG. 40 (1969), cited the FTC:

> A high priority is accorded those matters which relate to the basic necessities of life, and to situations in which the impact of false and misleading advertising, or other unfair and deceptive practices, falls with cruelest impact upon those least able to survive the consequences—the elderly and the poor.

Id. at 42.

[49]E. F. COX, R. C. FELLMETH, AND J. E. SCHULTZ, THE NADER REPORT ON THE FEDERAL TRADE COMMISSION (1969).

[50]*See*, M. PERTSCHUK, REVOLT AGAINST REGULATION: THE RISE AND PAUSE OF THE CONSUMER MOVEMENT (1982); W. G. MAGNUSON AND J. CARPER, THE DARK SIDE OF THE MARKETPLACE: THE PLIGHT OF THE AMERICAN CONSUMER (1968).

[51]This is not the cost of an individual product, but the cumulative loss created by the misrepresentations.

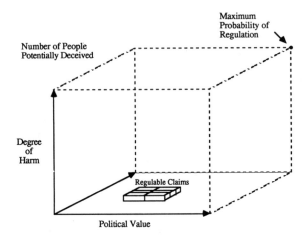

FIG. 2.1.   Marshalling resources.

based on deception."[52] Where the product is inexpensive, the degree of harm is certainly less, and the authorities might better apply their regulatory efforts and resources elsewhere.[53] However, if the product is expensive (e.g., automobiles) or can be dangerous to health (e.g., food and drug products), there is a greater incentive to tap the FTC's limited resources in an effort to curtail that likely harm.

Finally, the number of consumers likely to be deceived will have an influence on the decision to regulate. Although only a "substantial number" of the consumers to which an ad is directed is necessary for a claim to be regulable,[54] that number may be too small to justify the time of the FTC staff. If the ad is directed at a very small number of consumers, or the "substantial number" criterion is just barely met, the claim will be less likely to be addressed. If the ad, however, is aimed at a mass audience, or the percentage likely to be deceived is very substantial, regulation is more justifiable.

Figure 2.1 illustrates the relationship of these factors that play into the decision of whether or not to regulate the claim.

The farther the claim is pushed toward the upper right corner, the greater the probability the agency will act against that claim. None of these dimensions is independent of the others. Where there is a large number of users that are affected, there will very probably be a concomitant political value to invoke regulations, and the larger influence will

---

[52]*Policy Statement on Deception, supra* note 19.

[53]*Id.* Note, however, that where the product is widely distributed the cumulative loss could be substantial, thereby justifying greater Commission scrutiny.

[54]Preston and Richards, *supra* note 28, at 609-15.

likewise result in greater total harm to be avoided by regulatory intervention.[55]

The natural result of limited regulatory resources is that not all deceptive and material claims, although regulable, will actually be regulated.
The Commission staff must pick and choose only those cases it judges
most egregious, most politically advantageous, and most easily won.

DISTINGUISHING PUFFERY AND UNFAIRNESS

Although these qualifications define deception under the law, there are
two other closely related concepts, *outside* deception, that also deserve
brief mention. The first of these is *puffery*, which is viewed as an exception
to the rules of deception. It is a special category of claim that resembles
deception, but that has been singled out by the FTC and the courts for
special treatment, in accord with a long historical treatment of puffery
that pre-dates the creation of the Commission.[56] Puffery is defined as
"mere exaggeration" of a product's qualities, and is considered to be
offered and understood as an expression of the seller's opinion only, and
is not to be relied on by the buyer. Hyperbole like "the best," "fantastic,"
and "amazing" are all assumed to be harmless, and carry with them no
liability because of their subjective nature.[57]

The other associated classification, one that stems directly from the
Act, is *unfairness*. Unfairness is a seldom relied-on basis for prosecution
of an ad, although it has periodically arisen.[58] This principle has been a
tool that permitted the Commission to reach beyond the more strict
boundaries of deception, to right a variety of vaguely defined inequities
including immoral, unethical, oppressive, or unscrupulous conduct.[59] In

---

[55]Commissioners Perschuk and Bailey, while criticizing the Commission's *Policy Statement on Deception, supra* note 19, note that physical injury or large monetary loss may justify the FTC acting on smaller percentages of deceived consumers. *Id.* at 184 and 189.

[56]For a discussion of the legal development of puffery, *see generally,* Preston, *supra* note 32, at 8.

[57]*See* Colgate-Palmolive Co., 59 F.T.C. 1452, 1460 (1961); Carlay Co. v. FTC, 153 F.2d 493, 496 (7th Cir. 1946), *aff'd,* 380 U.S. 374 (1965); Tanners Shoe Co., 53 F.T.C. 1137, 1146 (1957); I.T.T. Continental Baking Co., 83 F.T.C. 865 (1973), *modified order,* 83 F.T.C. 1105 (1973), *modified,* ITT Continental v. FTC, 532 F.2d 207 (2d Cir. 1976), *modified order,* 90 F.T.C. 181 (1977); Pfizer, Inc., 81 F.T.C. 23, 64 (1972).

[58]*See, e.g.,* FTC v. Sperry & Hutchinson Co., 405 U.S. 233, 239 (1972); Pfizer, Inc., 81 F.T.C. 23 (1972); I.T.T. Continental Baking Co., *supra* note 57; International Harvestor Co., *supra* note 33.

[59]FTC v. Sperry & Hutchinson Co., *supra* note 58.

1980 the FTC, in a policy statement, redefined unfairness.[60] As it did recently with deception, the new position raised the threshold for what it considered impermissible activity, according potentially less protection to consumers.

Although unfairness was recently conceptualized by the FTC as the general classification of which "deception" is only a part,[61] this form of representation has been historically treated by the FTC and Congress as a separate area of Commission power.[62] The characterization of deception as a subset of unfairness is clearly inaccurate, however, since the Supreme Court declared otherwise in *Raladam*[63] and the Commission's own statements following that characterization[64] reveal that the standards of unfairness do not apply to deceptiveness. In spite of Commission declarations, deceptiveness and unfairness should more properly be considered discrete forms of regulation.

Although it is much more complex than need be explained here, a primary distinction between deception and unfairness is that although deception "focuses on 'likely' injury, unfairness cases usually involve actual and completed harms."[65] Because completed harm is required, and the practices falling under unfairness are much less well defined, this area of FTC authority is less critical to advertising regulation and less subject to systematic study. Unfairness may encompass such activities as preying on the loneliness of elder citizens or coaxing children to nag their parent to purchase a certain product. Because it is such a flexible catch-all concept, capable of covering so many different activities, it is probable that each of these activities would demand a separate theory and a unique measurement method. Consequently, unfairness will not play a major role in the discussions that follow.

ERRORS BY CONSUMER RESEARCHERS

An important aspect of behavioral researchers' interaction with the deception concept is that they have made some mistakes in understanding it. Deception for persons operating outside the legal context might be defined as intentional misstatements by advertisers or as cases of consum-

---

[60]Letter from the Federal Trade Commission to Senators Ford and Danforth, Dec. 17, 1980, attached as an appendix to International Harvestor Co., 104 F.T.C. 949 (1984).

[61]*Id.*, at 1060.

[62]*See discussion* of historical developments in Richards & Zakia, *Pictures: An Advertiser's Expressway Through FTC Regulation*, 16 GA. L. REV. 77 (1981).

[63]FTC v. Raladam Co., 238 U.S. 643 (1931), *aff'g*, 42 F.2d 430 (6th Cir. 1930).

[64]*Supra* note 60, at 1061.

[65]*Id.*

ers actually acquiring false beliefs.[66] Intent of the seller, however, is not a factor in illegal deceptiveness,[67] and no consumer need actually have been misled.[68] Such requirements may be viable for some purposes, and may be philosophically important in other contexts, but under the law they need not be present in order to find a violation.

Preston[69] noted that several advertising researchers have confused or failed to distinguish the legal and lay meanings when discussing deception in advertising. He comments that these authors "are discussing a meaningful concept and are doing so usefully. The problem is that readers are likely to derive the impression that by discussing deception they are discussing the requirement for what is legally violative. The surrounding contexts suggest that the authors indeed think that is the case."[70] As examples of this confusion, he pointed to several of the errors. These scientists are not simply misstating the law, there is a recurring theme in these errors: These researchers are often discussing reasonable concepts of inequity similar, but not identical, to regulable deceptiveness.

Jacoby and Small discussed misrepresentations falling within the bailiwick of the Food and Drug Administration (FDA), which derives from that agency's statutory authority under the rubric "misleading."[71] The authors stated:

> It is fortunate that the Federal Food, Drug and Cosmetic Act uses *misleading* as opposed to *deceptive*, the word favored by the FTC. According to the dictionary, *deceptive* implies a deliberate act on the part of the source of the message to lead the receiver of that message astray . . . being mislead is not necessarily due to any manipulation on the part of the advertiser.[72]

---

[66]According to WEBSTER'S NEW WORLD DICTIONARY OF THE AMERICAN LANGUAGE 2D COLLEGE EDITION 365 (1974), deception entails (a) the act or practice of deceiving, (b) the fact or condition of being deceived, and (c) something that deceives, as an illusion, or is meant to deceive, as a fraud or imposture. It delineates this concept from several synonyms:

Deception is applied to anything that deceives, whether by design or illusion; *fraud* suggests deliberate deception in dishonestly depriving a person of property, rights etc.; *subterfuge* suggests an artifice or stratagem used to deceive others in evading something or gaining some end; *trickery* implies the use of tricks or ruses in fraudulently deceiving others; *chicanery* implies the use of petty tricking and subterfuge, esp. in legal actions.
Id.

[67]FTC v. Algoma, 291 U.S. 67, 81 (1934).
[68]FTC v. Sterling Drug, Inc., *supra* note 23, at 674.
[69]Preston, *supra* note 25.
[70]*Id.* at 81.
[71]Jacoby and Small, *The FDA Approach to Defining Misleading Advertising*, 39 J. MKTG. 65 (Oct. 1975).
[72]*Id.* at 66.

Although the authors chose a dictionary definition of *deceptive*, and may not themselves be confused about its legal implications,[73] it seems ironic that in an article about misleading advertising they should mislead their readers. Their reference to the FTC certainly suggests to the reader that the agency's prosecutorial activities are restricted to deliberate acts of advertisers.

In similar fashion, David Gardner made this *faux pas*. He declared that "the present legal approach . . . focuses on the act of deceiving by the advertiser, rather than the effect of the message on the consumer."[74] This is wholly inaccurate. There is no focus whatsoever on the advertiser or its "acts."

Another common fallacy is that deceptiveness depends on consumers believing a claim.[75] Actual beliefs of consumers are irrelevant.[76] No one even needs to have *seen* the ad or claim! Examples where researchers may have misled readers, causing them to miss this subtle exclusion, are several.

Gardner, again, stated, "If an advertisement . . . leaves the consumer with an impression(s) and/or belief(s) . . . factually untrue or potentially misleading, then deception is said to exist."[77] Armstrong and Russ said, "For deception to occur it is not sufficient that the claims are false. They must also be believed."[78] Olson and Dover, in a similar remark, said

---

[73]Preston, *A Comment on "Defining Misleading Advertising" and "Deception in Advertising"*, 40 J. MKTG. 54 (July 1976), made this same criticism of Jacoby and Small. In a response, Jacoby claimed that the statement was not intended to be attributable to the FTC, but was merely chosen to provide insight. Jacoby, *A Reply* . . . , 40 J. MKTG. 57 (July 1976).

[74]Gardner, *Deception in Advertising: A Conceptual Approach*, 39 J. MKTG. 40 (Jan. 1975), Preston, *supra* note 25, likewise showed this inaccuracy. Gardner countered that the word "act" did not mean "deliberate action," but was rather meant to focus on the advertisement itself as opposed to concentrating on the consumer or receiver of the information. Gardner, *A Reply* . . . , 40 J. MKTG. 58 (July 1976). This, too, represents an inaccuracy by Gardner, because the Commission has made it quite clear that it focuses on the conveyed message rather than the claim itself in all cases except where the claim is explicit. This was true even at the time of Gardner's writing.

[75]*See, e.g.,* Aaker, *Deceptive Advertising*, in D. A. AAKER AND G. S. DAY, CONSUMERISM: SEARCH FOR THE CONSUMER INTEREST 137 (1974). This article appears to be the originator of the inaccuracy. It is the earliest to make this declaration, and is cited by many of its successors.

[76]International Harvestor Co., 104 F.T.C. 949 (1984), states, "[W]e do not go beyond likelihood to require evidence on the incidence of actual false belief." *Id.* at 1056.

[77]Gardner, *Deception in Advertising: A Receiver Oriented Approach to Understanding*, 5(4) J. ADV. 5, 7 (1976).

[78]Armstrong and Russ, *Detecting Deception in Advertising*, 23 MSU BUS. TOPICS 21 (Spring 1975). Five years later those same authors, joined by a third, continued to hold to this conviction: "In finding deception, the FTC depends on discovering that consumers (1) have perceived false claims and (2) believed them." Armstrong, Gurol, and Russ, *Defining and Measuring Deception in Advertising: A Review and Evaluation*, in J. LEIGH AND C. MARTIN,

"deception is considered to occur when consumers acquire demonstrably false beliefs as a function of exposure to an advertisement."[79] The problem is that these researchers are speaking of "deception," while failing to point-out to readers that the legal criterion is "deceptiveness." Although their remarks may have some utility in the researchers' own working context, which I more fully review later, their failure to indicate this crucial distinction threatens to confuse readers as to the legal requirements.

Another error frequently found in the scholarly literature is to assume that all deceptive claims are regulable under the law. Shimp, in accusing the FTC of failing to regulate misrepresentations that are the result of evaluative rather than factual appeals, concluded:

> Because cognitive structures vary from a receiver to receiver, the meaning evoked by a particular [evaluative claim] is also variable. In short, different receivers form different beliefs to the same advertising claim. Since not all beliefs are supportable in reality, all receivers who have formed incorrect beliefs have been deceived.[80]

That claims be deceptive is a necessary, but not sufficient, condition to regulation. Only where the mistaken impression is about something that is instrumental in their purchase decision (legally "material") does regulable deception exist.[81] It is true that consumers may be likely to be deceived, but the implication created by Shimp is clearly that this deceptiveness is always legally cognizable.

In a later article, Shimp acknowledged a distinction between these concepts:

> Two major conceptualizations of the nature of deception have been advanced. The more encompassing view holds that deception occurs when

---

CURRENT ISSUES AND RESEARCH IN ADVERTISING 1980 17 (1980). This is particularly egregious error, because the FTC neither finds "deception," nor does it depend upon *beliefs* (see *infra*, Chapter 5).

[79]Olson and Dover, *Cognitive Effects of Deceptive Advertising*, 15 J. MKTG. RES. 29, 30 (Feb. 1978).

[80]Shimp, *Social Psychological (Mis)Representations in Television Advertising*, 13 J. CONS. AFF. 28, 33 (1979).

[81]Cliffdale, *supra* note 19, at 165. Even those writers who understand that regulation requires both deceptiveness and materiality may be found misstating that requirements. Garfinkel said, "[I]n deception, there must be a misleading claim which injuriously affects buying behavior." Garfinkel, *A Pragmatic Approach to Truth in Advertising*, in R. J. HARRIS, INFORMATION PROCESSING RESEARCH IN ADVERTISING 175, 191 (1983). Although this clearly refers to materiality, it incorrectly states that the claim must injuriously affect buying behavior, when the actual requirement is that it must be *likely* to injuriously affect buying behavior.

either a false advertising claim or a true but unqualified claim is perceived and believed, thereby altering the receiver's cognitive structure in a fashion that a nondeceptive claim would not. A more rigorous conceptualization contends that deception results only if purchase behavior is affected. According to this latter view, an advertisement may deceive consumers into believing that a product will provide a trivial benefit. If, however, this benefit is not salient to consumers in their purchase decisions, it possesses no serious negative behavioral consequences, and thus "real" deception has not occurred.[82]

This statement provides only two views of misrepresentation, when, in fact, there are many. Shimp is still missing the legal concept of regulable deceptiveness, which is not that "deception results only if purchase behavior is affected," but rather that regulable deceptiveness results only if purchase behavior of a substantial number of people is *likely* to be affected.[83] He, too, failed to distinguish between deception and deceptiveness, referring to a claim being perceived and *believed*.

In 1978, an article by Shimp was published entitled, "Do Incomplete Comparisons Mislead?"[84] While I in no way mean to discount the value of this work, or of any of the others discussed here, this piece is particularly notable for its unequivocal statements evidencing a mistaken concept of the legal construct of deceptiveness. The major premise of this paper is: incomplete comparisons, those that claim a product is "better" or "will get your dishes cleaner," without specifically denoting to what the product is being compared, are "inherently susceptible to multiple interpretations, some of which may be false" and are consequently "misleading."[85] The idea, indeed, is an important one. However, this researcher repeatedly suggests that some consumers must inevitably be misled because every interpretation by every consumer cannot be accurate, and he concluded that "it is an insidious type of puffery that possesses the distinct capacity to deceive ... regulators should judge it an unacceptable advertising technique."[86]

The author, by this remark, made two major errors. First, he misunderstood the concept of puffery. By definition, a claim cannot be both puffing and have the capacity to deceive, and as soon as the advertiser makes a comparison, even one that is unqualified, it is no longer a "puff."

---

[82]Shimp, *Evaluative Verbal Content and Deception in Advertising: A Review and Critical Analysis*, in R. J. HARRIS, INFORMATION PROCESSING RESEARCH IN ADVERTISING 195, 199 (1983).

[83]Cliffdale, *supra* note 19, at 165.

[84]Shimp, *Do Incomplete Comparisons Mislead?* 18(6) J. ADV. RES. 21 (1978).

[85]*Id.* at 21.

[86]*Id.* at 27.

It is no longer mere opinion, because a definitive and measurable claim has been made. The advertiser is not stating what he or she believes, that the product is "great." It is impossible to determine what "great" means, because there is no point of reference. But an incomplete comparison that the product "will get your dishes cleaner" does have an implied point of reference. If the product does not "get your dishes cleaner" than *some* other product, it is certainly discoverable and probably deceptive.[87] In fact, if consumers can be shown to perceive this to mean "cleaner than all other cleaners," it is clearly an implied superiority that may be subject to regulation if it is likely to affect buying behavior.[88] Superiority claims, even without specific referents, have indeed been regulated by the FTC.[89]

The second error is that a "capacity to deceive" is sufficient to invoke regulatory action, without consideration of materiality. This is the same error that Shimp carried throughout his articles.

I do not intend by this analysis to be hypercritical of these researchers. These scholars are vulnerable to criticism primarily because they are some of the few brave consumer researchers who have discussed misrepresentation in advertising. On the other hand, their work cannot be maximally effective unless they operate from correct assumptions.

QUALIFICATION REGARDING TERMINOLOGY

The FTC is responsible for establishing and enforcing standards, within the confines of its statutory authority. Because its concern is for those standards, rather than the labels or semantics attached to them, its use of terminology is sometimes rather loose or ambiguous where the distinction does not substantively affect those standards. However, because the present study focuses on some behavioral issues not normally considered by the regulators, I have been forced to make some choices regarding the labels I apply. It is important that the reader understand these choices reflect my own interpretation of Commission remarks, and that other interpretations are possible.

The first example of this is my choice of the terms *deceptiveness* and *deception*, to denote a *likelihood* of deceiving versus *completed* deception.

---

[87]E. W. KINTNER, A PRIMER ON THE LAW OF DECEPTIVE PRACTICES 33 (1971).

[88]This can be seen, to some extent, in the recent rash of analgesics cases, which all claimed to be "better" or "stronger," although many of the claims offered vague referents (of 220 brands, ours is best). *See, e.g.,* Dancer-Fitzgerald-Sample, Inc., 96 F.T.C. 1 (1980); Sterling Drug, Inc., 102 F.T.C. 395 (1983).

[89]*See, e.g.,* Jay Norris, 91 F.T.C. 751, 847 at n. 20 (1978), *aff'd*, 598 F.2d 1244 (2d Cir.), *cert. denied*, 444 U.S. 980 (1979).

The terms I have chosen are adopted from the work of Preston.[90] The FTC, however, sometimes uses the term *deception* in reference to the likelihood to deceive,[91] and "actual deception" to mean completed deception.[92] It is important to realize that the standard is clear; it is only the labels used that are being interpreted here. Most importantly, I have made this choice of terms and use it consistently in the material that follows, to ensure that there is no question about the signified construct.

The second instance where this applies involves the question of whether deceptiveness *includes* materiality or if they are separate. The standard, again, is clear. A claim must be *both* likely to mislead and material to be regulated. But, it is unclear whether deceptiveness refers only to the likelihood to mislead or to both. The Commission's statements are unhelpful. For example, Chairman Miller remarked "the Commission will find . . ." a claim deceptive if it meets both criteria.[93] This can mean either that a claim is deceptive only if it has both elements, or that it will only be *regulated* if it includes both. Under the former interpretation, False Conveyed Meaning + Materiality = Deceptiveness, while under the latter, Deceptiveness + Materiality = Regulable Deceptiveness. The standard is the same, but the words differ. Because I take the position that a claim can be deceptive without necessarily being likely to affect action, I use the latter terminology. Again, I use these labels consistently throughout this book, for the sake of clarity. This selection, however, is certainly debatable.

---

[90] Preston, *supra* note 25.

[91] For example, Chairman Miller, in his recent explanation of Commission policy regarding deceptive advertising, stated, "[T]he Commission will find *deception* if there is a representation, omission or practice that is *likely to mislead* the consumer. . . ." Letter from Chairman Miller to Congressman Dingell, Oct. 14, 1983, appended to Cliffdale, *supra* note 19, at 176 (italics added).

[92] Chairman Miller explained, "The issue is whether the act or practice is likely to mislead, rather than whether it causes *actual deception.*" *Id.* (italics added).

[93] *Id.*

The Law's View of Deceptiveness as a Behavioral Concept

From the law's viewpoint, deceptiveness is fundamentally a legal concept. However, upon setting out to determine its existence, the law must treat it as a behavioral concept. Following the discussion in chapter 2 about the legal criterion for deception as being an advertisement's deceptiveness (i.e., its capacity or tendency or likelihood to mislead), I discuss in this chapter the facts the FTC finds and how it applies them to that criterion. Whereas the findings of law, which involve whether the facts found indicate the existence of a violation, are wholly within the expert domain of the lawyers, the facts themselves lie within the expert domain of the behavioral researchers, and the findings of such facts thus in many instances are delegated in significant part by the lawyers to the behavioral researchers.

That is because deceptiveness is a phenomenon that lies inside people's heads, and thus is an aspect of human behavior. As such, it is clearly the business of those who study such behavior, although it remains as well the business of those who must identify that behavior for legal purposes. It is within the domain of the behavioral researchers because they are the experts in studying, measuring, and identifying behavior, and yet it never leaves the domain of the lawyers because the law gives them the right to make such determinations either with or without the help of those experts.

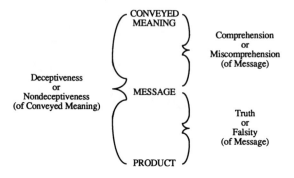

FIG. 3.1.   Types of evidence.

GETTING INSIDE CONSUMERS' MINDS

The specific behavioral evidence used to determine deceptiveness is that of the message conveyed to consumers by the advertisement. The function of conveyed meaning as evidence of deceptiveness is depicted in Fig. 3.1.[1] This illustration reveals three different types of evidence frequently used in FTC cases: (a) the product (or service) advertised and offered for sale, (b) the message about the product as contained in the advertisement, and (c) the conveyed meaning of the message as perceived by the consumer upon exposure to that advertisement.

A comparison of any two of these pieces of evidence may be useful to locate a form of error occurring in the communication of product information. Where the explicit message about a product attribute is compared to the actual product attribute, a difference is indicative of *falsity*. When comparing the conveyed, received, meaning to the explicit message, a difference would represent *miscomprehension*. Finally, if the conveyed meaning differs from the actual product attribute, the result is *deceptiveness*. Deceptiveness, therefore, may be caused by message falsity or consumer miscomprehension or a combination of the two.

False Advertising Is Not Always Deceptive

This distinction between falsity and deceptiveness is crucial because behavioral research plays no role in detecting falsity, and, because the legal criterion is deceptiveness, not falsity, in spite of colloquial reference to "false advertising." As Preston explained:

---

[1]This figure is taken from Preston and Richards, *Consumer Miscomprehension as a Challenge to FTC Prosecutions of Deceptive Advertising*, 19 J. MARSHALL L. REV. 605, 617 (1986).

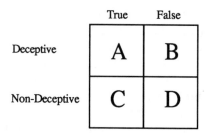

FIG. 3.2.   Deceptiveness versus falsity.

It is far easier to detect falsity than to detect deception. Falsity is objective, which means we can discover it by looking at nonhuman objects. We can check to see whether the product for sale matches the stories told about it. . . . Deception is different; it is subjective and it leaves considerable room for doubt. It is a property of human beings. We look for it within the mind of the consumer, the person who is considering the object. If the sales message makes the consumer believe the toothpaste contains something it doesn't, then it deceives him.[2]

The relationship of falsity and deceptiveness, as just defined, can be illustrated as shown in Fig. 3.2.

Because true–false represents the explicit message, and deceptive–nondeceptive is the conveyed message, blocks B and C are situations where there is no difference between explicit meaning and conveyed meaning, whereas blocks A and D are situations where conveyed meaning differs from explicit meaning. An example of block A would be a claim that "Efficin contains no aspirin."[3] Although this is explicitly true, it conveys meaning that Efficin has none of aspirin's side effects, which is false, and therefore the claim is deceptive. Block B is an expressly false claim that is deceptive, which is the typical notion of a "false advertisement." Block C encompasses most ad claims, being both true and nondeceptive. Block D would encompass "spoof" claims in ads, being explicitly false yet not conveying the false content as true but only as a joke. A current example of this is a series of ads for Isuzu automobiles, where the spokesman makes outrageous claims (e.g., this truck costs only $19.95, or this car does 0-60 mph in half a second). The claims are so grossly exaggerated, no reasonable consumer would believe them.

Accordingly, the Commission and the courts have acknowledged the difference between falsity and deceptiveness. The Tenth Circuit, in *Bock-*

---

[2]I. L. PRESTON, THE GREAT AMERICAN BLOW-UP: PUFFERY IN ADVERTISING AND SELLING 8 (1975).

[3]Adria Laboratories, 103 F.T.C. 512 (1984).

enstette v. FTC,[4] found deceptive a merchant's merely implied representation that he and the baby chickens he sold were certified by a government Record of Performance. This merchant's claims were absolutely true (i.e., there was no falsity), but the court felt consumers would comprehend something different than what was expressly claimed. The court decided that "[w]ords and sentences may be literally and technically true and yet be framed in such a setting as to mislead or deceive."[5] In fact, courts have determined that if a statement in an ad lends itself to more than one interpretation by the ordinary recipient of the ad, and *one* of those interpretations is deceptive, the representation will be construed to be deceptive *in toto.*[6]

A corollary to this is the doctrine that even silence can be deceptive.[7] In *P. Lorillard Co. v. FTC*[8] the court announced that "[t]o tell less than the whole truth is a well known method of deception; and he who deceives by resorting to such method cannot excuse the deception by relying upon the truthfulness per se of the partial truth by which it has been accomplished."[9] These ideas lead naturally to the consequence that "[t]he ultimate impression upon the mind of the reader arises from the sum total of not only what is said but also of all that is reasonably implied"[10] (i.e., the courts look not at a single sentence or claim, but to the total impression communicated by the advertisement).[11] An omission or a partial truth in one part of an ad can affect how the consumer interprets other parts in the ad. This has even been expressed by the Supreme Court, in *Donaldson v. Read Magazine, Inc.:*[12]

> Advertisement as a whole may be completely misleading although every sentence separately considered is literally true. This may be because things

---

[4]134 F.2d 369 (10th Cir. 1943).

[5]*Id.* at 371. *See, also,* Sebrone Co. v. FTC, 135 F.2d 676, 679 (7th cir. 1943); Kalwajtys v. FTC, 237 F.2d 654, 654-56 (7th Cir. 1956), *cert. denied,* 352 U.S. 1025 (1957).

[6]United States v. 95 Barrels, 265 U.S. 438, 442 (1924); Resort Car Rental Sys. v. FTC, 518 F.2d 962, 964 (9th Cir. 1975), *cert. denied* 423 U.S. 827 (1975); Chrysler Corp. v. FTC, 561 F.2d 357, 363 (D.C. Cir. 1977); Rhodes Pharmacal Co. v. FTC, 208 F.2d 382, 387 (7th Cir. 1953), *rehearing denied* (1954), *modified on other grounds* 348 U.S. 940 (1955).

[7]*See discussion* in International Harvester Co., 104 F.T.C. 949, 1057-59 (1984).

[8]186 F.2d 52 (4th Cir. 1950).

[9]*Id.* at 58.

[10]Aronberg v. FTC, 132 F.2d 165, 167 (7th Cir. 1942).

[11]Elliot Knitwear, Inc. v. FTC, 266, F.2d 787 (2d Cir. 1959); Spiegel, Inc. v. FTC, 411 F.2d 481 (7th Cir. 1969); Ford Motor Co. v. FTC, 120 F.2d 175 (6th Cir.), *cert. denied,* 314 U.S. 668 (1941); Perloff v. FTC, 150 F.2d 757 (3rd Cir. 1945); Murray Space Shoe Corp. v. FTC, 304 F.2d 270 (2d Cir. 1962); Thompson Medical Co., Inc., 104 F.T.C. 648, 790 (1984), *aff'd,* Thompson Medical Co. v. FTC, 791 F.2d 189 (D.C. Cir. 1986).

[12]333 U.S. 178, *upon reargument* (Black, J., 1948).

are omitted that should be said, or because advertisements are composed or purposefully printed in such a way as to mislead.[13]

Evidence of Consumer Understanding

Because deceptiveness rather than falsity is the legal criterion, and because deceptiveness is indicated by analysis of the conveyed meaning, which involves examining consumer behavior rather than messages, the question arises as to what the FTC considers to be acceptable methods of proving or disproving the existence of deceptiveness. In *Thompson Medical*[14] the Commission began by remarking that express claims are an easy case because they are unequivocally stated.[15] With such clear and undeniably false promises, the ad, alone, constitutes sufficient proof a claim is made. The literal message is taken automatically to constitute the conveyed meaning. There is no need to consider whether consumers actually believe the falsity, inasmuch as "the likelihood or propensity of deception is the criterion by which advertising is measured."[16] No one need actually have been deceived.[17] Where there is express misrepresentation, the Commission appears to assume a "fair probability" readers will be misled.[18] Conse-

---

[13]*Id.* at 188.

[14]Thompson Medical, *supra* note 11. This case concerned the promotion and sale of Thompson's "Aspercreme" rub-on pain reliever. The FTC staff alleged that the name and advertising for the product suggested to consumers that the product contained aspirin, that it was a newly developed product, and that it was scientifically proven more effective than orally ingested aspirin for relief of arthritis and other conditions. The Commission found those allegations supported by the evidence, and among other orders, forbade Thompson from using the name on any product not containing a significant amount of aspirin.

[15]*Id.* at 788.

[16]Beneficial Corp. v. FTC, 542 F.2d 611, 617 (3rd Cir. 1976).

[17]Jacob Siegel Co. v. FTC, 150 F.2d 751, 755 (3rd Cir. 1944); Feil v. FTC, 285 F.2d 879, 896 (9th Cir. 1960).

[18]The court in Regina Corp. v. FTC, 322 F.2d 765, 768 (3rd Cir. 1963), remarked that the mission of the FTC is preventative, not corrective, and FTC v. Sterling Drug, Inc. 317 F.2d 669 (2d Cir. 1963), declares:

In order to best implement the prophylactic purpose of the statute, it has been consistently held that advertising falls within its proscription not only where there is proof of actual deception but also when the representations made have a capacity or tendency to deceive, i.e., when there is a *likelihood or fair probability that the reader will be misled.*

Id. at 674 (italics added).

quently, empirical research is seldom a consideration where a claim is explicit.[19]

The analysis of implied claims, however, where the conveyed meaning is different from the literal message, is frequently more involved. Although the Commission will often conclude an ad contains an implied claim solely by evaluating the ad's contents and the circumstances surrounding it,[20] if it cannot confidently make a conclusion in this manner it will require the introduction of extrinsic evidence before finding an advertiser to have been deceptive.[21]

The FTC need not use extrinsic evidence in making determinations of deceptiveness. It need only use intrinsic evidence, which means nothing more than the ad itself.[22] This has been established by the courts, with the leading case being *Zenith*.[23] However, despite this privilege, the Commission has decided that under certain circumstances it will require extrinsic evidence. The FTC, in *Thompson Medical*,[24] announced:

> Implied claims are any claims that are not express. They range from claims that would be virtually synonymous with an express claim through language that literally says one thing but strongly suggests another to language which relatively few consumers would interpret as making a particular representation. . . . Because of this wide range, the Commission employs two different techniques in evaluating whether an advertisement contains

---

[19]Although the Commission does not need behavioral research to support a finding of deceptiveness in such cases, nor is it likely to be helpful in most of those instances, research could be useful to prove, e.g., that consumers realize the explicit claim is false and are therefore not likely to be deceived by it. It is also arguable that such evidence is needed in the event that the FTC challenges an explicit claim concerning an "evaluative" product attribute, which I discuss in following chapters. *See* Richards and Preston, Quantitative Research: A Dispute Resolution Process for FTC Advertising Regulation, 40 OKLA. L. REV. 593 (1987).

[20]Thompson Medical, *supra* note 11, at 789. "Logical" implications, for example, might be expected to fall into this category.

[21]*Id.*

[22]*See discussion* in Preston, *Data-Free at the FTC? How the Federal Trade Commission Decides Whether Extrinsic Evidence of Deceptiveness is Required*, 24 AMER. BUS. L. J. 359 (1986).

[23]Zenith v. FTC, 143 F.2d 29 (7th Cir. 1944), states:

> The Commission was not required to sample public opinion to determine what the petitioner was representing to the public. The Commission had a right to look at the advertisements in question, consider the relevant evidence in the record that would aid it in interpreting the advertisements, and then to decide for itself whether the practices engaged in by the petitioner were unfair or deceptive.

Id. at 31. This was acknowledged by the Supreme Court in FTC v. Colgate, 380 U.S. 374, 391 (1965).

[24]*Supra* note 11.

implied claims. One is to look at evidence from the advertisement itself. We often conclude that an advertisement contains an implied claim by evaluating the contents of the advertisement and the circumstances surrounding it. . . . If our initial review of evidence from the advertisement does not allow us to conclude with confidence that it is reasonable to read an advertisement as containing a particular implied message, *we will not find the ad to make the implied claim unless extrinsic evidence allows us to conclude that such a reading of the ad is reasonable.*[25]

This evidence can take several forms, including consumer surveys, dictionary definitions, generally accepted principles of marketing, expert witnesses, and consumer testimony.[26] Extrinsic evidence, therefore, has become common where the challenged claims are implicit.

Although each of these types of evidence might be of some value, the probative substance of consumer survey research far outweighs the alternatives. Only this approach directly assesses consumer perceptions of the particular ad in question. The testimony of a few isolated consumers chosen purposively to prove one side of a lawsuit, for example, is hardly generalizable to any larger population, and rather than *lead* to a

---

[25]*Id.* at 788–89 (italics added).

[26]The Commission states:

The extrinsic evidence we prefer to use and to which we give great weight is direct evidence of what consumers actually thought upon reading the advertisement in question. Such evidence will be in the form of consumer survey research for widely distributed ads. . . . Ads of that sort are directed at so large an audience that it is too costly to obtain the statements of enough individual consumers in another manner (e.g., by way of affidavits) to be reasonably confident that the consumers' views on the record of the proceeding were representative of the entire group to which the ad was addressed. . . .

Another type of evidence we will look at is evidence not specifically showing how consumers understood the advertisements at issue before us, but showing how consumers might ordinarily be expected to perceive or understand representations. . . . For example, we might look at the dictionary definition of a word to identify the word's common usages. Or we might look at principles derived from market research, as expressed by marketing experts, which show that consumers generally respond in a certain manner to ads that are presented in a particular way, and presume that consumer reactions to a particular ad before us would be consistent with the general response pattern. Where we apply such marketing principles, we will derive them from research presented in references generally accepted as reliable in the field of marketing. . . .

A third type of evidence we will consider is offered as the opinion of expert witnesses in the proceeding as to how an advertisement might reasonably be interpreted. . . .

Id. at 789. *See,* Preston, *Extrinsic Evidence in Federal Trade Commission Deceptiveness Cases,* 1987 COLUM. BUS. L. REV. 633 (1987).

determination of the issues it is more likely to *mislead*.[27] Use of expert witnesses is also of limited value, because no one can honestly be said to *know* what others think. Aside from survey research, each of these other fact-finding methods is no more than a best guess.

The Nature of Implications

For the FTC staff to locate claims that imply more than they state explicitly, it must have some general view of how consumers comprehend ad claims. That view is reflected in Preston's typology of implied deceptive claims attacked by the FTC, paraphrased here:[28]

1. *Proof Implication.* An explicit claim, often technical, scientific, or medical, about the features or performance of the advertised product or service, implies that proof exists for the claim. For example, the claim that an automobile tire will "stop 25% quicker" tied with the claim "It comes straight out of Firestone racing research" implied there was proof for the claim that Firestone tires would stop 25% quicker than any other tire under typical driving conditions.[29]

2. *Demonstration Implication.* Demonstration of one effect is taken as implying proof of another more impressive effect. A demonstration that Baggies keeps food dry even under water might be inferred to suggest that Baggies keep food fresh.[30]

3. *Reasonable Basis Implication.* Making a product claim falsely implies that the maker has a prior reasonable basis to believe it.[31] For example, a claim that Bayer Children's Aspirin is superior in terms of significant

[27]*See* discussion of individual testimony in Richards, *Obscenity and Film: An Empirical Dilemma*, 6 Loy. Ent. L. J. 7, 24 (1986).

[28]Preston, *The Federal Trade Commission's Identification of Implications As Constituting Deceptive Advertising*, 57 Cincinnati L. Rev. 1243 (1989). *See* an older formulation of this typology in Preston, *The FTC's Handling of Puffery and Other Selling Claims Made "By Implication"*, 5 J. Bus. Res. 155 (1977).

[29]Firestone Tire, 81 F.T.C. 398 (1972), *aff'd*, Firestone v. FTC, 481 F.2d 246 (6th Cir. 1973), *cert. denied*, 414 U.S. 1112 (1973). *See also*, American Home Products, 98 F.T.C. 375 (1981); Litton, 97 F.T.C. 1 (1981), *modified*, Litton v. FTC, 676 F.2d 364 (9th Cir. 1982).

[30]Colgate-Palmolive, 77 F.T.C. 150 (1970). *See also*, American Home Products, 81 F.T.C. 579 (1972); Ford Motor, 84 F.T.C. 729 (1974); Sun Oil, 84 F.T.C. 247 (1974); Standard Oil of California, 84 F.T.C. 1401 (1974).

[31]This allegation can be found as near boiler-plate language in almost every FTC advertising complaint. The case that introduced this form of implication to FTC history was Pfizer, 81 F.T.C. 19 (1972). A whole body of advertising regulation ha grown up around this area, and is called advertising "substantiation." It is a relatively recent development, and was upheld in Warner-Lambert Co. v. FTC, 562 F.2d 749 (D.C. Cir. 1977), *cert. denied*, 435 U.S. 950 (1978).

therapeutic effect to any other children's aspirin implied that Bayer had scientific evidence to support such a claim.[32]

4. *No Qualification Implication.* Explicit product claims broadly stated with no explicit qualification, implied that no material qualification exists. Firestone, for example, advertised its tire as "The Safe Tire," with descriptions of tests conducted in driving conditions beyond those encountered by typical consumers.[33] The Commission, however, felt that no tire is completely safe, given improper inflation, overloading, etc., and that consumers were misled by this implication.

5. *Ineffective Qualification.* A literal or implied claim is qualified by a literal but inconspicuous statement. The claim might be, for instance, "contains a real 17-facet diamond," implying a stone of some value, while buried in a copy block it describes the diamond as .25 pt. (1/400 carat), which is essentially diamond dust.[34] A qualification that is inconspicuous or otherwise ineffective is held not to be part of the conveyed message.

6. *Uniqueness Implication.* This is the claim that a product has certain features, accompanied by the concomitant implication that it is the *only* such product with those features (e.g., "Wonder builds strong bodies 12 ways!").[35]

7. *Halo Implication.* A true claim of superiority about one aspect of the product is alleged to imply to consumers that the product is superior in other ways. Sun Oil promoted its Sunoco 260 gasoline as "World's highest octane available."[36] Although the statement was factually true, the FTC challenged this claim, because its staff was concerned that it falsely implied this gasoline was uniquely able to supply power and performance.

---

[32]Sterling Drug, Inc., 102 F.T.C. 395 (1983).

[33]Firestone Tire, 81 F.T.C. 398 (1972), *aff'd*, 481 F.2d 246 (6th Cir. 1973). *See also,* Lorillard et al., 80 F.T.C. 455 (1972); Cynex, 104 F.T.C. 464 (1984); Porter and Dietsch, 90 F.T.C. 770 (1977), *modified*, 605 F.2d 294 (7th Cir. 1979), *modified*, 95 F.T.C. 806 (1980).

[34]*See, e.g.,* R. H. Macy, 79 F.T.C. 33 (1971). *See also,* Stauffer Laboratories v. FTC, 343 F.2d 75 (9th Cir. 1965); Beneficial, 86 F.T.C. 119 (1975), *remanded,* Beneficial v. FTC, 542 F.2d 611 (3rd Cir. 1976), *consent settlement,* 94 F.T.C. 425 (1979), *modified,* 108 F.T.C. 168 (1986); Warner-Lambert, 86 F.T.C. 1398 (1975), *aff'd,* 562 F.2d 749 (D.C. Cir. 1977), *modified,* 92 F.T.C. 191 (1978).

[35]ITT Continental Baking Company, Inc., 83 F.T.C. 865 (1973), *modified order,* 83 F.T.C. 1105 (1973), *modified,* ITT Continental v. FTC, 532 F.2d 207 (2d Cir. 1976), *modified order,* 90 F.T.C. 181 (1977). For other examples *see,* Dollar Vitamin Plan, Inc., 69 F.T.C. 933 (1966); Gulf Coast Aluminum Products, 71 F.T.C. 339 (1967); Swift, 79 F.T.C. 146 (1971).

[36]Sun Oil, 84 F.T.C. 247 (1974). For other examples *see,* General Motors, 84 F.T.C. 653 (1974); American Home Products, 98 F.T.C. 136 (1981), *modified,* 695 F.2d 681 (3rd Cir. 1982), *modified orders,* 101 F.T.C. 698 (1983), 103 F.T.C. 57 (1984), 103 F.T.C. 528 (1984).

8. *Confusing Resemblance Implication.* This implication involves using an unusual word or phrase that is similar to a more familiar one. Elliot Knitwear used the term "Cashmora" in association with a line of sweaters. The unusual term was charged as having a tendency to imply that the sweaters were made of cashmere.[37]

9. *Ordinary Meaning Implication.* In this case a word or phrase with an ordinary meaning is used for a different meaning, but implies to consumers the ordinary meaning. An example of this is Ocean Spray's use of the term "food energy" when advertising the merits of its fruit products.[38] Consumers might understand this term to mean the product is rich in nutrients, but in fact Ocean Spray was rich only in calories.

10. *Contrast Implication.* This concerns ads that contrast a product with a competitive product, truthfully showing one difference, but implying other differences. Anacin was advertised with the phrase, "only Anacin has this formula."[39] The statement was true, because this product was *only* aspirin, while its competition included other additives. The alleged implication, however, was that Anacin had unique ingredients, not fewer.

11. *Endorsement Implication.* When consumers or celebrities endorse a product, expressing their personal satisfaction, an ad may imply to readers or viewers that they will experience the same benefits. This is frequently seen in advertisements for weight-loss products, with testimonials leading consumers to expect large weight losses.[40]

12. *Expertise Implication.* This involves falsely implying that an "expert" used in an ad has expertise that is relevant to the accompanying claim. For example, an astronaut extolling the fuel savings of an automobile engine attachment is not necessarily an expert on automobile engines.[41]

13. *Significance Implication.* This is the suggestion that a true fact mat-

---

[37]Elliot Knitwear, 59 F.T.C. 893 (1961). For other examples *see*, Thompson Medical, *supra* note 11.

[38]Ocean Spray, 80 F.T.C. 975 (1972). For other examples *see*, Chrysler, 87 F.T.C. 719 (1976); National Commission on Egg Nutrition, 88 F.T.C. 89 (1976), *modified*, National Commission on Egg Nutrition v. FTC, 570 F.2d 157 (7th Cir. 1977), *modified order*, 92 F.T.C. 848 (1978).

[39]American Home Products, *supra* note 36. *See also*, Bristol-Myers, 102 F.T.C. 21 (1982), *aff'd*, 738 F.2d 554 (2d Cir. 1984).

[40]Porter and Dietsch, 90 F.T.C. 770 (1977), modified, 605 F.2d 294 (7th Cir. 1979), modified order, 95 F.T.C. 806 (1980). For other examples *see*, Cliffdale, 103 F.T.C. 110 (1984); Dr. Barry Bricklin, 106 F.T.C. 115 (1985); Beatrice Foods, 81 F.T.C. 830 (1972).

[41]Cooper, 94 F.T.C. 674 (1979). For other examples *see*, Mattel, 79 F.T.C. 667 (1971), *modified*, 104 F.T.C. 555 (1984); Standard Brands, 97 F.T.C. 233 (1981).

ters when it does not. For example, "Gainesburgers have all the milk protein your dog needs" suggests that dogs have a special need for milk protein.[42]

14. *Product-Specific Implications.* These are implications that deal with idiosyncratic attributes of the product or service. Medicines, for example, offer the opportunity for claims implying a cure through messages that explicitly claim only to provide relief from symptoms.[43]

The pool of implication types, of course, is subject to continuing expansion, as the FTC recognizes heretofore unnoticed implied claims and as inventive advertisers create new forms of appeal. This list, however, is indicative of the forms of implied claim with which the FTC has dealt in the past.

In each of these implication types can be seen a thread of commonality: consumers are expected to *expand* the meaning of the message, to connote more than is actually claimed. About implications, Preston remarked:

Typically they play the role of *expanding* a sales message beyond its explicit content to some additional implied content which the consumer finds sensible to see being conveyed. Such widening, which creates an increase in the value of the advertised item, does not necessarily create a deceptive message about the item, although of course that is what the FTC alleges in the cases it prosecutes.[44]

The Commission view of consumer comprehension of messages can be seen in this "expansion" assumption, but its understanding of this phenomenon is limited. In particular, this agency recognizes that claims falling within this list of implication types frequently may result in deceptiveness, but it reveals no knowledge of or interest in the underlying causes or cognitive processes involved. Preston continued:

The case records state virtually nothing as to *why* consumers see added content, such knowledge being irrelevant to the evidentiary burden. If deceptive content is conveyed, it is subject to prohibition no matter how it happened, apparently, and thus the FTC recognizes no incentive to determine underlying reasons.[45]

---

[42]General Foods, 84 F.T.C. 1572 (1974). For other examples *see*, P. Lorillard v. FTC, 186 F.2d 52 (4th Cir. 1950); Carnation, 77 F.T.C. 1547 (1970).

[43]*See, e.g.*, American Home Products, 70 F.T.C. 1524 (1966), *modified*, 402 F.2d 232 (6th Cir. 1968), *modified order*, 76 F.T.C. 81 (1969), *modified*, 421 F.2d 845 (6th Cir. 1970), *modified orders*, 77 F.T.C. 726 (1970), 107 F.T.C. 427 (1986).

[44]Preston, *The Federal Trade Commission's Identification of Implications as Constituting Deceptive Advertising*, 57 CINCINNATI L. REV. 1243 (1989).

[45]*Id.*

Therefore, the FTC's general view of implications is that they differ from explicit claims because the latter are conveyed without error, whereas the former are subject to an "expansion" error. That is to say, the meaning received by a consumer is the same as the meaning sent by an ad if the claim is explicit, but the meaning received is bigger than the one sent if the claim is implied. Why this occurs has not been a pressing concern of the Commission.

The Role of Opinion Claims

We now turn to an additional area of complexity in identifying deceptiveness, involving the fact that everything discussed in this chapter to this point involves ad claims that are explicitly or impliedly *factual*. Nonfactual claims (i.e., opinion claims) are treated differently.

Background.   Opinions are a special form of claim because the advertiser, rather than stating that the product has a certain attribute, is only claiming that *in his or her opinion* the product has a given attribute. An opinion is often stated where the underlying attribute is untestable. If, for example, a breakfast cereal is claimed to be "the best tasting" it is opinion because the attribute is not a matter of physical fact, and an assertion that it exists cannot be determined to be true or false. The advertiser may actually believe it tastes better than any other cereal, but there is no way to guarantee that every buyer will feel the same. For hundreds of years the law has considered such subjective claims nonactionable. This can be seen in a case more than 300 years ago, where a British court remarked, "An action will not lie for saying, that a thing is of greater value than it is . . . because value consists in judgement and estimation, wherein men many times differ."[46] Opinions, generally, were considered by courts to be nonfraudulent.

This is not to say that all statements of opinion in a sales transaction fell outside the legally circumscribed domain. Although the literal form of an opinion might contain no content testable as true or false, it is possible that such a statement might imply to consumers an additional conveyed meaning that has factual form and can be regarded as true or false. For example, the claim about the cereal's taste might cause consumers to see conveyed a factual claim that a majority or substantial portion of cereal users are of the opinion that the cereal is the best tasting. Although the literal statement as to the cereal's taste may be merely

---

[46]Ekins v. Tresham, 1 Lev. 102, 83 Eng. Rep. 318 (1963). For a more complete review, *see* Preston *supra* note 2, at 7.

opinion, the statement that certain consumers *hold* an opinion is a statement of fact that is either true or false.[47] In this way, among others,
opinion statements may be regulated on the basis of the falsity of facts
they convey by implication. Of course those opinion statements that imply
no such false facts remain free.

To state, however, that opinions implying false facts are regulable and
those implying no false facts are not is something of an oversimplification.
This would suggest there are no exceptions to this rule of thumb, or
special categories of opinion, carved out by judicial or administrative
precedent. That is simply not the case, as the next section explains.

Puffery as Nonregulable Opinion.   In the law of the marketplace there is
an additional concern involving the treatment of opinions. It involves
the existence of *puffery* as a form of opinion statement that is assumed to
convey no factual meaning to consumers and therefore to be immune
from the possibility just discussed of prosecuting opinions for the facts
they imply. Because opinion statements appearing in marketplace communication tend generally to be interpreted as constituting puffery, the
result is that the potential for prosecuting opinions, although remaining
viable outside the marketplace, has generally been negated within.

Following logically from the FTC view of truth and falsity outlined
earlier, if a claim is nonfactual opinion and expressly stated, conveying
to consumers no more than it expressly states, the puffery exemption is
justified. The claim states no facts about the product/service, the consumer comprehends no factual claim, therefore no testable fact is involved. If the claim carries any *implications*, however, the meaning may
be expanded. If expanded to encompass nonfactually based (subjective)
statements, the FTC assumption is also justified. If, on the other hand,
the claim is expanded to make a *factual* statement the assumption behind
the puffery exclusion is contradicted. Because facts are involved, they
can be proved or disproved.

Consequently, where a claim is labeled a *puff* by the Commission, and
thereby invulnerable to legal challenge, the commissioners are suggesting
not only that no facts are expressly claimed, but that the claim makes
no factual implications. The evidence, however, suggests many claims
labeled *puffery* by the Commission and the courts convey factual implications.[48] In fact, it is arguable that many of these claims make *explicit*
factual claims.

It appears that where the Commission expects explicit claims to convey
to consumers a meaning approximately equivalent to their words, and

---

[47]*Supra* note 2, at 109.
[48]*Id.*

expects implicit claims to expand the meaning of their words, it believes claims it labels *puffery* will convey *less* than they say (i.e., they contract the meaning.)[49] However, I suggest that this perspective on puffery is an anomaly resulting from improper classification of factual implications as puffery.

The Meaning of "Puffery."[50]   Allegations have been made, like that repeated by Rotfeld and Preston:[51]

> The argument has been made that, although it states no facts literally, puffery conveys facts by implication, that these facts are false, that puffery thus deceives a substantial portion of the public by implication, and that such claims, therefore, should be prohibited.[52]

Puffery, they contend, is wrongfully singled out for special treatment by the law. Judges and FTC commissioners, they believe, have mistakenly assumed that puffery does not deceive. Similar arguments have appeared elsewhere.[53]

This may indeed be true if one takes the position that puffery is what the FTC says it is (i.e., that every claim deemed a "puff" in a Commission decision is in fact a puff).[54] However, if one takes the position, as I do, that puffery is what FTC *policy* says it is:

> Puffing, as we understood it, is a term frequently used to denote the exaggerations reasonably to be expected of a seller as to the degree of quality of his product, the truth or falsity of which cannot be precisely determined.[55]

Although not all FTC expressions of puffery are this complete or explicit,[56] this definition reflects the general theme repeated throughout

---

[49]Preston, *supra* note 44.

[50]For a more extensive analysis, see Richards, *A "New and Improved" View of Puffery*, an unpublished manuscript, University of Texas at Austin, Department of Advertising (1989).

[51]Rotfeld and Preston, *The Potential Impact of Research on Advertising Law*, 21 J. ADV. RES. 9 (1981).

[52]*Id.* at 10.

[53]*See, e.g.*, Rotfeld and Rotzoll, *Puffery vs. Fact Claims—Really Different?*, 1981 CURRENT ISSUES & RES. IN ADV. 85; Preston, *The FTC's Handling of Puffery and Other Selling Claims Made "By Implication"*, 5 J. BUS. RES. 155, 177 (1977); Shimp, *Do Incomplete Comparisons Mislead?*, 18 J. ADV. RES. 22, 27 (1978).

[54]*See, e.g.*, Honigwachs, *Is It Safe to Call Something Safe? The Law of Puffing in Advertising*, 6 J. PUB. POL. & MKTG. 157 (1987), for an example of an article that starts form this premise.

[55]Better Living, Inc., 54 F.T.C. 648 (1957), *aff'd*, 259 F.2d 271 (1958).

[56]*See, e.g.*, Sterling Drug, Inc., 102 F.T.C. 395 (1983), in which the Commission merely states, "Puffing claims are usually either vague or highly speculative and, therefore, incapable of being substantiated." (Citing, as an example, the claim, "Bayer works wonders.") *Id.* at 749.

FTC decisions. I suggest that this fences true puffery into a small area: (a) those claims that reasonable people do not believe to be statements of fact, *and* (b) which cannot be substantiated as a true product quality. If either the truth of the product attribute can be determined by the advertiser, *or* consumers believe it to be a statement of fact (i.e., they believe the claim is substantiated), it is not puffery. In the former instance it would clearly be true or false, and in the latter it would be an implication subject to potential regulation. Many years ago, Millstein observed, "[I]f the superlative can be objectively disproved, the Commission may not consider it mere 'trade puffing.' "[57]

Although many other claims have frequently been assumed by the FTC to fall into this category, just as they apply their "expertise" to find other claims deceptive or nondeceptive without benefit of behavioral proof,[58] the fact that truly testable claims have been so labeled without testing does not negate the limited scope of this classification. Where claims were labeled puffery in Commission hearings, but fail outside this narrow area, it is simply because the FTC staff did not prove its case: insufficient evidence was proffered to convince the Commission those are deceptive implications.[59] Consequently, puffery is not deceptive because it is not believed. Although there is a legal presumption that "opinion" is puffery, it is a rebuttable presumption.[60] If it is *believed*, it is a regulable implication, not puffery. Puffery, therefore, differs from im-

---

[57]Millstein, *The Federal Trade Commission and False Advertising*, 64 COLUM. L. REV. 439, 469 (1964).

[58]*See, e.g.*, Richards and Preston, *supra* note 19.

[59]Sterling Drug, Inc., 102 F.T.C. 395 (1983), for example, finds puffery where there is no evidence to the contrary. *Id.* at 752. However, the Commission notes that "when extrinsic evidence is presented to assist in interpreting ads, that evidence must be considered." *Id.* at 748. It is likely, therefore, that an evidentiary showing that the claim was a deceptive implication, rather than a puff, would have altered that decision. In this case, also, it is possible that the Commission conceded the puffery defense regarding one claim because it did not need this "puff" to find deceptiveness in the challenged ads. Other challenged claims in this case were found clearly deceptive.

[60]Even FTC Chairman Miller, not known for expanding the protections afforded consumers by the Commission, acknowledged that not all so-called "opinion" statements will receive unquestioned protection from prosecution:

> [T]he Commission generally will not bring advertising cases based on subjective claims (taste, feel, appearance, smell) or on correctly stated opinion claims if consumers understand the source and limitations of the opinion. Claims phrased as opinions are actionable, however, if they are not honestly held, if they misrepresent the qualifications of the holder or the basis of his opinion *or if the recipient reasonably interprets them as implied statements of fact.*

Policy Statement on Deception, in the form of a letter from Chairman Miller to Congressman Dingell, Oct. 14, 1983, appended to Cliffdale, *supra* note 40, at 181 (italics added).

plicit or explicit-evaluative claims.[61] This is a debatable point, but I believe it is the only reasonable interpretation if one is to attempt reconciling the legal presumption regarding puffery with the empirical reality that many claims *called* puffery are as deceptive as other implications.

Consumer Understandings of "Unfair" Claims

Claims charged to be "unfair" are not subject to the same requirements as those alleged to be deceptive. It is worth noting, however, that unfair claims can also be either explicit or implied. Because analysis of unfair claims focuses on injury, rather than the message conveyed, the explicit-implied distinction is less important to unfairness cases. Behavioral evidence in these cases will more appropriately concern consumer actions resulting from a claim, rather than consumer understanding or belief of the claim. That is to say, the Commission in these cases is more concerned with evidence about what people do than what they think.

FTC THEORY OF CONSUMER INFORMATION PROCESSING

In addition to revealing how the FTC tests consumer deception the foregoing policies indicate that its agency, through its vast experience with deceptive advertising, has some theoretical or quasi-theoretical ideas about how consumers are deceived. Although no formal theory has ever been expressly stated, the underpinnings of a rudimentary information-processing theory can be derived from some of these policies.

After years of writing and revising its own policy in this area, the present Commission's approach to deception is summarized in *Cliffdale*:

---

[61]Some of these authors seem to misunderstand the meaning of a legal "defense." Oliver, arguing the inherent deceptiveness of puffery, remarked, "It is probably fair to say that the FTC . . . has adopted more stringent requirements for what may be construed as legal puffery although it should be noted that the Commission continues to recognize the puffing defense." Oliver, *An Interpretation of the Attitudinal and Behavioral Effects of Puffery*, 13 J. Cons. Aff. 8, 9 (Summer 1979) (italics added). However, to recognize a legal defense does not mean to remove such claims from all attack, (i.e., that any claim appearing to be a puff is absolutely protected). It merely means that when a respondent asserts the defense of "puffery" and tenders evidence to that effect, the burden of producing evidence to the contrary falls on the FTC staff. *See*, E. W. CLEARY, McCORMICK ON EVIDENCE 2D 783, et seq. (1972). The problem is not that the defense is recognized, but that the FTC frequently fails to meet its burden of producing evidence.

. . . the Commission will find an act or practice deceptive if first, there is a representation, omission, or practice that, second, is likely to mislead consumers acting reasonably under the circumstances, and third, the representation, omission or practice is material.[62]

This remark provides an operational legal definition of deceptiveness, discussed earlier, and simultaneously implies certain elements of an underlying theory about how consumers are misled. It suggests, for instance, that both active representations and those made passively, by omission, are capable of deceiving. However, that definition in isolation leaves many questions unanswered.

The statement in *Thompson Medical*,[63] distinguishing between explicit and implied representations is a further expression of the FTC's underlying theory, suggesting a message need not be explicit to be conveyed. A message may be received beyond that which is expressly stated.

Determination that there is a "representation, omission, or practice that . . . is likely to mislead consumers"[64] necessitates evidence of what message was actually *conveyed*, for implied claims, but needs only a showing that the claim was part of the ad where it is explicit, or nearly so.[65] An undercurrent of cognitive theory can also be seen in this policy; a theory that an implied claim invokes complex information processing, expanding upon the express statements. Explicit claims, it suggests, are conveyed to consumers with little modification as they travel through the cognitive mechanisms, making it possible to measure the falsity of the message sent rather than taking the more difficult route of measuring the deceptiveness of the message received. Stated another way, express claims require less interpretation by consumers than do implied claims, giving a high probability that the express false claim conveys a false meaning.

One other expression of theory is clear in *Thompson Medical*. The Commission summarized its "legal framework" explaining that, "Whether we are looking at evidence from the ad itself, extrinsic evidence, or both, we look at the overall, net impression made by an ad to determine what messages it reasonably can be interpreted as conveying to consumers."[66] The theory-oriented assumption here is that any claim may interact with other claims in the same ad, to form a net conveyed

---

[62]*Id.* at 164–65.
[63]*Supra* note 11, at 788–89.
[64]Cliffdale, *supra* note 40, at 165.
[65]*Supra* note 11, at 788–89.
[66]*Id.*, at 790.

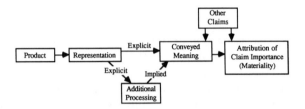

FIG. 3.3. FTC implied model of consumer information processing.

meaning that is greater than the sum of the parts: a sort of deceptiveness synergy.

Finally, looking back to the materiality requirement expressed in *Cliffdale*, that "[A] material representation, omission, act or practice involves information that is important to consumers, and, hence, likely to affect their choice of, or conduct regarding, a product,"[67] we can see one other theoretical expression. Implied, here, is the theory that a false conveyed meaning, alone, is insufficient to affect consumer purchase behavior, and that claims bear varying weights in the purchase decision process. Some claims are more important than others to this decision.

Summarizing these statements, it appears that the FTC's implied theory of information processing includes the following propositions: (a) claims can be either express or implied, (b) the cognitive processes for implied claims are more complex than for explicit claims, (c) the conveyed meaning of a claim may be affected by other claims in the ad, and (d) the probability that a deceptive claim will affect purchase behavior is a function of the importance of that claim to the purchase decision. Although this is not an exhaustive review of FTC policies, and their behavioral implications, these four points reveal the major structure and key components of the FTC view of how consumers process ad claims.

Obviously, any remark that there is *no* cognitive theory of deceptiveness is somewhat overstated. The FTC indeed implies such a theory. Reflecting the four points just enumerated, it can be represented as shown in Fig. 3.3. Attribute information originates with the product, is represented in the ad, and upon receipt by the consumer can take two different routes to culminate in a conveyed meaning. At this point meanings attached to other claims in the ad may have an impact on that conveyed meaning. The final step of this process, for FTC

---

[67]*Cliffdale, supra* note 40, at 165.

purposes, is the consumer's attribution of importance to the claim (materiality).

This theory, although useful as far as it goes, is not sufficiently developed to fully satisfy the needs of behavioral scientists attempting to judge the deceptiveness of specific ads when testifying in court,[68] or researchers trying to identify what types of formerly unsuspected claims may be deceptive. A more complete theory could help them make greater contributions to the regulatory process. The inadequately defined "additional processing," in particular, hinders identification of *why* certain claims cause deceptive inferences and limits ability to predict what claims will deceive.

SUMMARY

This chapter has reviewed the legal perspective of deceptiveness as a behavioral concept. It described the FTC's use of evidence to discover what consumers perceive, explained the Commission's justification for not using behavioral evidence in many cases, and distinguished its views regarding the behavioral aspects of puffery and unfairness. Finally, it summarized many of these regulatory policies into a coherent information processing model of how consumers are deceived.

The Commission's theory provides little insight into the cognitive processes of consumers that contribute to deception, or the problems that may arise when attempting to measure deceptiveness, nor does it significantly help behavioral researchers locate the best means of measuring deceptiveness. This theory, in effect, portrays the reasoning processes of consumers as a "black box." It offers no guidance to answer questions such as whether a disclaimer across the bottom of a television screen during a commercial is sufficient to correct any misimpression created by a spoken claim in the ad.

Although the agency's staff over the past 15 years has grown to extensively use behavioral researchers,[69] Commission decisions reveal no appreciable expansions of its theory. This condition should be unsatisfactory to researchers hoping to advance the state of advertising regulation. On the other hand, this represents a necessary starting

---

[68]The use of experts in lieu of survey evidence is a common and accepted form of evidence to identify the nature of a conveyed message before the FTC. *See*, Thompson Medical, *supra* note 11, at 790.

[69]Preston, *Researchers at the Federal Trade Commission—Peril and Promise*, 1980 CURRENT ISSUES & RES. IN ADV. 1, 3, (1980).

point for development of a more extensive theory. Regulators are unlikely to accept an approach to regulation that substantially differs from their own precedent, unless each of those differences is explained and justified.

The following chapter discusses the view behavioral scientists have of deceptiveness as a behavioral concept. That view is somewhat different from the one just presented, but is not wholly incompatible.

CHAPTER 4

Behavioral Researchers' View of Deceptiveness as a Behavioral Concept

This chapter extends the examination of deceptiveness. In chapter 2 we viewed the concept the way lawyers see it as a legal matter, and in chapter 3 it was shown how the lawyers see deceptiveness as a behavioral matter, the latter recognizing that deceptiveness properly exists within the domain of those who study behavior. Now, in this chapter, we examine the concept the way that behavioral researchers see it as a behavioral concept.

This view retains the orientation toward deceptiveness as a concept that should be prohibited by law, but it does not accept the limitations imposed on that viewpoint under its current legal treatment. The purpose is not to reject the behavioral thinking used by lawyers, but rather to introduce a wide range of concepts and analysis, drawn from behavioral theory and research, that has not heretofore been used by the lawyers. The question to be investigated is that of whether some or all of the additional analysis might reasonably be incorporated into the legal, or any other, treatment of deception.

BEHAVIORAL CONCERNS ABOUT DECEPTIVENESS

Unlike the FTC, behavioral scientists have a profound interest in *why* people are deceived. Their concerns derive not from the outcome, whether a particular ad is deceptive, but from the behavioral processes that contribute to deception (i.e., causation). They are interested, also, in the equities involved. Some feel strongly that public policy is too benign,

and that advertisers are too often permitted to lead consumers to erroneous purchases, whereas others view regulators as oppressors of free
enterprise. Their contributions are manicured to reflect their choice of
such positions. Whether the interest is equity or causation, their commonality is that both approaches tend to rely on behavioral theory and research to support their conclusions. They bring their behavioral expertise
to the dialogue regarding deceptiveness, adding new dimensions to our
potential understanding of this concept.

Growing out of these concerns, those behaviorally trained scholars
have a broader, and slightly different, perspective of deception. They
make statements and draw conclusions based on that divergent point of
view. As was indicated in chapter 2, this difference has caused some
legally erroneous remarks by behavioral researchers, but some positive
contributions have also sprung from it. Behavioral science has offered a
few new considerations as to what types of claim may cause deception
that could, and perhaps should, be considered by the FTC.

Even their errors have a positive side. They present considerations
derived from lay meanings of deception, more akin to a sense of equity
than to the law. Although inherently unrelated to the legal deceptiveness
criterion, no thorough dialogue of deception as a philosophical, ethical,
and policy concern in society would be complete if these considerations
were wholly excluded.

The next section pinpoints two concepts borne of behavioral research
that have not been, but perhaps should be, added to the FTC repertoire
regarding deceptiveness. This is followed with a section that outlines the
nonlegal factors belonging rightly to a broader view of deception as a
societal infirmity.

Equity in Regulation

Although behavioral scientists may have either consumerist or sellerist
leanings,[1] the preponderance of those addressing deceptiveness in the
scholarly literature appear to have a consumerist bias. These researchers
argue, in one manner or another, that the FTC systematically overlooks
many types of deceptive claims.

Factual Versus Evaluative Claims. It was pointed out in chapter 3 that
opinion claims are distinguished under the law by whether they are alleged
facts or nonfacts (i.e., whether they are objectively or subjectively based).

---

[1]For an extensive discussion of these classifications, and their implications, *see generally*,
I. L. PRESTON, THE GREAT AMERICAN BLOW-UP: PUFFERY IN ADVERTISING AND SELLING (1975).

The former are regulable, whereas the latter are not. Drawing that line between fact and nonfact, however, is difficult. Many behavioral researchers have taken exception to where the FTC has historically drawn that line.

Explicit factual claims are easily proved deceptive or nondeceptive, and although implied factual claims are more difficult, frequently requiring extrinsic evidence, the most troublesome evidentiary line of demarcation is the distinction between factual and nonfactual implied claims. One could speculate that because this area is so grey, and it is so difficult to prove that the line between fact and nonfact has been crossed, it would be natural for the Commission to draw that line conservatively to ensure that nonfactual claims are not accidentally regulated. This is the point of contention for many behavioral scientists, who argue that the FTC has erred too far in the direction of nonregulation, thereby creating a safe harbor for advertisers.

Shimp, a few years ago, argued:

> Regulatory agencies have generally assumed a more aggressive position in performing their statutory mandates: The FTC, for example, has expanded and intensified its efforts to regulate unfair and deceptive business practices. . . . The irony of the FTC's expanded regulatory activity is that there probably has not been any significant diminution in the extent of advertising deception. What has occurred instead is that *blatant deception has been replaced with subtle forms*. Regulatory pressure has likely led advertisers to resort to less discernible forms of advertising misrepresentation as a means of avoiding FTC detection.[2]

His argument is that advertisers are taking refuge in this safe harbor, which he followed with an argument that the FTC must begin to confront these subtle forms of deceptiveness:

---

[2]Shimp, *Social Psychological (Mis)Representations in Television Advertising*, 13 J. CONS. AFF. 28, 28-29 (1979) (italics added). Even one FTC Commissioner has speculated this may be the consequence of the Commission's regulatory efforts:

> The present public policy in advertising is to produce truth and honesty. An interesting question is whether the existence of that policy is pushing advertising away from direct product claims which can be validated and subject to the F.T.C. Act, into some of the less definable, less verifiable product claims and advertising themes including this kind of psychological associating with individual status and anxieties. I don't think that it is completely true, but we have to remember in formulating public policy that the so-called "cure" might push people into doing things which are more objectionable than the original problem to which the "cure" was designed to be applicable.

Jones, *The Cultural and Social Impact of Advertising on American Society*, 8 OSGOODE HALL L. J. 65, 87 (1970).

Puffery is the exemplar. Advertising messages are replete with opinions, superlatives, and other means of exaggerating product quality. Not only is puffery potentially deceptive, but as a by-product of its frequent use and because of the FTC's benign neglect, two additional undesirable consequences result. First, less objective product information is provided than might otherwise be the case. . . . A second consequence of the widespread use of puffery ". . . is the prevalence of various nonpuffing misrepresentations which sellers feel they can get away with by utilizing the protective *loophole* which the puffery rule provides."[3]

Although I have argued, in chapter 3, that puffery should not be considered deceptive, this comment illustrates the focus of behavioral researchers on the fact versus nonfact dividing line.

Shimp's article concerns what he called social–psychological representations, where an advertised product attribute exists only in the consumer's social environment or mind. These are attributes not intrinsic to the product, but to the consumer that uses it. In other words, these attributes are forms of opinion that are not factually based, and are therefore considered unregulable by the FTC. These claims, according to Shimp, are deceptive and should be regulated.[4]

Holbrook called such claims "evaluative."[5] He described "factual" claims as "logical, objectively verifiable descriptions of tangible product features," and "evaluative" claims as "emotional, subjective impressions of intangible aspects of the product."[6] He is unclear whether it is the objectivity of the description or the tangibility of the attribute that governs, but the two are highly correlated. I suggest focusing on attribute tangibility because it is more directly related to the proof of falsity of consumers' impressions. I adopt Holbrook's term *evaluative* for intangible, incorporeal, product attributes. A factual claim may say "X product contains no sugar," whereas an evaluative claim might state "X product will make you sexy."

---

[3]*Id.* at 29, citing Preston, *supra* note 1, at 274.

[4]*Id.* at 33.

[5]Holbrook, *Beyond Attitude Structure: Toward the Informational Determinants of Attitude*, 15 J. MKTG. 545 (1978). Non-factual forms of appeal have been called "social-psychological," Shimp, *supra* note 2, "evaluative," Shimp and Preston, *Deceptive and Nondeceptive Consequences of Evaluative Advertising*, 45 J. MKTG. 22 (1981), "feeling," Golden and Johnson, *The Impact of Sensory Preference and Thinking Versus Feeling Appeals in Advertising Effectiveness*, 10 AD-VANCES IN CONS. RES. 203 (1983), "arbitrary," Preston, *Theories of Behavior and the Concept of Rationality in Advertising*, 17 J. COMMUNICATION 211 (1967), and "social reality," Mizerski and Settle, *The Influence of Social Character on Preference for Social Versus Objective Information in Advertising*, 16 J. MKTG. RES. 552 (1979). I use the term *evaluative* here, because it seems to be a broader and more appropriate term.

[6]Holbrook, *supra* note 5, at 547.

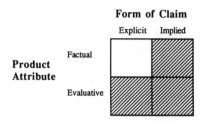

FIG. 4.1. Relationship of product claim and product attribute types.

Several articles by behavioral researchers have dealt with evaluative claims.[7] The point that each of them makes is that the FTC has regulated only factual claims, although evaluative claims may be equally deceptive. Holbrook's research even indicates that although factual messages may be most effective in favorably influencing some beliefs (at least for well-educated consumers buying relatively technical products), emotional appeals were barely distinguishable from the factual ones in their influence on the consumer.[8] This is confirmed by the work of Rotfeld and Preston.[9] In other words, it appears evaluative, nonfactual claims may be nearly as persuasive, and potentially as deceptive, as hard facts. Additional evidence suggests claims of this sort are common, if not predominant, in modern advertising.[10]

Although the FTC regulates explicit or implicit *factual* claims, these researchers argue that evaluative claims deserve equivalent regulatory attention. The Commission indicates that consumer research is useful for implied, but not explicit, claims, but the work of these researchers would suggest behavioral evidence would also be valuable for evaluative claims, whether explicit or implied (see the shaded area of Fig. 4.1).[11]

---

[7]*See, e.g.*, Shimp, *Evaluative Verbal Content and Deception in Advertising: A Review and Critical Analysis*, in R. J. HARRIS, INFORMATION PROCESSING RESEARCH IN ADVERTISING 195 (1983); Shimp and Preston, *supra* note 5; Richards and Preston, *Quantitative Research: A Dispute Resolution Process for FTC Advertising Regulation*, 40 OKLA. L. REV. 593, 597 (1987); Reed, *The Psychological Impact of TV Advertising and the Need for FTC Regulation*, 13 AM. BUS. L. J. 171 (1975); Reed and Coalson, *Eighteenth-Century Legal Doctrine Meets Twentieth-Century Marketing Techniques: F.T.C. Regulation of Emotionally Conditioning Advertising*, 11 GA. L. REV. 733 (1977).

[8]Holbrook, *supra* note 5.

[9]Rotfeld and Preston, *The Potential Impact of Research on Advertising Law*, 21 J. ADV. RES. 9, 12 (1981).

[10]Marquez, *Advertising Content: Persuasion, Information or Intimidation?*, 54 JOURNALISM Q. 482 (1977), found that twice as many ads consist of basic persuasion as those consisting of basic information. Although their interpretations differ, this data is supported by Pollay, Zaichowsky, and Fryer, *Regulation Hasn't Changed TV Ads Much!*, 57 JOURNALISM Q. 483 (1980) and Resnick and Stern, *An Analysis of the Information Content in Television Advertising*, 41 J. MKTG. 50 (1977).

[11]Figure taken from Richards and Preston, *supra* note 7.

Only claims that are both explicit and factual could effectively be assessed by the advertisement on its face.

Evaluative explicit claims are more difficult. The FTC lawyer must prove the claim was made, but with an explicit claim, again, this is no problem. However, the attorney must likewise prove that the product cannot live up to that claim. Unlike factual claims, evaluative ones have not been made subject to the "substantiation" requirements of the FTC,[12] which shift the burden of proof to the advertiser, so the burden would be on the FTC to prove the falsity of the claim. Because the product attribute concerned here is subjective, the best proof requires measuring the consumers' subjective evaluations.

This could reasonably be handled in two different ways. First, the subjective evaluations of the product attribute can be tested directly. This requires testing consumers that have tried the product, to discover whether or not they actually receive the promised subjective benefit.

Second, it might be "translated" to an implication. It could be treated as an implication that this subjective product attribute is an objective one. Does a consumer believe this attribute to be an *intrinsic* part of the product? In that case it would be *perceived* as a factual claim. If the claim cannot be verified as a fact, it would be false. If, on the other hand, the claim is perceived to be an *extrinsic* attribute, the consumer understands the alleged benefit results from influences beyond the product. Depending on their environments and their own self-images, individual consumers may or may not reap the purported extrinsic benefits. For some, the product may actually live up to the claim. The consumer who understands this attribute to be extrinsic, will not be deceived. Such claims are puffery because consumers understand they are not to be believed as fact. Clearly, in either approach, behavioral research is the best method of determining a subjective assessment of an evaluative product attribute.

Modes of Communication.   Little has appeared in the literature concerning the mode of presentation for conveying information,[13] but an increas-

---

[12]*See*, Federal Trade Commission Report, *Federal Trade Commission Policy Statement Regarding Advertising Substantiation Program*, 48 Fed. Reg. 10,471 (1983), 47 A.T.R.R. 234 (1984), appended to Thompson Medical, 104 F.T.C. 648, 839 (1984); FTC STAFF REPORT, EVOLUTION AND EVALUATION OF THE AD SUBSTANTIATION PROGRAM SINCE 1971 (Dec. 1, 1978); Comment, *Ad Substantiation Program: You Can Fool All of the People Some of the Time, But Can You Fool the FTC?*, 30 AM. U. L. REV. 429 (1981).

[13]Pollay and Mainprize remarked:

Most of the analysis [of advertisements] to date among social scientists, like the analysis by lawyers, has been focussed on the verbal component of an ad. This despite the fact that art takes up the majority of the space in the majority of print ads . . . art in print ads has been consistently increasing throughout the twentieth century,

ing body of behavioral research indicates that pictures may be as effective, or more so, as words for communicating information. This research has been interpreted to mean that the mechanisms used to comprehend and store information in human cognition are modality dependent.[14]

Although the FTC has limited its regulatory efforts primarily to verbal claims,[15] it is possible that visual illustrations can make both explicit and implicit claims, and they may be uniquely effective at conveying evaluative information.[16] It is equally likely that background music or sound effects, auditory information, in television or radio commercials are well equipped to convey information. If they are so equipped, it is also possible for them to convey *false* information.

In a remark similar to the one by Shimp cited earlier, Richards and Zakia argued, "An expressway has been developed through the archaic methods of the regulators of advertising. Claims about products are today made directly to the inner drives of the consumer, seldom parking where they can receive a ticket from the FTC patrol."[17] They state that much of today's advertising is dominated by pictorial information, which is confirmed by a later unpublished content analysis by Richards.[18] They make both legal and behavioral arguments in favor of the regulability of pictorial claims, and conclude that:

> If seventy-five percent of the communicative value of an advertisement is in its photographic content, current efforts regulating only the written (or

---

and has been accompanied by a corresponding shrinkage in verbal content, the ad copy. The art is larger, playing an evermore central role in the total communication we call an ad. It deserves closer examination.

Pollay and Mainprize, *Headlining of Visuals in Advertising: A Typology of Tactical Techniques*, 1984 PROC. OF THE AMER. ACAD. OF ADV. 24, 24 (1984).

[14] *See, e.g.*, Percy and Rossiter, *Mediating Effects of Visual and Verbal Elements in Print Advertising upon Belief, Attitude and Intention Responses*, in PERCY AND WOODSIDE, ADVERTISING AND CONSUMER PSYCHOLOGY 171 (1983); Childers, Houston, and Heckler, *Measurement of Individual Differences in Visual Versus Verbal Information Processing*, 12 J. CONS. RES. 125 (1985); Childers and Houston, *Conditions for a Picture-Superiority Effect on Consumer Memory*, 11 J. CONS. RES. 643 (1984); A. PAIVIO, IMAGERY AND VERBAL PROCESSES (1971); Shepard, *Recognition Memory for Words, Sentences, and Pictures*, 6 J. VERB. LEARNING & VERB BEHAV. 156 (1967).

[15] *But see* American Home Products, 98 F.T.C. 136, 290-91 (1981), *modified*, 695 F.2d 681 (3rd Cir. 1982), *modified orders*, 101 F.T.C. 698 (1983), 103 F.T.C. 51, 103 F.T.C. 528 (1984).

[16] Richards and Zakia, *Pictures: An Advertiser's Expressway Through FTC Regulation*, 16 GA. L. REV. 77 (1981).

[17] *Id.* at 132.

[18] Richards, *The Role of Evaluative and Pictorial Appeals in Advertising*, an unpublished manuscript (1985). An analysis of 318 ads appearing in *Time, Playboy*, and *Cosmopolitan* magazines were analyzed, finding that although 43.7% of the ads contained pictures that

spoken) word are no more than twenty-five percent efficient. If regulation is to continue at such a level of ineffectiveness, the pressing question becomes whether the fiscal expenditures currently employed to reach this end are justified. It seems quite unreasonable to funnel millions of dollars into a system of regulation that can be easily sidestepped by the high-technology methods now pervading the advertising industry.[19]

Although considerably more research is needed to determine the efficacy of pictures and sounds, behavioral evidence indicates these modes of communication may be capable of deception.[20] If this suggestion bears out, it would require another extension to current regulatory activity.

Coming from behavioral science, the desirability of exploring evaluative appeals and visual/auditory modes of expression has been raised for potential addition to regulatory efforts. Certainly, there may be other factors that could also be drawn from behavioral theory and research for FTC consideration, but the body of behavioral literature aimed at deceptiveness remains so small that few of the possible factors have yet been studied.

Nonlegal Factors Important to Society

To discuss deception as a legal concept is one thing, but to discuss it as a societal interest necessitates considering some factors that play no part in the legal deceptiveness criterion. Deception is a legal issue only as a derivative of an overriding societal concern for equity, or justice. It is an overworked truism, however, that states law and justice are two different things.

Behavioral researchers, in their legal mistakes, reveal concern for actions or responsibilities of the advertiser, a concern not adopted by the law. When Gardner referred to deception as "the *act* of deceiving by the advertiser, rather than the effect of the message on the consumer"[21] he suggested that the *source* of the message, through malice, negligence, or some other influence, serves some function in causing deception. This comports with the dictionary definitions of deception, fraud, subterfuge, trickery, and chicanery[22] that are parts of the broader social construct of

---

filled the entire ad, only 3.1% of them contained written copy that filled the entire ad. In fact, in 51% of the ads no more than *one quarter* of it was written copy.

[19]Richards and Zakia, *supra* note 16, at 133.

[20]This is suggested, e.g., by Olson and Dover, *Cognitive Effects of Deceptive Advertising*, 15 J. MKTG. RES. 29, 30 (1978).

[21]Gardner, *Deception in Advertising: A Conceptual Approach*, 39 J. MKTG. 40, 42 (Jan. 1975).

[22]WEBSTER'S NEW WORLD DICTIONARY OF AMERICAN LANGUAGE 2D COLLEGE EDITION 365 (1974).

"deceiving." Although intent is not a legal factor, it may be a justifiable social concern.

Researchers have also been concerned with the receiving end of the communication process: the consumer. When Shimp stated that "deception results only if purchase behavior is affected"[23] he implied that not only likely behavioral outcome but *actual behavioral effect* is in some way very salient to deception. After all, from a social perspective deception is nothing but "teasing" if no one is actually hurt by it. Actual purchase behavior is clearly inappropriate as a legal test of whether a claim was implied, given the prophylactic purpose of the FTC to stop misrepresentational claims before any purchase has ensued. But, although actual behavior is inconsequential to the law, it may have a place in a broader context. Therefore, actual behavioral impact of a claim should be included for this broader, nonlegal, conceptualization.

Finally, one other aspect of the consumer, attitude or *affect*, deserves insertion into this broad view of deception. Shimp and Preston[24] introduced the concept of "low-involvement" information processing to the discourse about advertising deception. For several years the predominant theories of advertising communications were "hierarchical," stating that consumer knowledge (cognition) precedes that consumer's formation of an attitude toward the product (affect), which precedes purchase behavior (the term *conation* is typically used by behavioral scientists, which includes not just the action but also the intent to act).[25] In 1965, however, Krugman posited a "low-involvement" theory, that when viewing advertising requiring only minimal cognitive activity *behavior may precede attitude*.[26]

Consumers highly involved with a product, such as where the product represents a major expense, are likely to spend time digesting information about that product, comparing its features to competing brands. This is a "high involvement" condition, where a hierarchical model would apply. Many products, however, require less cost or concern, because a "wrong" purchase decision is of minor consequence. Next time, the consumer can opt for a different brand. This small commitment suggests "low involvement."[27]

---

[23]Shimp, *supra* note 7, at 199.

[24]Shimp and Preston, *supra* note 5.

[25]*See, e.g.*, Lavidge and Steiner, *A Model for Predictive Measurement of Advertising Effectiveness*, 25 J. MKTG. 59 (1961); Palda, *The Hypothesis of a Hierarchy of Effects: A Partial Evaluation*, 3 J. MKTG. RES. 13 (1966).

[26]Krugman, *The Impact of Television Advertising: Learning Without Involvement*, 29 PUB. OPINION Q. 349 (1965).

[27]Richards, *Clearing The Air About Cigarettes: Will Advertisers' Rights Go Up In Smoke?*, 19 PAC. L. J. 1 (1987). *See, generally*, Ray, *Marketing Communication and the Hierarchy-of-Effects*, in P. CLARKE, NEW MODELS FOR MASS COMMUNICATION RESEARCH 147 (1973). *See, also*,

Shimp and Preston argued that consumers may regard evaluative claims as having limited usefulness, and that low involvement may be likely in such instances.[28] Although the difference between these two forms of involvement is predicted to occur after cognition, or conveyance of the message, making the distinction facially irrelevant to the legal deceptiveness issue, what this means for present purposes is that affect may be important to a broader view of deception. It is possible, for example, that a researcher might propose looking at attitude change caused by an alleged deceptive ad rather than at the knowledge obtained from the ad.

Affect is an improper measure for inferring illegal deceptiveness, because there are instances where a consumer may purchase products or services *before* forming attitudes about them.[29] To depend on evidence of affect would be ineffective in these "low involvement" circumstances. It would defeat the FTC's prophylactic purpose. Other problems are also to be expected when using affect as evidence. Affect is typically measured by "liking" for the product or ad, which reveals nothing about the underlying representations concerning the FTC. New methods of dissecting affectations would therefore be necessary. Also, affect may not be directly attributable to the ad, but to prior-held perceptions or evaluations. For the Commission to act on such evidence, it should be required to show a probable causal link between ad and affect. This would fall outside the current legal approach, but the researcher might argue that for reasons of equity the FTC should augment that approach (e.g., where evaluative claims are involved).

Although the FTC's deceptiveness process, including materiality, has only four components, the addition of these three behavioral components leaves us a seven-step process for the flow of information in this broader concept. That process is shown, in the hierarchical order, in Fig. 4.2.

FIG. 4.2.   Seven-step process for information flow.

Gardner, Mitchell, and Russo, *Low Involvement Strategies for Processing Advertisements*, 14 J. Adv. 4 (1985); Zaichowsky, *Measuring the Involvement Construct*, 12 J. Cons. Res. 341 (1985).

[28]Shimp and Preston, *supra* note 5, at 29.

[29]*Supra* note 26; Batra and Ray, *Advertising Situations: The Implications of Differential Involvement and Accompanying Affect Responses*, in R. J. Harris, Information Processing Research in Advertising 127 (1983); Ray, *supra* note 27; Greenwald and Leavitt, *Audience Involvement in Advertising: Four Levels*, 11 J. Cons. Res. 581 (1984).

This model represents a much more complete vision of how information travels from product attribute to eventual purchase.

FRAMEWORK OF FACTORS INVOLVED
IN THE BEHAVIORAL VIEW

It was shown in the previous section that behavioral researchers, when discussing deception, not only look at factors related to the legal criterion of deceptiveness, but look beyond those factors to others, seeing aspects that either should be added to that legal criterion or belong to some broader concept of deception. Although researchers might justifiably discuss any of those legal or nonlegal factors, or a combination of them, they should take care not to inadvertently imply that the nonlegal issues are recognized by law. As a heuristic device, to help identify which factors, or combination of them, are legally salient and which are not, a taxonomy of legal and behavioral factors fitting into this broader view is presented here.[30] From that taxonomy I separately extract those factors used to prove deceptiveness, and those directly involved in determining claim regulability.

The taxonomy is depicted in Fig. 4.3. Note that it is labeled a *global* taxonomy of deception because it includes not only those factors directly involved in FTC practice, but also those that fit into the broader range of concerns that might be discussed by researchers. The components have already been defined, but a brief definition of each follows the taxonomy. The factors most important to regulation are then isolated, to aid researchers hoping to affect public policy.

The taxonomy is composed of the several legal and behavioral factors discussed in this and the preceding chapter, grouped into five dimensions. The dimensions are crossed to show that each "block" of the taxonomy represents an intersection of other dimensions that might

---

[30]Just as behavioral researchers must understand the legal realities, it is arguable that a lawyer can not represent the best interests of a client in a deception case without some grasp of the behavioral variables of interest, because "deception" occurs only in the mind of the consumer or receiver. Although the present discussion is directed at consumer researchers, it might be equally useful for attorneys concerned with advertising deception. *See* explanation of the need for behavioral research as proof of deception in Richards and Preston, *supra* note 7. Brandt and Preston stated, "Marketers should retain lawyers who are well-trained not only in legal processes but also in interpreting and introducing behavioral data and in contracting for the research needed to produce such data." Brandt and Preston, *The Federal Trade Commission's Use of Evidence to Determine Deception*, 41 J. MKTG. 54, 61 (1977).

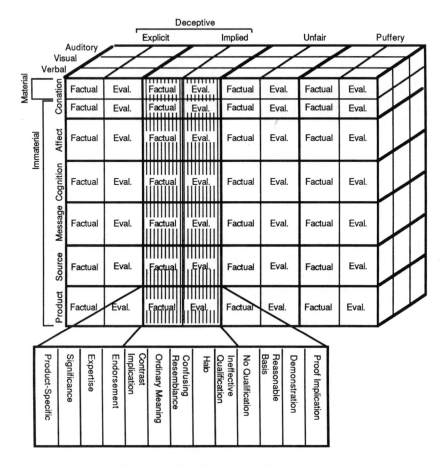

FIG. 4.3. Global taxonomy of deception.

potentially be addressed by a researcher. In the following discussion I attempt to highlight the areas of particular legal relevance.[31]

Claim-Type Dimension

This dimension depicted in Fig. 4.3, represents the primary classificatory system extant in FTC regulatory actions regarding advertisements. These four levels are, first and foremost, legal constructs. They derive from

---

[31]A word of caution, however, is in order. The various legal approaches upon which much of this discussion is premised are volatile to the extent that they are founded on contemporary legal interpretations and evidentiary biases. This, however, is not a serious problem, because the changes affecting the material discussed here have been few over the past several years.

FTC authority over "deceptive and unfair acts or practices."[32] Moving from left to right in the diagram, the regulation of these types of representation becomes more problematic.

Explicit Misrepresentation (Deceptive). Explicit misrepresentations are the most blatant forms of deceptiveness under the law, and have been defined by the FTC simply as "ones that directly state the representation at issue."[33] This is generally the most easily proved form of deceptive act, because the authorities need only show that an unmistakable claim has been made about a product/service.

Implied Misrepresentation (Deceptive). Implicit claims are ones that only *suggest* a benefit to be derived from the product/service.[34] Proof in this area is considerably more difficult; requiring consumer surveys, or less satisfying evidence such as "expert" testimony.[35]

Unfairness. It is rare that the FTC will attack a claim under this theory, because, unlike deceptiveness which focuses on "likely" injury, unfairness cases require a showing that someone has been actually and substantially harmed and could not easily have avoided the harm.[36] This typically requires no proof of a claim's meaning, because the claims are true. It is proving unscrupulous conduct and showing substantial injury that present the evidentiary hurdles.[37]

Puffery. This generally includes exaggerations or hyperbole, but puffery is defined here as those claims that (a) reasonable people do not

---

[32] 15 U.S.C. §45 (1982).

[33] Thompson Medical, 104 F.T.C. 648, 788 (1984), *aff'd*, Thompson Medical Co. v. FTC, 791 F.2d 189 (D.C. Cir. 1986).

[34] The concreteness of the suggestion can vary from claims that are very nearly explicit to those that may only be perceived by the subconscious of a consumer. Although the Commission refers to what "relatively few consumers would interpret as making a particular representation," thereby suggesting a conscious evaluation of product claims, there are strong arguments for the regulability of subconscious or subliminal appeals as well. *See, e.g.*, Richards and Zakia, *supra* note 16; Reed and Coalson, *supra* note 7; Comment, *Psychological Advertising: A New Area of FTC Regulation*, 1972 WIS. L. REV. 1097 (1972); Reed, *supra* note 7.

[35] Brandt and Preston, *supra* note 30, discusses the various forms of evidence used, and the relative frequency of application prior to 1973. *See, also, supra* note 33.

[36] International Harvester Co., 104 F.T.C. 949, 1061 (1984).

[37] *See* policy statement in the letter from the Federal Trade Commission to Senators Wendell H. Ford and John C. Danforth, December 17, 1980.

believe to be statements of fact, and (b) cannot be substantiated as a true product quality.[38]

Materiality Dimension

This is the second major factor instrumental in a legal discussion of ad regulation. The Commission's task regarding deceptive advertising is two part. First, it must decide whether the contested claim is "likely" to deceive. Then, if that likelihood is found, it must still determine whether the claim is material, or likely to affect consumer buying behavior.

Material Claims.   Materiality refers to the importance of the claim. The materiality of a particular claim depends both on the value of that product attribute to the consumer, and the relative value of other product attributes. This, essentially, represents a "weighting" process. A material representation or practice is one that is *likely* to affect a consumer's choice of or conduct regarding a product.[39]

Immaterial Claims.   Proof by a behavioral researcher that a particular form of appeal creates a mistaken impression in consumer's minds, without more, is insufficient. Researchers, ideally, should also prove this claim would be instrumental in consumer decision making. However, even the FTC is not overly dedicated to this requirement, rarely relying upon proof beyond the ad itself.

Materiality, more often than not, is presumed to exist where the FTC staff has proved deceptiveness.[40] The Commission in *International Harvester* states:

---

[38]Better Living, Inc., 54 F.T.C. 648 (1957), *aff'd*, 259 F.2d 271 (1958).

[39]*Supra* note 33. *See, also*, Moretrench Corp. v. FTC, 127 F.2d 792, 795 (2d Cir. 1942). Bockenstette v. FTC, 134 F.2d 369 (10th Cir. 1943), states:

It is not necessary. . .for the Commission to find that actual deception resulted. It is sufficient to find that the natural and probable result of the challenged practice is *to cause one to do that which he would not otherwise do.*

Id. at 371 (italics added).

[40]Chairman Miller stated, "The Commission considers certain categories of information presumptively material." He then offered a laundry list that includes: express claims; claims where seller intent is evidence; claims involving significant health or safety dangers; claims "central" to the product or service; claims involving the purpose, safety, efficacy, or cost of the product or service; and claims concerning durability, performance, warranties, or quality. Where materiality cannot be presumed, he concluded, external evidence such as consumer surveys may be required. *Policy Statement on Deception*, in the form of a letter from Chairman Miller to Congressman Dingell, Oct. 14, 1983, appended to Cliffdale, 103 F.T.C. 110, 182-3 (1984).

The Commission, however, presumes that all express claims are material, and that implied claims are material if they pertain to the central characteristics of the product, such as its safety, cost, or fitness for the purpose sold.[41]

This is perhaps more important as a means of *defense*, because any empirical showing that a challenged claim is immaterial would place on the FTC staff the burden of rebutting that evidence.[42]

Communication Process Dimension

This dimension represents legal and behavioral constructs involved in the communication process, discussed earlier.

Product.   This represents both products and services, and concerns the physical realities of the product or service.

Source.   This encompasses the sender of the message. That sender may be a manufacturer, a retailer, an advertising agency, or some other communicator. Any aspect of the source, such as advertiser *intent*, fits into this factor.

Message.   This stage concerns the structure and content of the physical advertisement, label, or package, and therefore represents the message that is sent. In contrast the following three terms concern the reception and processing of a conveyed message. In other words, they involve the message that is received.

Cognition.   This is an omnibus behavioral term for all consumer "thinking" responses that normally occur at the beginning of the purchase-decision process. It includes variables such as awareness of the advertisement, attention to it, awareness of the product, comprehension of the ad, and belief of the claim.[43]

---

[41]104 F.T.C. 949, 1057 (1984).

[42]The Commission in Thompson Medical, *supra* note 33, states:

[T]he very existence of the claim ordinarily is sufficient for us to conclude it is material. However, respondent is always free to counter this evidence either with arguments pertaining to the content of the ad itself or with extrinsic evidence.

Id. at 816, n. 45.

[43]*See, e.g.*, Ray, *supra* note 27, at 149.

Affect. This represents the "feeling" part of the purchase-decision process. Encompassed under this heading are interest in the ad or the product and conviction toward the product.[44]

Conation. Under this final umbrella term falls *intention* to act, as well as actual purchase or nonpurchase behavior (action).[45]

Product Attribute Dimension

It is this behavioral dimension that concerns the nature of the product attribute that is subject of the claim.

Factual. These are tangible product features.[46] These attributes are provable or disprovable by assessing the product itself.

Evaluative. These are intangible aspects of the product.[47] Claims about these attributes are much more difficult to prove or disprove, because they rely on subjective assessments by consumers.

Modality Dimension

This dimension has been included because it is possible, if not probable, that consumer perceptions may result in different forms of cognitive processing as the mode of the claim varies.

Verbal. Auditory or visually presented *words or text.* This is the most predominant form of regulated misrepresentation, and the most easily determinable form of claim.

Visual. Visually presented still or motion *pictures or illustrations.* A handful of FTC cases have involved visual deceptions,[48] but this remains relative virgin territory for the Commission.[49]

---

[44]*Id.* at 150.

[45]*Id.*

[46]Holbrook, *supra* note 5.

[47]*Id.*

[48]Colgate-Palmolive Co. v. FTC, 380 U.S. 374 (1965); Libbey-Owens-Ford Glass Co., 63 F.T.C. 746 (1963), *modified*, 69 F.T.C. 523 (1966); Ideal Toy Corp., 64 F.T.C. 297 (1964).

[49]Richards and Zakia, *supra* note 16.

Auditory.   Music, background sounds, and sound effects that are *not discernible words* fall into this category.[50]

AREAS OF LEGAL VALUE IN THE TAXONOMY

With this taxonomic structure as a basis, it is now possible to identify which factors are instrumental in regulation. These factors can be important in two different roles. First, some are important to prove deceptiveness and unfairness. Second, certain of them can be discussed in terms of claim regulability. All other portrayed factors have no significant value in FTC practice, and discussion of them should be avoided by researchers seeking to affect public policy.

Proving a Violation

The blocks of evidentiary value in the foregoing taxonomy vary depending on the nature of the advertising claim under scrutiny. The following explanations are offered to show how the principles discussed in the previous chapter are reflected in the shaded portions of Fig. 4.4.

Explicit–Factual.   As mentioned earlier, where claims are explicit, and refer to factual, intrinsic, product attributes, the attorney need merely show (a) the claim is present in the ad, and (b) the product cannot live-up to that claim. In Fig. 4.4 this is represented by the shaded blocks in the message and product rows.

Explicit–Evaluative.   Figure 4.4 is shaded under explicit–evaluative claims for both message and cognition. The former represents proof of the claim sent, as it did for explicit–factual claims. Cognition, however, is the appropriate measure from which to determine the product attribute. Product is also shaded, because it would still serve as a point of reference where no behavioral evidence is proffered, or where its scientific validity renders it of low probative value.

Implicit.   Behavioral (cognitive) research is preferable for *all* implied claims, to determine the message conveyed. Where the claim is about an

---

[50]Although there is very little research in this area, it is certainly possible to give a false impression as to the origin of a product by the music or background sounds used during a commercial. Alleged "subliminal" auditory sales techniques, being undiscernible by the average listener, would fall into this category.

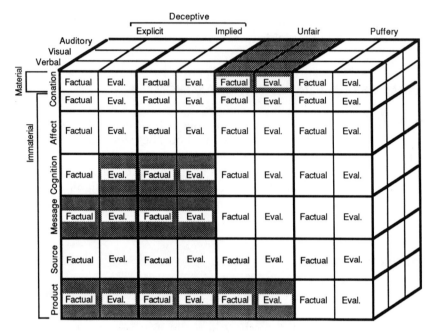

FIG. 4.4.   Area of evidentiary interest.

evaluative product attribute cognitive evidence may also be used to prove the existence or nonexistence of the product attribute.

Unfair.   Because the unfairness test espoused by the FTC requires actual and substantial injury to the consumer, only the conation stage of the taxonomy is common to each case. I have highlighted conation for that reason. On a case-specific basis, however, other forms of research might also be useful. Unfairness cases, however, are quite rare, so this should not be a major problem for consumer researchers. This rarity is evidenced in the fact that although the Commission described its unfairness policy in 1980[51] it was not applied in that form until 1984,[52] because no unfairness cases were pursued during that time.

Regulated Misrepresentation

For an ad claim to be regulable, it must be material (i.e., probable behavioral impact—conation).[53] The simple consequence of this legal limitation is that materiality exits only at the *conation stage*. Because *actual* conative

---

[51]Letter from the Federal Trade Commission to Senators Wendell H. Ford and John C. Danforth, December 17, 1980.

[52]*Supra* note 36.

[53]Cliffdale, *supra* note 40, at 165.

effect need not be shown for deceptive claims, and, conversely, *likely* conation is irrelevant to unfairness, only one-half of the conation level is shaded in both cases. We can eliminate puffery, because even material or important "puffery" will remain unfettered by regulators.

As can be seen from Fig. 4.5, the resulting areas of regulatory concern are but a small portion of the total taxonomy. Out of 168 blocks, only 18 remain significant to ultimately determine which claims are regulable.

SUMMARY

With this background into the legal and behavioral perspectives of deceptiveness as a touchstone, an information-processing theory of the deception process can be constructed. This theory is the next stage of the tripartite foundation for deception research. At this point our view of deception fully shifts to studying consumer behavior resulting from deceptive claims.

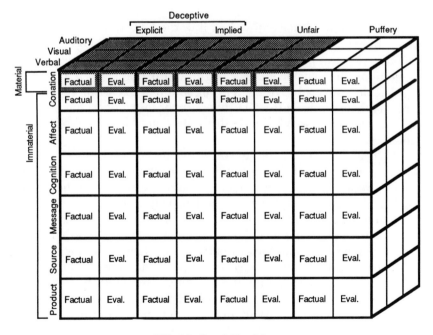

FIG. 4.5. Regulable claims.

A Proposed Theory and Definition of Deceptiveness

Up to this point we have discussed how the FTC views deception and what it does to prevent deception. We also have looked at how behavioral scientists view this public policy issue in a broader social context, and the suggestions they have made that might improve what the FTC does to regulate deceptive advertising. Throughout that discussion the primary focus has been on what the FTC has done or might do to minimize this social problem, by looking to both the law and behavioral science for guidance.

This chapter takes a somewhat different angle, looking to what behavioral researchers can do to improve their contributions to the law, beyond what they have already contributed. Because the domain of their expertise is the consumer, rather than the law, behavioral scientists are in a position to advance our understanding of the consumer's role in deception. To accomplish this goal, however, we must first develop a theory of how consumers mentally process advertising claims, that identifies the steps of that process which may contribute to deception. This chapter, therefore, presents such a theory, breaking cognition (thinking), affect (feeling), and conation (doing), identified in the previous chapter, into smaller constituent parts. With an enhanced understanding of the consumer we might better predict what types of claim are likely to deceive, thereby improving our contributions to the legal process.

Over the past two decades the FTC has revealed a progressive acquiescence to the need for behavioral evidence in its regulation proceedings.[1] During that period behavioral theories became a near integral part of the Commission's approach to regulation, being recited in FTC staff reports[2] and case decisions,[3] and became ever more popular in scholarly legal treatments of ad regulation.[4] Despite this confluence of law and behavioral theory, no general useful theory has emerged to describe how consumers attribute meanings to claims. Recalling Gardner's words, "it is not clear that the FTC, or anyone else, has an adequate understanding of deceptive advertising that is *based on a sound conceptual model* and backed with good research studies."[5] Little is known, by the FTC or by behavioral scientists, about what cognitive processes contribute

---

[1]Brandt and Preston, *The Federal Trade Commission's Use of Evidence to Determine Deception*, 41 J. MKTG. 54 (January 1977), found that prior to 1974 only 12 cases before the FTC involved surveys with some degree of scientific validity, but that the trend appeared to be toward greater use in the latter years. Preston, *Data-Free at the FTC? How the Federal Trade Commission Decides Whether Extrinsic Evidence of Deceptiveness is Required*, 24 AMER. BUS. L. J. 359, 361 (1986), determined that this presumed trend was borne-out in the years that followed.

[2]*See, e.g.*, FEDERAL TRADE COMMISSION, STAFF REPORT ON THE CIGARETTE ADVERTISING INVESTIGATION (1981); FEDERAL TRADE COMMISSION, FTC STAFF REPORT ON TELEVISION ADVERTISING TO CHILDREN (Feb. 1978).

[3]*See, e.g.*, American Home Products, 98 F.T.C. 136, 290 (1981); Firestone Tire and Rubber Co., 81 F.T.C. 398, 420 (1972); ITT Continental Baking Co., Inc., 83 F.T.C. 865, 955 (1973), *modified order*, 83 F.T.C. 1105 (1973), *modified*, ITT Continental v. FTC, 532 F.2d 207 (2d Cir. 1976), *modified order*, 90 F.T.C. 181 (1977). *See generally*, Preston, *Extrinsic Evidence in Federal Trade Commission Deceptiveness Cases*, 1987 COLUM. BUS. L. REV. 633 (1987).

[4]*See, e.g.*, Comment, *Psychological Advertising: A New Area of FTC Regulation*, 1972 WIS. L. REV. 1097; Reed, *The Psychological Impact of TV Advertising and the Need for FTC Regulation*, 13 AMER. BUS. L. J. 171 (1975); Reed and Coalson, *Eighteenth-Century Legal Doctrine Meets Twentieth-Century Marketing Techniques: F.T.C. Regulation of Emotionally Conditioning Advertising*, 11 GA. L. REV. 733 (1977); Richards and Zakia, *Pictures: An Advertiser's Expressway Through FTC Regulation*, 16 GA. L. REV. 77 (1981); Comment, *Federal Trade Commission Deceptive Advertising Regulation: A Proposal for the Use of Consumer Behavior Research*, 76 N.W.U. L. REV. 946 (1982); Barnes, *The Significance of Quantitative Evidence in Federal Trade Commission Deceptive Advertising Cases*, 46(4) LAW & CONTEMP. PROB. 25 (1983); Preston and Richards, *Consumer Miscomprehension as a Challenge to FTC Prosecutions of Deceptive Advertising*, 19 J. MARSHALL L. REV. 605 (1986); Richards, *Clearing the Air About Cigarettes: Will Advertisers' Rights Go Up in Smoke?*, 19 PAC. L. J. 1 (1987); Richards and Preston, *Quantitative Research: A Dispute Resolution Process for FTC Advertising Regulation*, 40 OKLA. L. REV. 593 (1987).

[5]Gardner, *Deception in Advertising: A Conceptual Approach*, 39 J. MKTG. 40, 40 (January 1975) (italics added). In a similar vein, Kuehl and Dyer, criticizing the case-by-case approach used in previous studies of corrective advertising, said:

> While such a focus may result in accurate statements of the implications inherent in current policies . . . it does little to advance knowledge in a normative sense . . . these studies were oriented more toward investigating existing legal theory and FTC policymaking actions vis-à-vis constructing and explaining innovative behavioral science concepts, theory, and variables related to corrective advertising.

to discrepancies between the message sent and its conveyed meaning. A theory of those processes is needed to advance our understanding of deceptive advertising.

NEED FOR A THEORY OF THE DECEPTION PROCESS

Theory, to any scientific endeavor, is fundamental. It serves as the researcher's road map, leading from cause to effect; helping identify intervening and confounding variables. This is an outgrowth of formal logic and philosophy of science. Modern science is premised primarily on deductive logic,[6] which maintains that theories generate hypotheses, which generate observations, which are then generalized to modify the theories from which they sprung.[7] Because it is impossible to absolutely prove any proposition *true*, science tends to posit theories and then try to prove them *false*.[8] Therefore, theory is a requisite of good science.

Calder and Tybout asserted:

> No amount of empirical observation allows us to induce a theory. Observation itself presupposes theory, and inductive proof is logically impossible. . . . The key features of scientific knowledge are that there have been empirical attempts to refute a theory and that the theory has performed better than any available competitors. Refutation necessarily comes from empirical data. . . . the goal of research is to expose a theory to possible refutation to give alternative theories a chance.[9]

Kuehl and Dyer, *Applications of the "Normative Belief" Technique for Measuring the Effectiveness of Deceptive and Corrective Advertisements*, 4 ADVANCES IN CONS. RES. 204, 204 (1977).

[6]Beveridge explained:

> Logicians distinguish between inductive reasoning (from particular instances to general principles, from facts to theories) and deductive reasoning (from the general to the particular, applying a theory to a particular case). In induction one starts from observed data and develops a generalization which explains the relationships between the objects observed. On the other hand, in deductive reasoning one starts from some general law and applies it to a particular instance.

W.I.B. BEVERIDGE, THE ART OF SCIENTIFIC INVESTIGATION 113 (1950). *See, also,* T. D. COOK AND D. T. CAMPBELL, QUASI-EXPERIMENTATION: DESIGN AND ANALYSIS ISSUES FOR FIELD SETTINGS 1 (1979).

[7]*See, generally,* W. L. WALLACE, THE LOGIC OF SCIENCE IN SOCIOLOGY (1971).

[8]Cook and Campbell, *supra* note 6, at 1.

[9]Calder and Tybout, *What Consumer Research Is . . .*, 14(1) J. CONS. RES. 136, 137-8 (1987).

FIG. 5.1.   Inductive FTC process.

A scientific study of deceptiveness or deception, consequently, requires deduction, and deduction requires a theory to refute.

The typical FTC procedure is primarily inductive. That process can be depicted as shown in Fig. 5.1. The FTC staff monitors advertising, and when an observed claim is suspected to be deceptive (or when a substantial number of complaints is received) a simple hypothesis is retro-fitted to support litigation.[10] If litigation is successful, challenge of similar claims in other ads is imminent, based on the tentative conclusion that all such claims are deceptive.

A deductive approach would be organized quite differently (see Fig. 5.2). In this instance, theory leads to observation rather than the reverse.[11] The hypotheses, based on theory, predict which claims will be deceptive. Predictions are not possible with the inductive mechanism of the normal regulatory process.

Suppose a certain claim does not appear deceptive to FTC staff members. Suppose, however, this particular claim actually does deceive many consumers. This is not inconceivable. FTC staff members can obtain better product information than typical consumers. They can, therefore, normally determine when they, themselves, have been deceived, but *only* if they are suspicious enough to ask for that information. And, if they are not deceived by a claim, they must decide whether it would deceive others. This is a difficult task. FTC staff members are probably among

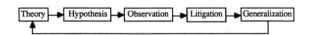

FIG. 5.2.   Deductive proposed procedure.

---

[10]*See, e.g.,* discussion in G. E. ROSDEN AND P. E. ROSDEN, THE LAW OF ADVERTISING, § 32.06 et seq. (1984).

[11]E. R. BABBIE, THE PRACTICE OF SOCIAL RESEARCH 7-9, 372-76 (1975). The deductive process is frequently depicted with the so-called "Wheel of Logic," as seen in Wallace, *supra* note 7:

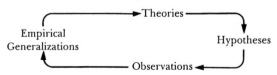

Id.

the consumers least susceptible to deception, given their training and experience. If just anyone could spot deceptive claims, then how could they be deceptive? This means in many if not most circumstances the claims do not fool them, and they are forced to *guess* whether others would be deceived. They may overlook certain subtle forms of deception. It is prediction of these subtle deceptions that is the greatest worth of deductive reasoning. The following section reviews the few attempts by consumer researchers, to date, to develop a theory of the deception process, and reveals the shortcomings of those theories.

PREVIOUS THEORIES

The only attempts to construct a formal theory of deception have been meager, and none of them, to date, has made clear any relationship of those theories to the legal deceptiveness criterion. By far the most cited theories come in the form of mathematical models, drawing on the Fishbein multiattribute attitude model.[12] For example, Gardner presented the theoretical expression shown in Fig. 5.3.[13]

Although this theoretical expression does not specifically refer to deception, Gardner justified its use by (erroneously) stating, "It should be clear that when referring to deception in advertising, we are dealing primarily with attitudes."[14] He then applied this theory to conclude:

It seems probable that deception can occur in either of two ways:
- by the promotional communication influencing the probability of a particular belief being associated with an attitude toward a brand.
- by influencing the evaluation of a particular belief associated with a brand.[15]

---

[12]Fishbein, *A Behavior Theory Approach to the Relations Between Beliefs about an Object and the Attitude Toward the Object*, in M. FISHBEIN, READINGS IN ATTITUDE THEORY AND MEASUREMENT 389 (1967). A product or service is a multi-attribute object. As Wilkie and Pessemier, *Issues In Marketing's Use of Multi-Attribute Attitude Models*, 10 J. MKTG. RES. 428 (Nov. 1973), stated, "Overall affect is posited to reflect the net resolution of an individual's cognitions (beliefs) as to the degree of which given objects possess certain attributes weighted by the salience (importance) of each attribute to the individual."

[13]Gardner, *Deception in Advertising: A Receiver Oriented Approach to Understanding*, 5(4) J. ADV. 5, 9 (1976). *See, also,* Adams, *Evaluation of An Expectancy Screening Model for Federal Trade Commission Reviews of Advertising Deception*, in J. C. MALONEY AND B. SILVERMAN, ATTITUDE RESEARCH PLAYS FOR HIGH STAKES 254 (1979).

[14]Gardner, *supra* note 13, at 9. This is somewhat misleading, since we are dealing with beliefs, i.e., individual components of attitudes, not attitudes *per se*.

[15]*Id.* at 10.

$$A_{jk} = \sum_{i=1}^{n} I_{jk} B_{ijk}$$

where   i = attribute or product characteristic
             j = brand
             k = consumer or respondent

such that: A_{jk} = consumer k's attitude score for brand j.

            I_{jk} = the importance weight given to attribute i
                 by consumer k.

            B_{ijk} = consumer k's belief as to the extent to
                 which attribute i is offered by brand j.

FIG. 5.3.　Gardner's deception theory.

This model has little merit, but it identifies belief and importance weight of the attribute as the *quid pro quo* of deception and materiality, and suggests regulable misrepresentations result from the product of the two.

One shortcoming of this model is that it suggests only a means of measuring deception, through belief and importance, without illuminating what variables contribute to that result. This omission is especially important because it adds nothing to our ability to predict which claims will deceive. A second problem is that it identifies deception in lieu of deceptiveness. Gardner's real contribution is the fact that he was one of the first researchers to ask *how* consumers are deceived.

In a similar approach, Armstrong, Kendall, and Russ[16] provide that deception from a claim is as is shown in Fig. 5.4.

For the perception score, subjects were shown an ad and then presented a pre-selected set of claims. They were next asked to indicate the probability that each of those claims was made by the tested ad (conveyed meaning). The claims were then rated for how much they were believed to be true, and for how important the attribute would be in the consumer's decision to buy the product. The precise nature of the scaling was undisclosed.

This model differs from Gardner's in three important respects. First, it does not sum across all product attributes, but rather separates the deceptive tendencies of the various attributes. This is particularly important, because under the Gardner model the deceptive effect of one important attribute could be subjugated by a large number of nondeceptive attributes of minimal importance to the consumer. The Armstrong et al. model, therefore, is more in accord with the FTC approach. Gardner,

---

[16]Armstrong, Kendall, and Russ, *Applications of Consumer Information Processing Research to Public Policy Issues*, 2 COMM. RES. 232, 234 (1975).

$$D_{ijk} = P_{ijk} B_{ijk}$$

where D_{ijk} = consumer i's deception score for claim k of ad j.

          P_{ijk} = consumer i's perception score for claim k of ad j.

          B_{ijk} = respondent i's belief (or expectancy) score for claim k of ad j.

and $$D^*_{ijk} = P_{ijk} B_{ijk} W_{ijk}$$

where D^*_{ijk} = salient deception for consumer i on ad claim k of ad j, and

          W_{ijk} = the importance (salience, value) of claim k to respondent i.

FIG. 5.4.   Armstrong, Kendall, and Russ' deception theory.

himself, admitted that, "[i]t seems inappropriate to focus primary attention to A_{jk} because it reflects the multiplication of weights and their respective beliefs which are summed."[17] It is true the FTC does not determine deceptiveness of a single claim out of context, but from the total impression caused by the ad.[18] As can be seen in the implied FTC theory presented in chapter 3, that does not mean the effects of all claims should be summed, but rather that there is a possible interaction of claims impinging on interpretation of consumers' attribute-based beliefs.

Second, Armstrong et al. substitute D_{ijk}^* (salient deception) for A_{jk} (attitude). Attitude as a measure of deception suggests an affective component directed at the product/service as a whole, which, as mentioned in the last chapter, is difficult to reconcile with advertising theories that place affect after purchase.[19] Deception must occur, if at all, before purchase, so attitude is an inappropriate measure of deceptiveness.

Finally, this model adds "perception" to its calculation of deception. Consequently, one contributing variable notably absent in Gardner's model is added, accounting for at least part of the reason *why* certain claims create deceptive beliefs. However, because this is a measure of conveyed meaning, it would be more appropriate to call this *comprehen-*

---

[17]Gardner, *supra* note 13, at 10.

[18]Thompson Medical, 104 F.T.C. 648, 790 (1984), *aff'd*, Thompson Medical Co. v. FTC, 791 F.2d 189 (D.C. Cir. 1986).

[19]*See, e.g.*, Krugman, *The Impact of Television Advertising: Learning Without Involvement*, 29 PUB. OPIN. Q. 349 (1965).

sion.[20] Unfortunately, like Gardner's model, the focus is on deception without indicating how that relates to the legal deceptiveness criterion.

Although a mathematical representation is seductive, it can also be misleading. It is no more than a research nicety to imply that "perception" is something capable of being multiplied. A consumer's perceptions are not strictly quantifiable; they are categorical at best. A consumer can perceive a claim to mean the advertised product is "big" or "green" or that it will perform some function, but there is no meaningful way to assign numbers to those perceptions so that they can be multiplied. The mathematical model is merely for operational convenience.

Additionally, although identification of perception (comprehension) as part of the process is valuable, it should not be multiplied by belief because the two variables are confounded. A "belief" score necessarily incorporates the effect of "perception," as they use the term. If consumers are uncertain a claim was made, their belief of that claim will probably be lower than if they were positive the claim was made. The two variables interact. To then multiply the two is to introduce the effect of perception twice, exaggerating its effect!

Finally, both mathematical models require multiplying belief and importance. Multiplication of any two variables requires ratio scaling of both, and neither of these is a ratio variable: both are ordinal. Multiplication of nonratio scales is common in multi-attribute attitude discussions, and it carries a sense of conceptual accuracy. However, operationally, especially in a legal setting, it presents some very real obstructions. Those inaccuracies present little difficulty to theoreticians, but they are unworkable as evidence in court. If a scientist, acting as an expert witness in an FTC hearing, was to offer such a theory to explain his or her conclusions on the deceptiveness of a claim, opposing counsel could easily destroy the scientist's credibility by pointing to this significant problem.

Another theory is in the form of an iconic model, by Armstrong and Russ,[21] two authors of the prior model. Essentially, this model is a pictographic representation of that previous mathematical model (see Fig. 5.5). This appears to be the most satisfying model of the three.

The problems with the mathematical models made this iconic model the superior theoretical expression. However, even this model is of little utility to a researcher attempting to hypothesize what forms of claim are

---

[20]J. JACOBY AND W. D. HOYER, THE COMPREHENSION AND MISCOMPREHENSION OF PRINT COMMUNICATIONS: AN INVESTIGATION OF MASS MEDIA MAGAZINES 32 (1987). Note, also, that Jacoby and Hoyer referred to this concept more specifically as "communication beliefs," i.e., the probability with which consumers believe the claim was made. *Id.* at 17. *See, also,* Preston and Richards, *supra* note 4.

[21]Armstrong and Russ, *Detecting Deception in Advertising*, 23 MSU BUS. TOPICS 21, 24 (1975).

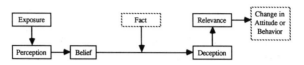

FIG. 5.5.   Armstrong and Russ' deception theory.

inherently deceptive, if one believes that behavioral variables other than comprehension play a role in the consumer's belief.

The last available theory, more complete than its predecessors, was presented by Shimp and Preston.[22] This conception incorporates variables not addressed by the simpler theories, and avoids most of the pitfalls identified in those theories. They explain that where deception occurs:

1. The claim is *attended* to by the consumer,
2. The claim (or implication therefrom) *affects beliefs*,
3. The claim (or implication therefrom) is *important*,
4. The important claim (or implication therefrom) becomes represented in *long-term memory*,
5. The claim (or implication therefrom) is *objectively false*, and
6. *Behavior* is influenced as a result of either the deceptive claim or the implication derived from the claim.[23]

Like the preceding model, these researchers incorporate belief and claim importance, although they miss comprehension. They go farther in other areas, however, by adding attention, long-term memory, objective falsity, and effect on behavior.

"Attention" is certainly an appropriate addition, as a condition precedent to belief. If consumers pay no attention to a given claim, it will be difficult for them to form a belief about that claim.[24]

The inclusion of long-term memory (LTM) is valuable. Even deceived consumers cannot act on that misconception if they have no representations of that claim in memory when making their purchase decisions. From a practical standpoint, of course, it may often be difficult or even impossible to determine whether a specific belief is represented in LTM,

---

[22]Shimp and Preston, *Deceptive and Nondeceptive Consequences of Evaluative Advertising*, 45 J. MKTG. 22 (Winter 1981).

[23]*Id.* at 25. *See, also*, Shimp, *Evaluative Verbal Content and Deception in Advertising: A Review and Critical Analysis*, in R. J. HARRIS, INFORMATION PROCESSING RESEARCH IN ADVERTISING 195, 199 (1983).

[24]*See models in* J. P. PETER AND J. C. OLSON, CONSUMER BEHAVIOR: MARKETING STRATEGY PERSPECTIVES 51 (1987); K. A. LONGMAN, ADVERTISING 255 (1971); J. Jacoby and W. D. Hoyer, *supra* note 20, at 37.

such as those resulting in a "sleeper" effect.[25] It is important to remember the representation in LTM resulting from a deceptive claim may not be recall of the claim itself, but of some consequence of that deceptive belief such as negative affect toward the product. Therefore, although this component is important to a theory of deception, the allegation by Shimp and Preston that the belief must be "represented" in LTM should not be taken to mean *recall* of that belief.

The addition of "objective falsity" is likewise advantageous. This gives a point of comparison for the obtained beliefs not heretofore presented. This, however, is somewhat narrow, and does not account for objectively true claims that have no substantiating basis, which is an area regulated by the FTC as deceptive.[26]

Finally, they add a provision that consumer behavior must be affected by the deceptive claim. When regarding regulable deceptiveness this is, quite clearly, erroneous. As discussed earlier, behavior need not be altered by the claim for it to be regulable.[27] But, these researchers, unlike their predecessors, clearly and specifically state they are *not* defining the legal construct.

Although this last theory comes much closer to a useful conception, it is also too abbreviated and contains certain inadequacies, like excluding comprehension and not accommodating the legal deceptiveness standard. However, this theory, along with the FTC's apparent theory of consumer behavior, can serve as bases for a more complete theory.

A PROPOSED MODEL

In constructing this theoretical model, I have the luxury of using insights from those preceding theoreticians. At the same time the model should be composed with cognizance of the FTC perspective, to ensure regulatory applicability of any resulting research. This process of integration permits both an extention to variables not considered in prior models and a more stringent specification of how those variables relate to one another.

---

[25] *See, e.g.*, Percy, *Some Questions on the Validity of Recall Testing as a Measure of Advertising Effectiveness*, 1978 CURRENT ISSUES & RES. IN ADV. 121; Moore and Hutchinson, *The Effects of Ad Affect on Advertising Effectiveness*, 10 ADVANCES IN CONS. RES. 526 (1983).

[26] *See*, Preston, *Description and Analysis of FTC Order Provisions Resulting from References in Advertising to Tests or Surveys*, 14 PEPPERDINE L. REV. 229, 252 (1987); Note, *The F.T.C. Advertising Substantiation Exclusionary Rule*, 27 AM. U. L. REV. 76 (1977); *FTC Policy Statement Regarding Advertising Substantiation*, 48 Fed. Reg. 10471 (1983), reprinted as appendix in Thompson Medical, 104 F.T.C. 648, 839 (1984).

[27] The "materiality" requirement demands only a likelihood that the claim would affect conduct regarding the product. Cliffdale, 103 F.T.C. 110, 165 (1984).

The theoretical model presented here (see Fig. 5.6) has several components, but they are distilled into three separate levels. Level A represents product and message. At this level the true product/service attributes are discoverable. The "objective falsity" touchstone referred to by Shimp and Preston can be assessed here, as can any lack of substantiation for a claim. The outcome of this level (the claim) can be compared to those "facts" to assess the facial validity of the claim (falsity). At Level B are components attributable to consumer cognition. The comprehension step of this level can be compared to the product/service attributes of Level A for discrepancies between fact and the message received (the typical measure of deceptiveness). The belief step can be compared to the product/service attribute of Level A to find actual deception.

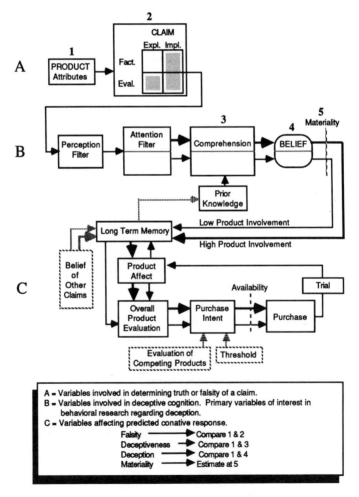

FIG. 5.6. Model of the deception process.

Level C consists of both affect and conation. These components are unnecessary to determine deceptiveness, and so are conceptually uninteresting to normal regulatory activities. However, inasmuch as we must predict the effect of claims on conation (materiality), these parts are essential to a more complete theory of the whole deception process. It is through the potential confounds in Level C that we must attempt to forecast effect on behavior.

Levels A and B differ from Level C in another important respect: *They are at different levels of analysis.* Consumers' purchase decisions are seldom, if ever, formed on the sole basis of a single claim about a product/service attribute. Each advertisement contains multiple factual or evaluative claims, most products are promoted by multiple ads, and most products are subject to competition and competitors' advertising. A plethora of claims, therefore, may play a role in the purchase decision, including those from interpersonal communications with friends and acquaintances. Consequently, Levels A and B focus on the conveyance and cognitive processing at the individual claim level of analysis, whereas Level C concerns the composite effects of all claims bearing upon purchase behavior.

Each of the levels are discussed here. The components are explained, and their roles in the deception process are more fully explained.

Level A: Product and Claim

Objective Truth. At this level come determinations of the true features or attributes of a product or service. This is the "input" to the system, and any finding of deceptiveness is predicated upon the "output" diverging significantly from the input.

Substantiation. At this level issues of "substantiation" also arise.[28] Where the ad states or implies the advertiser has a reasonable basis for a claim, the advertiser can be liable for deceptiveness if no reasonable basis exists. Level B, involving consumer perceptions, might become an additional issue where the ad merely *implies* existence of tests or surveys as substantiation,[29] but it is here all affirmative claims that "tests prove" a product attribute are ultimately resolved.

---

[28]*See generally, Federal Trade Commission Policy Statement Regarding Advertising Substantiation Program,* 48 Fed Reg 10471 (1983), 47 A.T.R.R. 234 (1984), appended to Thompson Medical, 104 F.T.C. 648, 839 (1984); Comment, *Ad Substantiation Program: You Can Fool All of the People Some of the Time But Can You Fool the FTC?,* 30 Am. U. L. Rev. 429 (1981).

[29]*See,* Preston, *supra* note 26.

Factual–Explicit Claims. Finally, at this level explicit factual claims would be assessed by the FTC, without regard for consumer perceptions.[30] The model reflects that practice (note that the factual–explicit claim is unshaded) and offers no recommendation for change. The Commission's assumption that unequivocal false statements of fact are "likely to deceive" can be empirically tested, but the FTC's position seems theoretically reasonable. Although there is undoubtedly potential for inaccuracy in this assumption, the variance inherent in this approach is probably much less than in a system of empirical testing, and it is especially doubtful that any marginal benefit from behavioral assessment could overcome its cost.

Level B: Cognitive Response

This second level is the most important to consumer researchers. It represents cognitive responses of a consumer to an *individual claim* in the ad under scrutiny, and all constituent components of cognition salient to deceptiveness. I submit that most future theoretical developments concerning deception should be at this level of the model. It is particularly important to note Level B concerns processing of an individual claim. Assessment of the product/service as a whole becomes important only later.

Seven elements are presented:

1. Perception Filter,
2. Attention Filter,
3. Comprehension,
4. Prior Knowledge,
5. Belief,
6. Materiality, and
7. Product Involvement.

A model with greater detail and more steps is certainly possible, but unnecessary and superfluous to the present purpose. For example,

---

[30]"Express claims are ones that directly state the representation at issue. Because the message is stated unequivocally, it is reasonable to interpret the ads as intending to make the claim." *Supra* note 18, at 788. This technique is also used where the claim is implied but very nearly explicit. *Id.* at 789.

Broadbent,[31] Norman,[32] and Treisman[33] have each presented different complex models of attention, but there is still no consensus on how attention works. Consequently, the model presented here reduces these into just perception and attention filters, which conforms adequately to all three concepts of attention. This model also echos the essential structure of several general models of the advertising process.[34]

The seven steps are discussed here. Accompanying the explanation of each variable, where appropriate, are examples of previous research fitting that variable and suggestions for additional research.

Perception Filter. *Perception*, as used here, deals with the sensory process, or what enters the consumer's "sensory register."[35] This sensory store is a form of memory, and is practically unlimited in the amount of information it can hold, but the information must be within the sensory field and can be stored for only about one quarter of a second. Where an ad claim or part of it is not seen or heard, it cannot be processed by the consumer. Factors like speed of presentation, size of stimulus, volume, and even motion may all contribute to inadequate processing of a message, as can personal characteristics like faulty vision or hearing. If not perceived, a claim cannot be comprehended or believed. Perception acts as a filter, potentially attenuating all or part of an ad claim, inhibiting conveyance of its meaning.

The implications of this step of the model on deceptiveness may not be readily apparent. To illustrate its importance, we might question the adequacy of a small Surgeon General's Warning at the bottom of a large billboard promoting cigarettes.[36] If the warning is too small to be read by a person with normal vision moving at highway speeds, it will not be perceived. Consequently, consumers will receive insufficient warning of health hazards, potentially deceiving them about the safety of cigarettes.

The only research to seriously address perception as a potential cause of deceptiveness is the body of literature concerned with "subliminal"

---

[31]D. E. BROADBENT, PERCEPTION AND COMMUNICATION (1958).

[32]Norman, *Toward a Theory of Memory and Attention*, 75 PSYCHOL. REV. 522 (1968).

[33]Treisman, *Verbal Cues, Language and Meaning in Selective Attention*, 77 AMER. J. PSYCHOL. 215 (1964).

[34]*See, e.g.*, Preston and Thorson, *The Expanded Association Model: Keeping the Hierarchy Concept Alive*, 24 J. ADV. RES. 59 (1984); K. A. LONGMAN, ADVERTISING 255 (1971). Longman's model, for instance, includes EXPOSURE → ATTENTION → COMPREHENSION → BELIEF → MOTIVATION → ACTION.

[35]Atkinson and Shiffrin, *Human Memory: A Proposed System and Its Control Processes*, in K. W. SPENCE AND J. J. SPENCE, ADVANCES IN THE PSYCHOLOGY OF LEARNING AND MOTIVATION RESEARCH AND THEORY 2D (1968).

[36]Richards, *supra* note 4.

appeals.[37] This research suggests claims may be perceived by the preconscious even though it is not consciously perceived. Unfortunately, little other deceptiveness research has dealt with perception. The greatest need for additional work is regarding disclaimers, health warnings, and other affirmative disclosures in television commercials and on billboards where perceptual fields and exposure time are limited.

Attention Filter. By way of definition, William James stated nearly a century ago:

> Every one knows what attention is. It is the taking possession by the mind, in clear and vivid form, of one out of what seem several simultaneously possible objects or trains of thought. Focalization, concentration, of consciousness are of its essence. It implies withdrawal from some things in order to deal effectively with others.[38]

This variable consists of stimulus recognition, choice of elements to process, and storage in short-term memory.

Only a small portion of what is perceived is actually processed, and what is processed depends on the ad elements to which consumers attend.[39] Although the senses can (depending on perceptual limitations) very briefly store all or a large part of an ad, Sperling found that a person's "span of apprehension," the number of items recalled from a brief exposure to a group of stimuli, was only about four to five elements.[40] Even where information from an ad claim successfully passes through the perception filter, it stands a significant risk of attenuation by the attention filter.

Although Gardner did not account for this element in his mathematical model, he recognized it plays a vital role in forming a belief from a deceptive claim:

---

[37]*See, e.g.*, Moore, *Subliminal Advertising: What You See Is What You Get*, 46 J. MKTG. 38 (1982); W.B. KEY, SUBLIMINAL SEDUCTION (1973); W. B. KEY, MEDIA SEXPLOITATION (1976); Richards and Zakia, *supra* note 4, at 118; Goodkin and Phillips, *The Subconscious Taken Captive: A Social, Ethical and Legal Analysis of Subliminal Communication Technology*, 54 S. CAL. L. REV. 1077 (1981); Kramer, *Judicial Recognition and Control of New Media Techniques: In Search of the "Subliminal Tort*," 14 J. MARSHALL L. REV. 733 (1981).

[38]W. JAMES, THE PRINCIPLES OF PSYCHOLOGY 403-4 (1890), cited in D. A. NORMAN, MEMORY AND ATTENTION: AN INTRODUCTION TO HUMAN INFORMATION PROCESSING 2D 6 (1976). For an overview of the concepts involved in attention, see chapters 1–4 in Norman, *Id.*

[39]Preston and Thorson, *supra* note 34, include this in their model, under the rubric "Ad Elements Awareness."

[40]Sperling, *The Information Available in Brief Visual Presentations*, 74(11) PSYCHOL. MONOGRAPHS (1960).

[I]t is clear that all stimuli do not enter into the individual's view of the world. . . . Advertisers are well aware it is necessary to get the attention of the receiver before the message can be categorized. . . . Personal factors such as span of apprehension, mental set, emotions and wants operate in a manner such that the number of objects that can be perceived vary from moment to moment and from individual to individual. These personal factors also result in receivers being selectively sensitized to stimulus objects and furthermore often resulting in the distortion of various stimuli so that they "fit" the personal factors of the receiver.[41]

Several potential threats to accurate comprehension may occur at this stage. If viewing a picture immediately prior to viewing an ad causes consumers to attend to the ad's illustration rather than its text, this "modality priming"[42] may prevent consumers from receiving text-based information vital to proper understanding. If bright colors or large elements of the ad divert attention away from crucial material, a structural interference may result. Mechanical features such as layout, headline, and illustration may direct viewer attention to one part of an ad, and away from others. Ad complexity may present too much information for consumers to process under normal viewing conditions.[43] Placement of the ad in a given context may direct attention toward certain ad elements at the expense of others. For example, positioning in a desert a billboard that depicts a beach scene may cause people to look at the picture rather than the text. These are all attentional factors in the deception process. If attention is directed away from information important to the purchase decision, consumers may premise that decision on incomplete information, and thereby be deceived.

A few studies bearing on the role of attention in regulation, deserve mention. Shimp, Dyer, and Divita studied effects of "premiums" in ads directed at children.[44] The FTC had alleged, in part, that:

The very purpose of the premium advertisement is to focus the child's attention on a factor that is almost always completely irrelevant to merits

---

[41]Gardner, *supra* note 13, at 6.

[42]*See,* Johnston and Dark, *Selective Attention,* 37 ANN. REV. PSYCHOL. 43, 46 (1986).

[43]Recognizing this problem, Maloney, *Is Advertising Believability Really Important?*, 27(4) J. MKTG. 1 (1963), stated:

In trying to fill his advertisements with more and more information about his product or service, the advertiser can easily diminish his chances of leaving a clear, unitary impression of his product or service in the consumer's mind.

Id. at 5.

[44]Shimp, Dyer, and Divita, *An Experimental Test of the Harmful Effects of Premium-Oriented Commercials on Children,* 3 J. CONS. RES. 1 (1976).

of the principal product, thereby greatly increasing the likelihood that the child's response to the ad will reflect confusion.[45]

The charge, therefore, was that perceived importance of the premium would cause children to selectively attend to the premium information to the exclusion of product attribute information. Resulting comprehension about product attributes, consequently, would be based on inadequate and therefore inaccurate information. Attention is a causal variable for deceptiveness in such situations, though this case alleged "unfairness." However, these researchers did not find support for the FTC's argument, upon comparing recognition of product attributes in experimental and control groups.[46]

In the same general line of thought, Scammon addressed the effects of comparative claims in ads.[47] Although she did not provide an answer, she suggested comparative ads may divert consumer attention to irrelevant product attributes.[48]

Morris and Millstein looked at effects of varied formats for precautionary notices in drug ads.[49] Although this study was not directed at deception, efficacy of informational notices in ads has implications for deceptiveness (e.g., affirmative disclosures mandated by the FTC).[50] A portion of their findings indicated risk information in bold typeface was marginally superior to a normal typeface for communicating health dangers, but the use of subtitled warnings on television commercials, combined with auditory announcements, proved less efficacious than fully integrating the information into the commercials. Bold print apparently diverted the attention of some viewers, but the formats used for television were insufficient to attract attention away from the primary ad message.[51] For example, a commercial promoting an over-the-counter drug may

---

[45]*Id.* at 2.

[46]*Id.* at 6. They concluded, "A relatively short presentation of a premium object in a commercial will not interfere with children's processing of product information and, perhaps, might even encourage children to rehearse and retain product information so that it may provide the basis for more acceptable purchase urgings to parents, and thereby the desired premium object may be obtained." *Id.* at 7.

[47]Scammon, *Comparative Advertising: A Reexamination of the Issues*, 12 J. Cons. Aff. 381 (1978).

[48]*Id.* at 389.

[49]Morris and Millstein, *Drug Advertising to Consumers: Effects of Formats for Magazine and Television Advertisements*, 39 Food, Drug & Cosmetic L. J. 497 (1984).

[50]Wilkie reviewed the use of affirmative disclosure requirements by the FTC from 1970-77. Wilkie, *Affirmative Disclosure: Perspectives on FTC Orders*, 1 J. Mktg. & Pub. Pol. 95 (1982). *See, also,* Wilkie, *Affirmative Disclosures at the FTC: Objectives for the Remedy and Outcomes of Past Orders*, 4 J. Pub. Pol. & Mktg. 91 (1985); Wilkie, *Affirmative Disclosure at the FTC: Strategic Dimensions*, 5 J. Pub. Pol. & Mktg. 123 (1986).

[51]Morris and Millstein, *supra* note 34, at 503.

cause consumers to overlook a notice about dangerous side effects by printing that notice across the bottom of the screen, thereby deceiving them.

Consequently, attention may be a greater factor in the deception process for television advertising than for print in some circumstances. At least it illustrates the importance of attention to understanding of how deception occurs. Cohen concluded, "Thus, 'full disclosure' cannot be a completely effective control mechanism when its main purpose is to protect the consumer from using a particular product or service, for the consumer may simply ignore these disclosures."[52]

Attention, like perception, has been all but ignored in deceptiveness literature. All of the attentional factors previously listed, including modality priming and structural interference, deserve further research. Unlike perception, this variable holds *many* threats to accurate comprehension. Any ad that implies one claim and disclaims it elsewhere, is potentially deceptive if consumers can have their attention diverted away from the disclaimer.

Comprehension and Prior Knowledge.   Comprehension is the typical dependent measure used to assess deceptiveness (likelihood of deception) in FTC proceedings.[53] *Prior knowledge* equates roughly to Preston and Thorson's *prior perception.*[54]

Comprehension is conceptualized as a workspace in the mind.[55] It is defined as "the act of grasping with the intellect; understanding."[56] It receives incoming data and searches prior knowledge for related information to aid in categorizing the new data. Peter and Olson remarked:

---

[52]Cohen, *The Federal Trade Commission and the Regulation of Advertising in the Consumer Interest,* 33 J. MKTG. 40, 42 (1969).

[53]*See generally,* Preston and Richards, *supra* note 4.

[54]This is only a rough equivalent. Preston and Thorson, *supra* note 34. Garfinkel argued:

Clearly, it is extremely important to notice the significance of prior knowledge to a treatment of deception. Such knowledge (e.g., whether it is safe to use a product, whether a specific characteristic is unique to a product, that it is necessary to spend money to get that product) will determine whether or not the audience makes a particular deduction that may later on be proven to be true or false.

Garfinkel, *A Pragmatic Approach to Truth in Advertising,* in R. J. HARRIS, INFORMATION PROCESSING RESEARCH IN ADVERTISING 175, 178 (1983).

[55]Wyer and Srull, in their human information-processing model, separate comprehension into several constituent parts, of which a "work space" is only a temporary repository, of input information and prior knowledge, associated with several processing units that work on that data. This has been greatly simplified in the present model. Wyer and Srull, *Human Cognition in Its Social Context,* 93 PSYCHOL. REV. 322, 324 (1986).

[56]Jacoby and Hoyer, *supra* note 20, at 2.

Differences in interpretation occur because meanings are heavily influenced by each consumer's prior knowledge structures. Because no two consumers have had exactly the same past experiences, they will not have identical knowledge structures in memory and are not likely to form identical meanings.[57]

Prior knowledge, therefore, includes both semantic and episodic long-term memory.[58] At this stage, long-term memory is represented only in terms of retrieval. The encoding function is placed in the next level of the model.

Under the umbrella of these two components lie several additional opportunities for inaccurate processing of product information. The two previous stages acted to *filter* potentially valuable information from being processed, which could lead to deceptive impressions, but it is here that *meaning* is attached to the data that passed through those filters.[59] This meaning derives from access to semantic and episodic memory. As a result, factors like semantic priming,[60] where preceding a message with a different message can affect the meaning attached to the later one, might create deceptiveness. A semantic *interference* is also possible. For example, suppose a photograph of a tiny diamond, greatly enlarged to make its facets visible, is qualified with a clear statement that the diamond is .25 pt. in size. In this case the enlarged photograph might interfere with the qualifying statement, causing consumers to read it as .25 ct., thereby deceiving them to expect a much larger diamond!

Harris, Dubitsky, and Bruno empirically tested comprehension of ad implications.[61] Their results suggested "subjects draw inferences from the claims in ads and remember them as facts."[62] If we take as correct the FTC "theory" that explicit and implicit claims involve different cognitive processes it appears the two separate routes may merge at comprehension, after drawing upon prior knowledge to derive meaning. Beyond this point it may be possible to treat the two as equivalent. If so, we could

---

[57]Peter and Olson, *supra* note 24, at 77.

[58]Tulving, *Episodic and Semantic Memory*, in E. TULVING AND W. DONALDSON, ORGANIZATION OF MEMORY 385 (1972).

[59]A very recent opus by Jacoby and Hoyer, *supra* note 20, does a credible job of ferreting out the intricacies of comprehension, offering the most comprehensive and insightful view to date of the relationship between comprehension and mediated communications.

[60]*See, e.g.*, Carr, McCauley, Sperber, and Parmelee, *Words, Pictures, and Priming: On Semantic Activation, Conscious Identification, and the Automaticity of Information Processing*, 8 J. EXPER. PSYCHOL.: HUMAN PERCEPT. & PERFORM. 757 (1982).

[61]Harris, Dubitsky, and Bruno, *Psycholinguistic Studies of Misleading Advertising*, in R. J. HARRIS, INFORMATION PROCESSING RESEARCH IN ADVERTISING 241 (1983).

[62]*Id.* at 246.

expect deceptiveness of explicit and implied claims to be equivalent, as well as the resulting *belief.*

Shimp studied a specific type of implication he termed "incomplete comparisons."[63] These claims use comparatives, such as "better" or "cleaner," but without a comparative referent. Shimp hypothesized a claim like "Brand X is better" would imply a referent to consumers. Although explicit use of that referent might be regulable as deceptive, these implications have historically been treated as nondeceptive. He conducted an experiment, testing that hypothesis, and concluded "receivers of an ad comprehend (or read into the ad, so to speak) more than what is actually contained,"[64] and concluded receivers of ads are conditioned to expect grandiose claims from sellers.[65] This tendency of consumers to expand the meaning of what is stated in a claim is confirmed through an earlier study by Preston and Scharbach.[66] This tends to substantiate the FTC's assumption that implied claims are expanded by consumers.

Studies that dealt more specifically with prior knowledge are those involving "corrective" advertising.[67] Corrective ads are intended to *correct* the residual effects of deceptive claims (i.e., to rectify inaccuracies retained in prior knowledge).

Semenik studied the relative effectiveness of corrective ads versus the traditional FTC remedy of ordering advertisers to "cease and desist" from making the deceptive claims.[68] He found corrective ads were, in fact, better equipped to dispel preconceptions resident in long-term memory.[69] This suggests prior knowledge can be modified more quickly with the *presence* of accurate information than with the *absence* of deceptive information.

Perhaps more important, to the advertiser, Semenik discovered it is possible to formulate effective corrections without a carry-over that adversely impacts overall brand image.[70] This threat of comingling a change of prior knowledge attached to one attribute with prior knowl-

---

[63]Shimp, *Do Incomplete Comparisons Mislead?*, 18 J. ADV. RES. 21 (Dec. 1978).

[64]*Id.* at 24.

[65]*Id.* at 26.

[66]Preston and Scharbach, *Advertising: More Than Meets the Eye?*, 11 J. ADV. RES. 19 (June 1971).

[67]Warner-Lambert Co. v. FTC, 562 F.2d 749 (D.C. Cir. 1977), *cert. denied*, 435 U.S. 950 (1978). *See, also,* Faller, *The Federal Trade Commission Has the Power to Order Corrective Advertising in Cases Where the Lingering Effect of Prior Advertising Influences Future Consumer Decisions*, 47 U. CIN. L. REV. 129 (1978); Cornfeld, *A New Approach to an Old Remedy: Corrective Advertising and the Federal Trade Commission*, 6 IOWA L. REV. 639 (1976).

[68]Semenik, *Corrective Advertising: An Experimental Evaluation of Alternative Television Messages*, 9(3) J. ADV. 21 (1980).

[69]*Id.* at 26.

[70]*Id.* at 30.

edge of other attributes, or of the product as a whole, has serious policy implications and deserves additional research. Craswell argued that regulatory remedies are not intended to be punitive, but they frequently may have halo effects that negatively affect perception of nondeceptive product claims.[71] Semenik's results tend to indicate legally mandated corrective claims can be accomplished without these adverse effects.

Hunt addressed a similar question in an earlier study.[72] He looked specifically at the potential role of inoculation theory in corrective advertising. An advertiser anticipating government-mandated corrective claims, he suggested, could use two separate strategies to minimize adverse carry-over from corrective claims. The advertisers could either bolster supportive claims (supportive inoculation) hoping to strengthen consumer beliefs so these consumers would later minimize their belief of the corrections, or consumers could be given small doses of the refutational arguments in advance of corrections to "disprove" them (refutational inoculation), lending consumers the means to resist later corrective claims.[73] He discovered refutational inoculation was effective where corrections occurred that made explicit attacks about the deceptive claim.[74] This suggests, in our present context, that belief of corrective messages can be reduced by preparing ready counterarguments in the prior knowledge of consumers. As shown in the model, these counterarguments are drawn out of storage in prior knowledge and first affect comprehension, making consumers aware of information disputing the corrective message, which then minimizes belief of the correction. Again, prior knowledge plays an important role in deceptiveness.

Because comprehension occurs at this stage, *mis*comprehension also resides here. Preston and Richards examined the role of miscomprehension in prosecuting deceptiveness.[75] Their aim was to defuse efforts to convince regulators that much of what is termed *deceptive* is only miscomprehension, unavoidable by advertisers.[76] The work of Jacoby, Hoyer, and Sheluga,[77] had threatened to add fuel to that fire, but Preston and Richards found several fallacies in that work and note that miscomprehension can be intentionally *induced* by advertisers. The recommenda-

---

[71]Craswell, *Interpreting Deceptive Advertising*, 65 B. U. L. Rev. 660 (1985).

[72]Hunt, *Effects of Corrective Advertising*, 13 J. Adv. Res. 15 (Oct. 1973).

[73]*Id.* at 16.

[74]*Id.* at 20.

[75]Preston and Richards, *supra* note 4.

[76]As Garfinkel recognized, " 'Deception' seems to place the burden of the problem on the shoulders of the advertiser and 'misunderstanding' places it on the shoulders of the consumer." Garfinkel, *supra* note 54, at 191.

[77]J. Jacoby, W. D. Hoyer, and D. A. Sheluga, Miscomprehension of Televised Communications (1980).

tion implied by Jacoby et al. was for the FTC to establish a miscomprehension threshold typical to all communications. and to prosecute only advertisers that demonstrably exceed that threshold. Preston and Richards explained Jacoby's position as follows:

> With people typically erring in an average of thirty percent of instances, deceptiveness should properly be attributed only to messages for which the observed miscomprehension figure is higher than thirty percent. If the figure in a given instance, for example, were forty percent, then only the last ten percent should be defined as deceptive.[78]

However, they countered that advertisers are professional communicators, capable of phrasing claims so as to manipulate miscomprehension levels of those claims. They stated, "Suggesting that miscomprehensions may be induced implies that they may be avoided. That, in turn, implies that advertising claims may be written in alternative ways that produce higher or lower rates of miscomprehension."[79] Therefore, the terms *ineradicable miscomprehension* and *eradicable miscomprehension* were proposed to distinguish the lowest possible level of miscomprehension for a claim from higher levels for which advertisers should be held responsible.

There remains the problem of how to deal with ineradicable miscomprehension. This is "noise" inherent in communication. In a follow-up study, Preston and Richards[80] found it possible to rewrite most implied claims to reduce miscomprehension, substantiating the presence of eradicable miscomprehension, but they also found some miscomprehension was not eliminated.[81]

This means, ideally, a researcher should subtract (or control for) errors in comprehension attributable to ineradicable miscomprehension, when calculating deceptiveness of a claim. Researchers should take care not to confound these two dependent variables.

Unfortunately, we know relatively little about how consumers construct or attach meaning to a statement or illustration. Most consumer

---

[78]Preston and Richards, *supra* note 4, at 609.

[79]*Id.* at 630. Pollay, many years ago, charged that "advertisers are able to take advantage of the consumer's readiness to misperceive, as in the case where ads are deceptive despite the literal truthfulness of each statement." Pollay, *Deceptive Advertising and Consumer Behavior: A Case for Legislative and Judicial Reform*, 17 KAN. L. REV. 625, 632 (1969). Hunt stated, "If professionally created communications lead to or reinforce erroneous beliefs, it is the professional's fault and responsibility." Hunt, *Decision Points in FTC Deceptive Advertising Matters*, 6 J. ADV. 28, 28 (1977).

[80]Preston and Richards, *Consumer Miscomprehension and Deceptive Advertising: A Response to Professor Craswell*, 68 B. U. L. REV. 431 (1988).

[81]Another notable finding was that there was no detrimental carry-over from the rewritten claims, to adversely affect comprehension of other claims in the ads.

research deals with ad *efficacy*, without significant concern for consumer *understanding*.[82] Comprehension is central to deceptiveness, however, and demands greater attention if the sophistication of deceptiveness research is to progress.

Belief. Once a claim is comprehended it may or may not be believed. If a false impression of the product attribute is believed, then actual deception has occurred, but if not believed there is no deception. Belief, therefore, is the appropriate dependent measure of actual deception. The legal criterion, deceptiveness, is the prediction ("likelihood") that inaccurate belief will ensue.

Although I borrow from multiattribute attitude theories, positing belief as a condition precedent to affect, I use *belief* in a more narrow sense. Multiattribute theories conceptualize belief as a multidimensional state.[83] Level B involves processing of a single claim, and we are concerned only with deception, so belief, here, is the consumer's evaluation of the *probability* a claimed attribute is associated with the product or service advertised.[84]

Like the other components, belief is affected in several ways. "Source credibility" circumscribes much of this area, because believability of an endorser, or of the publication in which the ad appears, may affect consumer belief of the ad.[85] Also, several claims in an ad may interact, with a single outlandish claim casting doubt on the believability of other claims in the ad. Prior knowledge about manufacturer, product, or other ads for the product may affect first comprehension and then belief of the claim. Finally, the ad's composition may have an effect, with an amateurish layout and design making the claim less believable. Maloney stated, "[B]elievability is not an inherent property of the advertisement

---

[82]Mick, *Consumer Research and Semiotics: Exploring the Morphology of Signs, Symbols, and Significance*, 13 J. CONS. RES. 196 (1986), remarked:

> [U]ntil recently consumer behavior theorists and researchers have tended to treat signs and their functions indiscriminately. Moreover, meaning has been merely ancillary to the inquiry on fundamental human behavior we choose artificially to call consumer behavior.

Id. at 205.

[83]*See, generally*, M. FISHBEIN AND I. AJZEN, BELIEF, ATTITUDE, INTENTION AND BEHAVIOR: AN INTRODUCTION TO THEORY AND RESEARCH (1975).

[84]Jacoby, Hoyer, and Sheluga referred to these as "Referent Beliefs." Jacoby, Hoyer, and Sheluga, *supra* note 77, at 17.

[85]Armstrong and Russ, *supra* note 21, at 28. *See also*, R. E. PETTY AND J. T. CACIOPPO, ATTITUDES AND PERSUASION: CLASSIC AND CONTEMPORARY APPROACHES 62 (1983).

itself. . . . Different people have different expectations about the trust-worthiness of various kinds of advertising. . . ."[86]

Belief was a central factor in the famous "sandpaper shaving" case, *Colgate Palmolive Co. v. FTC.*[87] This case concerned use of a "mock-up" in a television commercial for Colgate's *Rapid Shave* product. The commercial's announcer declared, "To prove *Rapid Shave*'s super-mois-turizing power, we put it right from the can on this tough, dry sandpaper. It was apply . . . soak . . . and off in a stroke,"[88] demonstrating the shaving cream's softening power by shaving sandpaper. Unknown to the audi-ence, however, this demonstration substituted, for the sandpaper, plexi-glass covered with sand. This was done because, although the cream *would* shave sandpaper, the required soaking time was about 80 minutes. Consumers, consequently, were given a false impression that they were seeing an actual test or demonstration. The Court focused its analysis on the implied representation that viewers were seeing the test for them-selves. It determined use of this undisclosed prop was deceptive and warned that, hereafter:

> [W]hen the commercial not only makes a claim, but also invites the viewer to rely on his own perception, for demonstration proof of the claim, the respondent will be aware that the use of undisclosed props in strategic places might be a material deception.[89]

The deceptiveness here was not the express claim that Rapid Shave could shave sandpaper, because it could. The Court might have focused on the implication that Rapid Shave could not only shave sandpaper but shave it during the short time of the commercial, although this is not what concerned the Court. Instead, it was concerned that viewers would think they were seeing the actual test; an implied claim that did not directly concern any product attribute, but involved manipulating con-sumer *belief* of a true claim. The Court apparently assumed consumers, thinking they were experiencing an actual test, would be more inclined to believe the claim (i.e., props or mock-ups could be used to modify belief). No empirical data was forthcoming, however, to dispute or sub-stantiate this assumption.

Some previous deception research applies to belief, and much of the literature regarding persuasion rightfully impacts our understanding of this area.[90] Olson and Dover looked specifically at posttrial belief

---

[86]Maloney, *Is Advertising Believability Really Important?*, 27(4) J. MKTG. 1, 1 (1963).
[87]380 U.S. 374 (1965).
[88]*Id.*
[89]*Id.*
[90]*See, e.g.,* Petty and Cacioppo, *supra* note 85.

persistence.[91] Although trial, as shown in the model, is not directly relevant to deception, it was used to assess the *consequences* of deceptive messages. These researchers showed subjects three mock ads extolling a coffee brand's lack of bitter taste, and then had them taste the coffee. The coffee was purposely made quite strong, to give it a more bitter taste. Pretrial and posttrial beliefs about its bitterness were then compared. Their conclusions stated:

> [T]rial experience with the product did not entirely eliminate the influence of the deception. Even after actually tasting the somewhat bitter coffee, the exposed group still had a stronger belief than the substantiation group that the coffee was "not-at-all-bitter" . . . and a weaker belief that the coffee was "fairly bitter". . . .[92]

Once a belief is formed, it seems, it is not easily changed. Even actual experience conflicting with that belief may not correct the detrimental effects of a misrepresentation. Any public policy measure designed to prevent or remove deception would probably, therefore, work best if gauged to effect a change before a belief has been formed.

"Puffery" research should also fall under belief.[93] As discussed earlier, puffery is not deceptive because it is not believed. If it is likely to be *believed*, it is a regulable implication, not puffery.

An aspect of puffery deserving greater attention is whether actual statements of opinion are frequently believed by consumers to be statements of fact. True puffery may be nonexistent in the real world. Another issue of belief deserving attention is whether consumers, even though they recognize a claim to be opinion, are abnormally swayed by a manufacturer's opinion vis à vis the opinions of others (i.e., a source credibility effect). Consumers may see the manufacturer as an expert of sorts, whose opinion is more credible. This might give large and particularly credible manufacturers an unfair advantage over smaller and less well-known sellers, and may create a deceptive implication that there is a substantiating basis for that opinion.

Clearly, there are many other aspects of belief, as it pertains to deceptiveness, needing research. One issue of particular importance, given the FTC's dependence on comprehension as the predictor of deception, is

---

[91]Olson and Dover, *Cognitive Effects of Deceptive Advertising*, 15 J. MKTG. RES. 29 (Feb. 1978).

[92]*Id.* at 36.

[93]Rotfeld and Rotzoll, *Puffery vs. Fact Claims—Really Different?*, 1981 CURRENT ISSUES & RES. IN ADV. 85; Rotfeld and Preston, *The Potential Impact of Research on Advertising Law*, 21 J. ADV. RES. 9 (1981); Preston, *The FTC's Handling of Puffery and Other Selling Claims Made "By Implication"*, 5 J. BUS. RES. 155, 177 (1977).

whether there is a significant difference between comprehension and belief of ad claims. Comprehension might prove a poor estimator of belief, making the traditional FTC approach a questionable measure of deceptiveness. This issue is addressed in chapter 7.

Materiality. As mentioned earlier, materiality refers to the importance of the claimed product attribute to the consumer's purchase behavior.[94] Arguably, this step could be placed earlier in the model, because a claim's materiality may affect whether or not consumers attend to that claim, but that early attribution of importance is qualitatively different from legally significant materiality, and is too far removed from the purchase decision to be a good predictor of conation. Early determination of salience may, but need not, be based on the same criteria as judgment of claim importance after its substance is comprehended. It is the weight of claims *as understood* (and as potentially believed) that is of legal concern. Early valuation of the claim may be behaviorally consequential, however, so it is presented in the model as differing levels of product involvement.

Materiality is depicted as a filter between the second and third levels of the model. Even where consumers hold demonstrably false beliefs, if the attribute is of low importance to their purchase decision its impact on that decision will be insignificant. Materiality, therefore, attenuates the relationship between belief and purchase, making it pivotal in predicting conative effects of deception.

To estimate the impact of a claim, we must predict all the way through the cognitive mechanism. To do this we make two separate estimations. First is deceptiveness, which estimates the difference between true attribute qualities and consumer belief. The second, materiality, estimates the correlation between belief and behavior (see Fig. 5.7). From a practical standpoint, estimating deceptiveness is easier than estimating materiality, with any degree of accuracy. Although we can empirically assess product attributes and comprehension to predict deceptiveness, I show in the

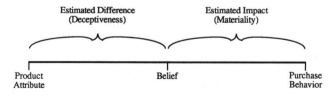

FIG. 5.7.   Estimating the effects of a claim.

---

[94]Materiality is highly correlated with the concept of "relevance," discussed by behavioral researchers in the context of the purchase decision process. Peter and Olson, *supra*, note 24, at 242.

discussion of Level C that there are numerous confounding variables making it unwise to measure purchase or purchase intent to assess its correlation with belief. Not only does the materiality component of the model illustrate its filtering, or weighting, function, this seems the most practical point in the process to estimate that correlation.

A researcher, therefore, should measure at three points in the process in order to estimate the deceptive effects of an ad claim: (a) product attribute, (b) comprehension, and (c) materiality. Of course, to implement the FTC's prophylactic purpose we normally attempt to intercept the process before belief has been formed. In that instance materiality would be measured before, not after, belief. Later, I explain how it is possible to measure belief rather than comprehension to estimate deception, without violating FTC purpose, thereby placing materiality after belief, as depicted in the model.

Academic researchers, like the FTC, have concentrated on deceptiveness/deception to the exclusion of materiality. No research is available on this part of the regulatory standard. That does not mean, however, that none is needed. Research is needed to determine the validity of materiality, at this early point in the process, as a predictor of purchase behavior. Seldom does the FTC empirically assess materiality, relying primarily on presumptions of claim importance, so a relatively accurate predictor may be needed to sway this agency toward empirical measures. Self-report is the natural starting point to test materiality, but research should also consider means of improving test methodology in this area. The Commission should be encouraged to abandon presumptions in favor of empirical evidence, but that evidence must be more accurate than those presumptions before that argument will be convincing. This issue, too, is considered in chapter 7.

Involvement. As mentioned in chapter 4, advertising researchers frequently distinguish messages by the "involvement" of consumers with the purchase decision, message, or product at issue.[95] Where involvement is low consumers are said to employ an information-processing mechanism distinguishable from that used for high-involvement situations.[96] Because the route taken by information will theoretically vary, that distinction is reflected in the model by separate lines of different widths.

A major problem with involvement is that it is a somewhat amorphous concept, with a plethora of meanings.[97] In the present context involve-

---

[95]Zaichowsky, *Measuring the Involvement Construct*, 12 J. Cons. Res. 341, 341 (1985).

[96]*See, generally,* Gardner, Mitchell, and Russo, *Low Involvement Strategies for Processing Advertisements*, 14 J. Adv. 4 (1985).

[97]Laurent and Kapferer, *Measuring Consumer Involvement Profiles*, 22 J. Mktg. Res. 41, 41 (Feb. 1985).

ment is not defined to include media or message involvement; only involvement with the product. Specifically, involvement is consumer interest in, or cognitive arousal invoked by, a particular product or product class. In high involvement, the consumer's expected benefit of a correct purchase decision, the cost of a wrong decision, or both, is greater than in low involvement. Therefore, product (or service) price is frequently, although not always, a crucial factor in involvement. Borrowing from Smith and Swinyard, "low involvement products are normally inexpensive and thus trial may be the favored information source."[98]

Involvement's role in message cognitions is still uncertain. It is reasonable to assume there may be substantial differences (e.g., at the preconscious level) in how consumers form beliefs at varying involvement levels. Therefore, a line is drawn through the center of attention filter, comprehension, and belief, to permit later refinements of this model, separating high and low involvement. Although involvement is represented as dichotomous, however, it is more likely continuous, with different products invoking multiple shades of arousal.

At this time, involvement can be expected to have at least two notable effects in the model. First, as Smith and Swinyard implied in the previous statement, the product purchase threshold may be lower if involvement is lower. Therefore, lower levels of belief and/or materiality may be necessary to cause purchase where involvement is low. Where the cost of an erroneous decision is minimal, the benefits derived need not be as great, and consumers may more readily purchase the product even though they have some doubts about the veracity of a claim. Second, as discussed earlier, product affect is expected to precede purchase in high involvement, but follow purchase where involvement is low.[99] These differences are reflected by diverging paths in Level C.

Shimp and Preston[100] took the view that low involvement "is a cognitive state characteristic of a situation where consumers are inattentive due to insufficient arousal to process information."[101] Accordingly, these two different levels of attention are shown in the model by a separation of involvement routes at the attention filter.[102] These writers further

---

[98]Smith and Swinyard, *Information Response Models: An Integrated Approach*, 46 J. MKTG. 81, 89 (1982).

[99]Smith and Swinyard, *id.* at 83.

[100]Shimp and Preston, *supra* note 22.

[101]*Id.* at 29.

[102]These researchers distinguish, further, two types of low involvement. One is the more traditional "attention-limited" form, where less perceived or anticipated goal-satisfying value of a message results in lower involvement in processing the ad as a whole. The second type is "strategy-limited," where consumers attend to nonbrand ad content in preference to brand-specific information. Both of these types represent a division of processing mechanisms beginning at attention. *Id.* at 29. *See, also*, Gardner, Mitchell, and Russo, *Chronometric*

proposed that factual and evaluative claims can be characterized by their levels of involvement, hence separating modes of processing applied to each:

> The essential point is that consumers learn from experience which product categories and brands provide useful information. Assuming that consumers regard evaluative advertising content as having limited usefulness, attention- or strategy-limited low involvement likely will be engaged upon exposure to ads for those products or brands which are known as being predominantly evaluative in nature, since involvement is a function of prior expectations concerning the usefulness (goal-satisfying value) of impending information.[103]

The factualness/evaluativeness of a claim, therefore, may directly affect involvement, which controls attention and results in two different processing channels. These two channels potentially may cause different response mechanisms at later information-processing stages. It is important to separate high and low involvement at each later stage until empirical research can determine their characteristics at each step.[104]

If evaluative claims do fall under the rubric of low-involvement processing, numerous studies about information content in ads may affect our view of low-involvement processing. Shimp explored evaluative claims he called "social-psychological representations" (SPRs).[105] He suggested such claims are deceptive, because they are subjective and receivers must introduce their own expectations to obtain meaning from these claims.[106] His content analysis of 243 commercials, containing 1,450 assertions, revealed that 58.5% were SPRs. A content analysis by Pollay, Zaichkowsky, and Fryer supports this conclusion.[107] They found 48% of 615 commercials contained no more than one factual piece of information,

---

Analysis: An Introduction and an Application to Low Involvement Perception of Advertisements, 5 ADVANCES IN CONS. RES. 581 (1978).

[103]Id. at 29. In low involvement, consumers may attend more to non-brand cues. Petty and Cacioppo, Central and Peripheral Routes to Persuasion: Application to Advertising, in L. PERCY AND A. WOODSIDE, ADVERTISING AND CONSUMER PSYCHOLOGY 3 (1983).

[104]Under Petty and Cacioppo's Elaboration Likelihood Model, structural ad components or cues may be processed through a route different from that used by highly involving information. These cues may require little attention to be effectively integrated into our comprehension of other claims in the ad. See, generally, Petty and Cacioppo supra note 103.

[105]Shimp, Social Psychological (Mis)Representations in Television Advertising, 13 J. CONS. AFF. 28 (Summer 1979).

[106]Id. at 33.

[107]Pollay, Zaichkowsky, and Fryer, Regulation Hasn't Changed TV Ads Much!, 57 JOURNALISM Q. 438 (Autumn 1980). See, also, Marquez, Advertising Content: Persuasion, Information or Intimidation?, 54 JOURNALISM Q. 482 (Autumn 1977), which found 65.7% of 600 print ads relied more on persuasion than information.

presumably relying primarily on evaluative claims for their impacts. To understand the deceptive potential of more than half the claims made in modern ads, it appears we must have a better understanding of how low and high involvement differ. Therefore, both routes to deception deserve attention by researchers.

Level C: Purchase Decision (Product Level)

Where the prior levels concerned a single claim, this level integrates all claims from an ad into the *overall* evaluation of the product or service. A single claim may not affect or determine the purchase decision, which is why we must have a measure of materiality. At this level, all claims contribute their various weights to the purchase decision.

Long-Term Memory.   Comprehension and belief are encoded from working memory to long-term memory (LTM) at this step. LTM is also hypothesized to act as a buffer between product affect (Do I like this product?) and comprehension (What does the claim mean?).

LTM is, effectively, a permanent store of world knowledge and life experiences.[108] It is from this memory that product information is retrieved at the time a purchase decision is consummated. The information retrieved may be an imperfect representation of the information encoded,[109] which may increase or decrease the effects of earlier deceptions, especially because LTM integrates belief of this claim with stored beliefs from other claims and sources (e.g., interpersonal communications).

Product Affect.   This is attitude toward the product as a whole. As previously indicated, product affect precedes purchase only in high involvement, permitting attitude toward the product to enhance or detract from purchase intent. For low-involving products, affect follows purchase and trial, affecting only repurchase decisions and post-purchase contentedness.

A reverse arrow in the model leads from affect to LTM. This is added to explain effects of certain preconscious processes, where comprehension and belief are effectively bypassed to cause a greater impact on affect

---

[108]Atkinson and Shiffrin, *Human Memory: A Proposed System and its Control Processes*, in K. W. SPENCE AND J. T. SPENCE, ADVANCES IN THE PSYCHOLOGY OF LEARNING AND MOTIVATION RESEARCH AND THEORY, VOL. 2 (1968).

[109]*See, e.g.*, Tversky and Kahneman, *Availability: A Heuristic for Judging Frequency and Probability*, 5 COGNITIVE PSYCHOL. 220 (1973).

than on its antecedents. Classical conditioning[110] and so-called "halo effects" are examples of such processes.[111]

This highlights two fallacies of measuring affect with the intent of determining materiality: (a) it incorporates all claims rather than a single questionable claim,[112] making it difficult to separate affect attributable to the claim at issue; and (b) prior to purchase it assesses only high-involvement products. Affect, therefore, is inappropriate for a test of materiality.

Overall Product Evaluation.   This component represents an integration step, where all of the feelings about the product and all of the beliefs, from whatever source, are aggregated to compose the overall product evaluation (i.e., Is it a good or bad product?).

Purchase Intent, Threshold, and Competing Products.   Purchase intent is the last step of the decision process prior to purchase. Once the consumer's overall product evaluation is formed, it becomes part of the purchase decision process. Overall product evaluation weights one side of the decision scale,[113] but potential counterweights are evaluation of compet-

---

[110]*See*, McSweeney and Bierley, *Recent Developments in Classical Conditioning*, 11 J. Cons. Res. 619 (1984); Allen and Madden, *A Closer Look at Classical Conditioning*, 12 J. Cons. Res. 301 (1985); Nord and Peter, *A Behavioral Modification Perspective on Marketing* 44 J. Mktg. 36 (1980); Bierley, McSweeney, and Vannieuwkerk, *Classical Conditioning of Preferences for Stimuli*, 12 J. Cons. Res. 316 (1985).

[111]Oliver, *An Interpretation of the Attitudinal and Behavioral Effects of Puffery*, 13(1) J. Cons. Aff. 8 (1979), declares:

[C]hanges in attitude caused by extraneous factors (e.g., social influences), conditioning, and even hypnosis frequently result in concomitant revisions in the underlying belief and evaluation levels in the absence of primary information inputs.

Id. at 12.

[112]Wilkie stated:

Brand attitudes are overall measures of like-dislike . . . and are too general to be attributed to exposures to specific messages . . . [the] measure is too aggregative for the FTC to rely upon [since] they measure consumers' net responses to previous experiences with brand usage as well as various stimuli quite distinct from advertising.

Wilkie, *Research on Counter and Corrective Advertising*, paper presented at the American Marketing Association Conference on Advertising and the Public Interest (1973), cited in Kuehl and Dyer, *supra* note 5, at 205.

[113]Bettman concluded, "The weight of evidence appears to be that attitude generally affects behavior indirectly through intentions, in accord with Fishbein and Ajzen." Bettman, *Consumer Psychology*, 37 Ann. Rev. Psychol. 257, 268 (1986).

ing products and a basal purchase threshold.[114] Where overall evaluation of another product is greater, it probably will be chosen over the one being studied. Likewise, where none of the products achieve a sufficiently high evaluation (or sufficiently low cost), it is unlikely that *any* purchase is imminent. This balancing process is represented as purchase intent.[115]

At this stage, during evaluation of competing products, prepurchase external search for additional information occurs.[116] This confounding aspect of purchase intent, inhibits accurate prediction of purchase behavior with materiality.

This illustrates the complexity of the process, and the inherent inaccuracies of predicting purchase from belief. I do not mean to suggest projection of purchase likelihood from materiality is fatally flawed, only that it is imperfect. Evaluation of competing products and purchase threshold are intervening variables representing "overhead" in the system.

Because we estimate only *likelihood* of affecting choice of, or conduct regarding, a product, we are concerned only with whether there is a significant increase in probability of affecting purchase behavior, not whether any resulting increase will *surpass* evaluation of competing products and the purchase threshold. Put another way, materiality requires we show *increased* likelihood of effect on conation resulting from the claim, not *probable* conative effect. In the former we must prove the claim a factor in purchase behavior; the latter demands we account for how much weight consumers give each competing product. If the standard was otherwise, regulability of misrepresentations would depend on product *competition*, making outright lies unregulable when products have strong competition and minor exaggerations regulable for products with virtual monopolies. Deception is, and should be, a product of a defective ad claim not of the quality of unchallenged products or services.[117]

---

[114]The threshold presented here does not attempt to delineate or specify a particular choice of integration process. This detail is theoretically uninteresting to the deception process. Consequently, various alternatives, whether multi-attribute, conjunctive, lexicographic, or other models, could fit the present model to some extent. For a review of these various models, *see* BETTMAN, AN INFORMATION PROCESSING THEORY OF CONSUMER CHOICE (1979).

[115]For an explanation of how beliefs and knowledge are integrated to form a behavioral intention, *see* Peter and Olson, *supra* note 24, at 229. *See, also,* Cohen, Miniard, and Dickson, *Information Integration: An Information Processing Perspective,* 7 ADVANCES IN CONS. RES. 161 (1980).

[116]Beatty and Smith, *External Search Effort: An Investigation Across Several Product Categories,* 14 J. CONS. RES. 83 (1987); Bloch, Sherrell, and Ridgway, *Consumer Search: An Extended Framework,* 13 J. CONS. RES. 119 (1986).

[117]This general policy of judging the merits of an ad without reference to the product's competition is reflected in the remarks of the Commission in *Sterling Drug:*

A restriction gauged by the breadth of market competition would be discriminatory, favoring products with greater competition over monopolistic products. This would pit deceptiveness regulation squarely against the First Amendment prohibition of content-based restrictions.[118] In regulation of speech, including regulation of advertising,[119] all speakers must be treated equally.[120] In other words, purchase intent is important from a theoretical perspective, but it would be an inappropriate measure of materiality because of this interaction with evaluations of competing products.

Purchase and Trial. The FTC materiality criterion does not require showing "actual" effect on purchase behavior to prove adverse impact of a claim.[121] Not only would that requirement defeat the agency's prophylactic purpose, it would have the same problem as measuring purchase intent. Such a policy would pin regulation of deceptiveness on strength of competition rather than the nature of the claim. It is important to note that even experiments aimed at simulating purchase situations to predict deceptive likelihood and materiality, while preserving the Commission's prophylactic goal, would violate this principle of independence from other products.

Implications of the Model

Choice of a Dependent Variable. I have emphasized that comprehension measures deceptiveness, and belief assesses actual deception. Indeed, comprehension is the dependent variable typically used in Commission

---

Sterling argues that its ads must also be examined in light of the advertising of its competitors to which it was attempting to respond. Although such a comparison may be helpful in interpreting advertising, it cannot excuse the failure to adequately substantiate the claims which are clearly made in Sterling's ads. Sterling is accountable for the advertising which it promulgated . . . and it cannot justify its failings by pointing to the conduct of its competitors.

Sterling Drug, Inc., 102 F.T.C. 395, 748-49 (1983). *See, also,* Chrysler, 87 F.T.C. 719, 752 (1976), at n. 43.

[118]Hudgens v. NLRB, 424 U.S. 507, 520 (1976); Virginia Pharmacy Board v. Virginia Consumer Council, 425 U.S. 748, 771 (1976).

[119]Virginia Pharmacy, *supra* note 118, at 771.

[120]*See discussion* in Richards, *supra* note 4, at 37. *See generally,* Karst, *Equality as a Central Principle in the First Amendment,* 43 U. CHI. L. REV. 20 (1975); Karst, *Why Equality Matters,* 17 GA. L. REV. 245 (1983); Tussman and tenBroek, *The Equal Protection of the Laws,* 37 CALIF. L. REV. 341 (1949).

[121]Cliffdale, *supra* note 27, at 165.

proceedings to measure "likelihood of deception," but this does not mean it is the only option, or even the best. I suggest that belief can and should be used to determine *deceptiveness*, and that this can be accomplished without violating FTC policy.

Comprehension is a poor estimator of deception if consumers understand a misleading claim but do not believe it. It reveals a *possibility* (capacity) of deceiving, but certainly not a *probability* (likelihood). Garfinkel remarked, "[D]eception would be unlikely if consumers did not believe the claims that were made in the commercial in question."[122] Wilkie asserted:

> [Beliefs] . . . represent precisely the level at which deception is presumed to occur and persist. These measures are specific to each brand attribute and reflect a consumer's expectations as to the degree that a given brand offers a particular benefit.[123]

Unless every comprehended message is also believed, which would eliminate use of humor in ads, belief is the better measure of deceptiveness. The problem, of course, is measuring belief (actual deception) without waiting for consumers to be deceived.

The FTC does not *require* testing belief: Only comprehension differing from the reality of the product attribute need be proved. Many surveys used in FTC cases ask only what the respondents saw the ad to claim, not what they believe about the true product/service attributes.[124] To ignore belief in measuring deceptiveness, however, could result in prohibiting "spoofs," where consumers *comprehend* a falsity, but do not believe it. The prediction in Fig. 5.8 can be made about the relationship of conveyed falsity and deception. As the falsity of a conveyed message increases, it causes a corresponding increase in false belief, but only to a point. As the conveyed falsity becomes more extreme beliefs will no longer increase, and at some point the message will become so outrageous that beliefs will actually diminish, until beliefs are at such a low level that they will be recognized under the law as "spoofs." Given the Commission's recent shift of the deceptiveness standard from a "capacity or tendency" to a "likelihood" it is arguable that a measure of comprehension is inadequate to meet this new standard.

Although comprehension is sufficient, measurement of a belief repre-

---

[122]Garfinkel, *supra* note 54, 191.

[123]Wilkie, *Research on Counter and Corrective Advertising*, paper presented at the American Marketing Association Conference on Advertising and the Public Interest (1973), cited in Kuehl and Dyer, *supra* note 5, at 205.

[124]In Thompson Medical, *supra* note 18, for example, respondents were asked, "What ingredient or ingredients, if any, did the commercial say Aspercreme contained?" *Id.* at 694. *See discussion* of open-end versus forced-choice questions in Preston, *supra* note 3.

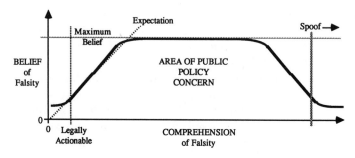

FIG. 5.8.   Relationship of belief and comprehension.

sents an improvement toward more valid evidence. And, by moving closer to the purchase action of the consumer, we improve the accuracy with which we can predict the "likelihood" that consumers would act on a misrepresentation.

Earlier deception models failed to separate comprehension from belief. This comingling of concepts may lead researchers to misinterpret their work or the work of others. For example, although Preston and Scharbach[125] studied consumer *comprehension* of ad claims, their work might easily be misinterpreted to have implications about *belief* if the two steps are not kept conceptually distinct. Preston and Scharbach presented a series of ads to subjects, in the form of news stories, business memoranda, personal letters, and ads. Subjects were then given statements, including inaccurate and logically invalid statements, and asked to indicate whether those statements were accurate or inaccurate restatements of what was stated or implied in the former message (*not* what they believed as a result of those statements). Their results indicated, "[A]dvertisements were significantly higher in acceptance of logically invalid restatements than each of the other message forms."[126] Their conclusions follow:

> The conventional wisdom on this matter is that many citizens report they are intolerant of much ad content and, therefore, discount the statements made therein. But this study appears to demonstrate expansion rather than contraction of perceived ad content—seeing more rather than seeing less—showing a certain tolerance rather than intolerance.[127]

Although they dealt only with comprehension, and made no allusion to belief, it would be easy to interpret their results to mean readers tend

---

[125]Preston and Scharbach, *Advertising: More Than Meets the Eye?*, 11 J. ADV. RES. 19 (June 1971).

[126]*Id.* at 21.

[127]*Id.* at 23.

to be more deceived by ads than other messages. This is a quantum logical jump. Consumers may expect more impressive claims in ads, expanding the comprehended meaning. Even so, this does not mean that they believe those extravagant claims. It may be at belief that consumers "discount" ad claims, understanding ads to promise the world but believing none of it!

This assumption can be seen in a study by Shimp.[128] Following a procedure resembling Preston and Scharbach's, and citing that study, he explored meanings attached to incomplete comparative statements in ads, such as "Brand X is better." He showed ads containing such claims to subjects, and followed viewing by presenting subjects with the same incomplete statements, asking them to "complete the statement as it actually appeared in the ad."[129] Shimp, by this instruction, tested what subjects comprehended the claims to mean, not what they *believed* about the product as a result of viewing the ad. They might not have believed *any* of those claims. Shimp's stated objective, nonetheless, was "to evaluate the potential misleading nature of incomplete comparatives."[130] This goal is partially fulfilled by revealing errors in information processing prior to belief, but without a showing of belief this "potential" remains remote from actual deception. Yet, in his conclusions, Shimp alleged that incomplete comparisons possess "the distinct capacity to deceive." I think it is clear in this instance that comprehension may be a rather poor predictor of deception. Although Shimp's conclusion comports with FTC practices, actual deception may be unlikely from such claims.

Although the Commission maintains, "[W]e do not go beyond likelihood to require evidence on the incidence of actual false belief,"[131] this should not be interpreted to mean belief is an *improper* measure of deceptiveness. What the Commission means is that deceptiveness *can* be stopped long before consumers have formed a belief. In fact, no consumer need yet have *looked* at the challenged ad.

It is possible to measure belief before consumers have formed beliefs, though, using experimental subjects rather than survey respondents. Deceptive belief of *consumers* is not to be confused with deceptive belief of experimental *subjects*, because those subjects are in an artificially-induced-viewing situation. Unlike most surveys, experiments permit simulation of the outside world, without waiting for the world to be affected. Measuring belief, under these circumstances, could still be preventative.

Although belief is an appropriate measure for experimental purposes,

---

[128]Shimp, *Do Incomplete Comparisons Mislead?*, 18 J. ADV. RES. 21 (Dec. 1978).
[129]*Id.* at 22.
[130]*Id.*
[131]International Harvester Co., 104 F.T.C. 949, 1056 (1984).

it is not useful in most true surveys. True surveys do not artificially induce viewing. For example, penetration or brand awareness surveys depend on normal, ecologically valid, viewing. To measure belief in such circumstances would presuppose viewing and belief formation by consumers, in direct contravention of Commission policy. This is not to say survey results would be worthless if they assessed belief. Indeed, if the survey discovered significant false belief it would indicate presence of actual deception, and the claim would clearly be regulable *if* it can be shown that the claim caused that belief. However, those surveys would be insensitive to a mere "likelihood," making them less valuable to the Commission.

FTC dependence on comprehension rather than belief thus is dictated by the methods used. Survey procedures are neither preventative, when they measure belief, nor do they typically use controls that would be necessary to separate the belief derived from the challenged claim from beliefs derived through other sources. In order to use belief for the regulation of a claim it is essential to show causation (i.e., that the false belief was the direct consequence of the challenged claim).[132] With surveys, the latest point in the process for predicting deception without serious threat of confounding influences is comprehension. With experimental approaches it would be possible to simulate actual deception, as a measure of deceptiveness, and introduce controls to allow causal inference. Jacoby and Hoyer recognized this fact:

> The regulatory agencies have adopted a less stringent approach. Instead of relying on carefully controlled experimental tests to convincingly demonstrate that an erroneous belief was due to the communication in question and nothing else, they focus on the communication's *potential* to mislead. . . . Under these circumstances, "it would follow that the appropriate research question would be 'Does the ad convey this statement?' rather than 'Do you believe this statement.' "[133]

Contrary to their implication, however, an experimental test of belief, like a survey of comprehension, would test the *potential* to mislead the public at large, but it would be a better estimation.

Where survey methods are used, comprehension is an appropriate and necessary dependent variable for testing deceptiveness. Experimental methods permit measuring belief, while still meeting FTC goals. This is

---

[132] Jacoby and Small, *The FDA Approach to Defining Misleading Advertising*, 39 J. MKTG. 65 (1972); Olson and Dover, *Cognitive Effects of Deceptive Advertising*, 15 J. MKTG. RES. 29 (1978).

[133] Jacoby and Hoyer, *supra* note 20, at 60, citing Preston, *Research on Deceptive Advertising: Commentary*, in R. J. HARRIS, INFORMATION PROCESSING RESEARCH IN ADVERTISING 289 (1983).

a better test of deceptive *likelihood*, because only credible claims will be targeted for regulation, while comprehension ignores credibility.

Placement of Affect in the Model. Putting affect outside the chain of factors bearing directly on belief, and hence deception, may at first blush seem trivial. However, this presents one potentially profound consequence. Just because information must flow through comprehension and belief steps before reaching affect does not ensure that each step will be equally affected, and this arrangement suggests that if an ad claim favorably alters product affect without significantly impacting belief, it may be possible to "trick" consumers into purchasing the product without the claim being deceptive. As inequitable as that ad may seem, it does not cause deceptiveness or deception. No false comprehension or belief exists. Such practices, if they exist, rightfully fall under "unfairness" rather than deceptiveness.

Given this premise, many forms of claim the FTC was heretofore criticized as erroneously overlooking for deceptive potential, are in fact nondeceptive. Evaluative claims, classical conditioning, and subliminal appeals might all take peripheral (low-involvement) routes to affect without substantial impact on comprehension or belief, thereby setting them outside deceptiveness. If this is the case, the FTC has not been in error for failure to regulate these claims as deceptive. It might be argued that this agency is negligent for not pursuing them under "unfairness," but that is a difficult argument under the current policy view of unfairness.

Conclusions

This section, representing the lion's share of this chapter, has presented an information-processing model to describe how consumers process deceptive ad claims. The model represents a substantial step toward a theoretical dialogue concerning deception and deceptiveness. It identifies steps of potential importance to the regulatory arena, including those suggested in earlier models and some not previously discussed in this context.

Out of this model also comes a recommendation for the point at which deceptiveness can best be measured. Although comprehension is normally the point of assessment, belief clearly offers greater face validity for measuring "likelihood of deception," but this requires experimental methods rather than surveys.

Likewise reflected in this model is the desirability of measuring materiality, in accord with FTC requirements. Without some estimate of the contribution a particular claim belief makes to overall product evaluation, it is difficult to accurately project any "likelihood" of affecting purchase behavior.

A DEFINITION

Before proceeding to a means of testing deceptiveness, it seems useful to define regulable deceptiveness from the behavioral viewpoint expressed in the model. Because an experimental method, testing belief rather than comprehension, is the better approach, this definition will apply strictly to experiments, and should not be used where survey methods are chosen.

Nearly every researcher addressing some issue in deceptive advertising creates a definition of deception. Where those definitions are strictly for operational purposes this multitude of conceptualizations is to be expected, but most are offered as behavioral interpretations of FTC policy. Without exception they fail to explain whether their intent is to define deception or deceptiveness, and they threaten to mislead readers to believe they are defining the legal criterion. To date no single definition has been adopted by consumer researchers, and this lack of agreement has borne criticism by some.[134] This criticism is not unjustified. If we cannot define it, we can hardly expect to measure it. Olson and Dover speculated:

> [A]t the time the author's study was conducted, not a single empirical investigation had been reported in which the presence of deception or its impact on consumers' behavior was measured. One likely reason for this paucity of research is the lack of a compelling conceptual and operational definition of deception in terms of its impact on the exposed consumer.[135]

Several different definitions are listed here:

Howard and Hulbert said that "advertising deception is defined as the case where a set of symbols is susceptible to two or more interpretations and one interpretation is false."[136]

---

[134]Armstrong and Russ, *supra* note 21, at 22; Armstrong, Gurol, and Russ, *Defining and Measuring Deception in Advertising: A Review and Evaluation*, 1980 CURRENT ISSUES & RES IN ADV. 17, 20 (1980); Barbour and Gardner *Deceptive Advertising: A Practical Approach to Measurement*, 11 J. ADV. 21 (1982).

[135]Olson and Dover, *Cognitive Effect of Deceptive Advertising*, 15 J. ADV. RES. 29, 29 (1978). Jacoby and Small suggested, ". . . to empirically determine whether a given advertisement is misleading, one must first have a clear definition of what constitutes having been misled." Jacoby and Small, *The FDA Approach to Defining Misleading Advertising*, 39 J. MKTG. 65, 66 (1975).

[136]HOWARD AND HULBERT, ADVERTISING AND THE PUBLIC INTEREST 24 (1973).

According to Gardner deception is as follows:

> If an advertisement (or advertising campaign) leaves the consumer with an impression(s) and/or belief(s) different from what would normally be expected if the consumer had reasonable knowledge, and that impression(s) and/or belief(s) is factually untrue or potentially misleading then deception is said to exist.[137]

Haefner said that deception "refers to the individual's ability to evaluate the 'truthfulness' of an advertisement stimulus independent of experts, such as engineers or chemists."[138]
Aaker said that:

> Conceptually, a deception is found when an advertisement is the input into the perceptual process of some audience and the output of that perceptual process (a) differs from the reality of the situation and (b) affects buying behavior to the detriment of the consumer.[139]

According to Gaeth and Heath [misleading is] "defined to be a discrepancy between the factual performance of a product and the consumer's *beliefs* generated by the advertisement."[140]
Olson and Dover said that "deception is considered to occur when consumers acquire demonstrably false beliefs as a function of exposure to an advertisement."[141]
Armstrong and Russ believed that "deception occurs when a consumer perceives and believes an advertising claim (explicit or implied) that is false, but that deception is of little concern unless the claim is relevant."[142]
And, concerning just prescription drug ads, Jacoby and Small said the following:

> A misleading prescription drug advertisement is one which causes—either through (1) its verbal content, (2) its design, structure, and/or visual artwork, or (3) the context in which it appears—at least n percent of a represen-

---

[137]Gardner, *supra* note 13, at 7; Gardner, *supra* note 5, at 42.

[138]J. E. Haefner, *The Perception of Deception in Television Advertising, An Exploratory Investigation 26,* a Ph.D. dissertation, University of Minnesota (1972).

[139]Aaker, *Deceptive Advertising,* in D. A. AAKER AND G. S. DAY, CONSUMERISM: SEARCH FOR THE CONSUMER INTEREST 2D 139 (1974).

[140]Gaeth & Heath, *The Cognitive Processing of Misleading Advertising in Young and Old Adults,* 14 J. CONS. RES. 43, 43 (June 1987).

[141]Olson and Dover, *Cognitive Effect of Deceptive Advertising,* 15 J. ADV. RES. 29, 30 (1978).

[142]Armstrong and Russ, *supra* note 21, at 24.

tative group of practicing physicians to have a common impression or belief regarding the advertised drug which is incorrect or not justified.[143]

Finally, these remarks should be compared to the legal definition given by the FTC [deceptiveness]:

> the Commission will find an act or practice deceptive if first, there is a representation, omission, or practice that, second, is likely to mislead consumers acting reasonably under the circumstances, and third, the representation, omission, or practice is material.[144]

Recurrent themes run through these definitions, but there are notable differences between them. All except Haefner's to some extent follow the model previously presented, but most omit several steps. These definitions run from the very abbreviated explanations of Olson and Dover and of Gaeth and Heath, to the more detailed specifications of Gardner and of Jacoby and Small. Only material deceptiveness, not actual deception, is important to us, but each of these definitions seems to confuse the concepts. Figure 5.9 shows a breakdown of their various components.

Inappropriate Definitions. Two of these can be dismissed as unhelpful in designing a more complete and specific behavioral definition. Haefner's approach can be eliminated as bearing no resemblance to the legal standard. His concept of deception is based on consumer perceptions of an ad's "truthfulness" rather than their beliefs about the underlying product or service.[145] In a sense, his view of deception is the *inverse* of the legal one. Where consumers disbelieve a claim, Haefner called it deceptive, but under the law a lack of belief constitutes evidence that *no* deception occurred. This is the premise behind permitting advertisers to use spoofs and puffery. Consequently, Haefner contributed nothing to our definition.

The Aaker definition is also flawed. Although parts of it are accurate, those parts are included in other definitions. It is wrong in its addition of effect on buying behavior, however, because only the *likelihood* of impact on behavior is of legal concern. It, too, can be ignored.

Legal Basis. The FTC definition is a legal construct rather than a behavioral one. As with the model, legal considerations are central to the

---

[143]Jacoby and Small, *The FDA Approach to Defining Misleading Advertising*, 39 J. MKTG. 65, 66 (1975).

[144]Cliffdale, *supra* note 27, at 165.

[145]J. E. Haefner, *The Perception of Deception in Television Advertising, An Exploratory Investigation 26*, a Ph.D. dissertation, University of Minnesota (1972).

Model	Input	Causes	Comprehension	Belief	Materiality	Comparison to Facts	Prediction	Purchase
FTC	Represent, Omission, Practice				Material	False	Likely While Acting Reasonably	
Howard/ Hulbert	Set of Symbols		Two or More Interpretations					
Gardner	Ad		Impression and/or Belief			Untrue or Misleading. Differs from Expectation wit Knowledge		
Haefner	Ad					Evaluate Truthfulness Independent of Experts		
Aaker	Ad			Output		Differs From Reality		Affects Buying Behavior
Gaeth/ Heath	Ad			Belief		Differs From Fact		
Olson/ Dover	Ad			Beliefs		Demonstrably False		
Armst./ Russ	Explicit or Implicit Claim		Perceives and Believes		Relevant	False		
Jacoby/ Small	Ad	Content, Structure, Context	Impression and/or Belief			Incorrect or Unjustified	N %	

FIG. 5.9. Comparison of definitions.

definition for it to be useful to most researcher's primary concern: affecting public policy. This, then, can serve as a base for the definition, but it is insufficient to describe the cognitive aspects of deceptiveness.

Input and Materiality.   Armstrong and Russ offer the best starting point for a definition. It is not the ad that is the appropriate unit of analysis, but the explicit or implicit *claim.* This is the FTC standard, but these researchers state that fact more clearly than the Commission. Their definition is also the only one outside the FTC to explicitly include Materiality as a factor.

Outcome Variable.   Most of the definitions tend to blur the outcome variable of import, mixing comprehension (or perception) with belief. I suspect this is because they are uncertain about the difference between deception and deceptiveness. Only belief need be considered in experimental settings. The Gaeth–Heath and Olson–Dover definitions are the only ones limited to belief, but neither of them makes it clear that this would be applicable only to experimental testing, or to deception rather than deceptiveness.

Causation and Prediction.   The Jacoby–Small definition, alone, contributes some suggestion of causal variables. This can help to direct the researcher, but we must be cautious not to be overly restrictive, preventing exploration into causes not considered in the model. This definition is likewise the only one, outside the FTC's, to include some mention of the probabilistic nature of deceptiveness, with its "N percent" criterion.

Comparison.   All the models indicate, more or less, the outcome variable must be compared to the product attribute to discover whether the belief is true or false. Jacoby–Small add to this the term *not justified,* apparently to encompass the need for claim substantiation.

Gardner's idea, however, stands out as both unique and interesting. He suggested that output of consumer cognitions be compared to that of adequately informed consumers, as well as to the product attribute. This is a divergence from FTC practice, and so, perhaps, should not be adopted as part of the present definition. It is arguable, however, that where adequately informed consumers would hold beliefs deviating from the reality of the product attribute, this deviation should be subtracted from the difference between the product attribute reality and the beliefs of those viewing the ad claim. The inaccurate beliefs of the well-informed are the product of "ineradicable miscomprehension" inherent in communication.[146] Therefore, although this is not part of present FTC practice, it is an inadequacy that probably results from the Commission's lack of knowledge about how communications are processed by consumers. Some consideration for this threshold of comprehension should be part of the definition.

A Behavioral Definition. Given the aforementioned considerations, from a behavioral perspective deceptiveness occurs when:

1. an explicit or implicit claim,
2. mediated by consumer perception, attention, comprehension, prior knowledge, other beliefs, or some other cognitive activity,
3. conveys a belief,
4. about a product/service attribute,
5. which is demonstrably false or unsubstantiated as true,
6. where it is likely that this belief will affect purchase behavior,
7. of a substantial percentage of consumers, *except where*
8. that false belief could not reasonably be eradicated by the advertiser.

Note the last item is not currently recognized by the FTC, and is included as a recommended enhancement of present policy.[147] This definition is less ambiguous than its predecessors, it combines the beneficial contributions of each, and it echos the structure of the theoretical model.

SUMMARY

This chapter represents an effort to construct a more complete and cogent cognitive theory of the deception process than those presented or applied to date, along with a definition based on that theory.[148] This model takes a pragmatic approach, identifying three points (attribute, belief, and materiality) at which measurement is appropriate for application to the regulatory process, while simultaneously filling some theoreti-

---

[146]*See discussion* in Preston and Richards, *supra* note 4, at 630.

[147]*Id.*; Preston and Richards, *Consumer Miscomprehension and Deceptive Advertising: A Response to Professor Craswell*, 68 B. U. L. REV. 431 (1988).

[148]It should be noted, however, that, "Any single theoretical representation will be flawed in that it will be incomplete; it will not capture all of the aspects of the phenomenon." Olson, *Presidential Address—1981: Toward a Science of Consumer Behavior*, 9 ADVANCES IN CONS. RES. v., vii (1981).

cal gaps by adding components that help explain why deception may result from certain forms of claims.

The final step in this tripartite research foundation is to create a method to test deceptiveness. The next chapter attempts this feat, using the model as its starting point. I addressed, earlier, one severe deficiency in using true survey methods to test deceptiveness. Consequently, this method will take an experimental approach.

A Design for the Measurement of Deceptiveness

Chapter 5 addressed what behavioral scientists can do to improve their contributions. It suggested they engage in a theoretical dialogue concerning the role of consumer information processing in the receipt of a deceptive message, and proposed one theory of that process. This chapter illustrates one benefit of this theoretical approach, by offering a new method of testing deceptiveness based on that theory. Development of a more valid and efficient method will not only benefit regulatory practice, but can serve to facilitate testing theoretical propositions.

The foregoing theory establishes the inadequacies of measuring comprehension as a test of deceptiveness, and hence the relative insufficiency of survey methods adapted to that purpose. It also substantiates belief as the optimum dependent measure of deceptiveness *when using experimental methods*. The method offered here adheres to that theoretical premise. Perhaps more important, it is specifically designed to measure *only* deceptiveness, and not to gauge some other aspect of ads or their efficacy. To date, methods used or proposed by behavioral researchers, whether for the FTC or for purely academic purposes, not only assess comprehension rather than belief, which the preceding model suggests is a qualitatively inferior dependent measure, but they are each subject to limitations that threaten their validity for measuring deceptiveness. By tailoring the technique to deceptiveness, it is possible to avoid those problems, and to achieve an enhanced sensitivity of the measurement instrument. Before presenting this method, I review the evidentiary norm in FTC cases, and discuss alternative methods used or proposed by behavioral scientists.

Of the several forms of external evidence considered in FTC cases, surveys represent the most probative means of assessing deceptiveness, so a review of cases exemplary of this fact-finding method should illustrate ad regulation at its best. The number of cases implementing this "best" evidence in the past was few[1] but its popularity in the past 15 years has yielded a substantial case selection. The following section does not attempt an exhaustive review of these cases, but provides a few examples indicative of the typical surveys used.[2] Although I repeatedly refer to "surveys," as does the FTC, some of the studies used in regulatory proceedings are more properly classified as quasi-experiments.[3]

FTC PROOF OF DECEPTION

Two survey types appear most frequently in FTC cases. The first is the in-home, day-after recall test, like that commonly conducted by Burke Marketing Research Company (Burke). The second is the out-of-home, or in-theater, presentation recall test, such as the Audience Reaction Tests administered by Audience Studies, Inc. (ASI). These two methods are described here. They are offered only for purposes of understanding the general approaches, because many surveys presented in FTC cases are not conducted by Burke or ASI but are very similar to them.[4]

Burke and ASI

Burke. The Burke test for television commercials permits respondents to see the test commercials under the normal viewing conditions in their homes, thereby conducting the survey in a natural viewing environment.[5]

[1]Brandt and Preston conducted a content analysis of 3,337 FTC cases from 1914 through 1973, and found that only 206 of those cases involved any showing of consumer perception, and 194 of those were simply instances of hand-picked consumers testifying. Only 12 cases involved surveys of consumer perceptions. Fully 94.7% of the cases involved "internal" Commission evidence; primarily the opinion of the Commissioners. Their conclusion, however, is that there was a major swing toward greater use of surveys, evident in the early 1970s. Brandt and Preston, *The Federal Trade Commission's Use of Evidence to Determine Deception,* 41 J. MKTG. (Jan. 1977). Preston, *Data-Free at the FTC? How the Federal Trade Commission Decides Whether Extrinsic Evidence of Deceptiveness is Required,* 24 AMER. BUS. L. J. (1986), shows that this upward trend continued through the next decade.

[2]For a more exhaustive review, see, Preston, *Extrinsic Evidence in Federal Trade Commission Deceptiveness Cases,* 1987 COLUM. BUS. L. REV. 633 (1987).

[3]T. D. COOK AND D. T. CAMPBELL, QUASI-EXPERIMENTATION: DESIGN & ANALYSIS ISSUES FOR FIELD SETTINGS 6 (1976). *See, e.g.,* ITT Continental, 83 F.T.C. 865, 977 (1973), *modified order,* 83 F.T.C. 1105 (1973), *modified,* ITT Continental v. FTC, 532 F.2d 207 (2d Cir. 1976), *modified order,* 90 F.T.C. 181 (1977).

[4]For a more exhaustive comparison of survey types used in FTC cases, *see* Preston, *supra* note 1.

[5]A. FLETCHER AND T. BOWERS, FUNDAMENTALS OF ADVERTISING RESEARCH 212 (1983).

Interviewers call randomly selected names from telephone directories until they find approximately 200 persons who claim to have watched the particular program into which the ad had been inserted the night before. Interviewers confirm the respondents watched the program, then give product or brand cues to test whether the commercials are recalled. If the commercials are remembered, a series of questions are administered to determine exactly what viewers recall. Besides recording recall of specific points in each ad, interviewers record comments or "verbatim" remarks of each respondent.[6]

The Burke approach to print advertising is very similar to the one used for television commercials. It involves sending copies of a magazine to respondents, into which have been attached the subject ads. The test ads are inserted to appear like regular ads.[7] Approximately 200 of these magazines are given to persons meeting specific criteria,[8] in high-traffic areas like shopping malls. Telephone calls are arranged for the following day on the pretense that respondents are participating in a magazine readership survey. The next day, interviewers telephone respondents and confirm the magazine was read. At that point the questioning proceeds in the same manner as the television commercial tests.[9]

One case that used the Burke method was *Warner-Lambert Co.,*[10] in which the company's product, Listerine mouthwash, was allegedly claimed to prevent or even cure colds and sore throats. The express claims made statements like, "Cold-catching season is here again! Nothing can cold-proof you—but Listerine Antiseptic gives you a fighting chance!" The product, in truth, would not prevent or cure colds or sore throats. As a result of the Burke test, it was discovered that substantial percentages of those surveyed perceived the message that Listerine was effective against colds and sore throats and, more specifically, *prevented* these maladies.[11] Placing apparent weight on this evidence, the administrative law judge (ALJ) stated:

> This high recall is even more significant in view of the fact that the surveys were made on the basis of a one-time showing of the commercial, and the

---

[6]Average recall, very similar to print advertising, is about 22–24%.

[7]*Supra* note 5, at 236.

[8]The chosen respondents have not read the test issue, they have read a comparable publication, and they meet certain demographic (age, sex, economic status, etc.) requirements.

[9]On average, only 22–25% of those that read the magazine can correctly recall at least one element of a test ad.

[10]86 F.T.C. 1398 (1975), *modified,* 562 F.2d 749 (D.C. Cir. 1977), *cert. denied,* 435 U.S. 950 (1978).

[11]*Id.* at 1416.

percentages were of individuals who had an opportunity to view of the commercial, but who, in fact, may not have watched or listened to it. With repeated exposure, it is to be anticipated that respondent's message would get across to more listeners and viewers.[12]

On review, the Commission did not *rely* on this evidence. It concluded that "in view of [the other evidence] we need no additional evidence . . . and therefore, we do not reach the question of whether the Burke test adds additional support."[13] However, Warner-Lambert was found liable for the implied claim, and this method has, since, gained full recognition in FTC regulatory proceedings.[14]

A Burke test was also introduced in *Ford Motor Company*.[15] A charge was made that Ford's advertising of its automobiles, by stating gasoline mileage figures for each automobile being promoted, implied to consumers that these figures were obtainable by the ordinary driver under typical long-distance driving conditions. If, in fact, this claim was implied, it would be factually inaccurate. Ford submitted a Burke survey, in an attempt to disprove the allegation. Although an analysis by surveyors supported that defense, the verbatim responses were found by the ALJ to support the existence of an implied claim. The initial decision in this case states:

> It should be pointed out that in the interpretation placed on the advertisements in the complaint is somewhat conservative, in that the allegation is limited to mileage claims for long or cross-country ("highway") trips. This gives the benefit of the doubt to respondent. Actually the Burke Research Report, and the verbatim responses therein, indicate that a large number of the interviewees did not qualify their understanding of the mileage claims to highway driving.[16]

On appeal, the Commission agreed with this factual determination by

---

[12]*Id.*

[13]*Id.* at 1488, n. 4.

[14]In Sterling Drug, 102 F.T.C. 395 (1983), it was stated, regarding the Burke method:

> The copy tests . . . were performed in a standard and reliable fashion. These tests or tests substantially identical to them were and are relied upon by large numbers of businesses . . . for purposes of making normal business decisions. . . . [They] are reliable and probative evidence of consumer recall of advertising content for ads challenged in this proceeding.

Id. at 462. *See,* Preston, *supra* note 2, at 646.

[15]87 F.T.C. 756 (1976).

[16]*Id.* at 779.

the ALJ.[17] The Burke survey proved instrumental in assessing consumer understandings.

ASI. ASI tests take a slightly different tack. Rather than opting for the natural environment of the home, these tests are conducted in a theater.[18] Audience members are recruited by telephone or in person, with an offer to attend a free preview of television programs.[19] They are given seats in a theater, half of which contain dials to record the audience's instantaneous reactions to the commercials, and before the showing each audience member is given a questionnaire, including a list of products and a question as to which they would prefer to receive as a door prize. A television program is then shown, followed by a series of commercials, and audience members are asked to fill out a questionnaire about the ads. This is followed by another television program, a questionnaire about the program, and another choice of products that may be offered as door prizes. They are finally shown a cartoon, then asked to complete a recall questionnaire including a request to write down everything they recall about the five commercials. Door prizes are then awarded.

As an example of this method, *American Home Products Corp.*,[20] concerned claims about the efficacy of Anacin pain reliever and Arthritis Pain Formula, including an alleged implication of superiority over competing products. Twenty ASI Audience Reaction Tests were entered in the record.[21] The tests had been conducted for American Home's advertising agency, Ted Bates and Company, to evaluate the persuasiveness and memorability of the ads, prior to the institution of the FTC challenge. The tests, in this case, helped confirm the ALJ's finding that the ads were deceptive in their impact.[22]

Problems With Burke and ASI. The Burke method has several weaknesses when used to test deceptiveness. Although in both cases just mentioned it was sensitive enough to detect deceptiveness, the comments of the ALJ in *Warmer-Lambert* serve to highlight an inadequacy of this

---

[17]The case was remanded on other grounds.

[18]In-home viewing is generally accepted to be a more "valid" method, since people may view commercials differently in the comfort of their own home, e.g., playing with their children or reading or eating meals, than they do in the more "forced" viewing environment of a theater.

[19]A good discussion of this technique appears in American Home Products Corp., 98 F.T.C. 136, 170 (1981).

[20]98 F.T.C. 136 (1981).

[21]*Id.* at 170.

[22]In two related analgesics cases, 17 ASI tests were used in Bristol-Myers, 102 F.T.C. 21, (1983), and two in Sterling Drug, 102 F.T.C. 395 (1983).

method for determining deceptiveness. There is no guarantee with this measure, that survey respondents *attended* to one specific commercial on one specific evening. This has a tendency to dilute the sensitivity of the instrument to detect any deception that might actually exist. The reason for this deficiency is that the survey was not designed for this purpose; it was intended to measure recall of a message in a real-world situation, rather than the conveyed meaning. *Recall* is a test of memory, whereas *deceptiveness* requires a test of meaning attribution. Memory is not really the step of information processing in which we are interested. Although the Burke tests have been useful in *Ford* and other cases,[23] there is no assurance that they will always find deception where it exists.

Although the ASI tests are somewhat vulnerable to the same criticism, they involve a "forced-exposure" that tends to secure a higher probability that the commercial will be given some attention. In addition, the time span between viewing the ad and responding to the questionnaire is much shorter for ASI, giving less time for dissipation of recall, and making this a more sensitive measure. These two factors make ASI far superior to Burke for testing deceptiveness.

However, both tests heavily rely on "verbatims." That measure is probably the least sensitive of survey techniques. Verbatims, the responses to open-ended questions, are nothing more than volunteered comments representing only top-of-mind recall of the conveyed message. They are unlikely to unearth more than a small percentage of what respondents comprehended or believed as a result of exposure to the ads.

The initial decision in *Thompson Medical* considered the worth of verbatims in detecting deceptiveness:

> It is accepted in marketing research that an open-ended question is not representative of everything stored in respondents' minds . . . open-ended questions lead most respondents to play back only one theme or point. They do not draw out a complete or exhaustive list of all things respondents may have on their minds. Rather, respondents will play back the dominant theme or primary impression and, having done that, will probably stop.[24]

---

[23]*See also,* ITT Continental Baking Co., Inc., *supra* note 3, at 890, which considered the evidence of 15 on-air (Burke-type) commercial tests, and Sun Oil Co., 84 F.T.C. 247, 257 (1974), where Russell Marketing Research conducted a Burke-type study. In both of these cases the challenged advertisers were found responsible for deceptive implications in their promotions. California Milk Producers Advisory Board, 94 F.T.C. 429 (1979), placed emphasis on Burke-type survey results in the initial decision by the ALJ, but the Commission decided the claim that "Every body needs milk" was substantially true for all but a small fraction of the population that is allergic to it.

[24]Thompson Medical Co., 104 F.T.C. 648, 697 (1984), *aff'd,* Thompson Medical v. FTC, 791 F.2d 189 (D.C. Cir 1986). *See, also,* Bristol-Myers, 102 F.T.C. 21, 215 (1983), *aff'd,* 738

If the alleged deceptive claim is not the first thing on the consumers' minds, the deceptiveness of the claim will not be detected. In spite of this weakness, Preston found that "Open-end questions have been used more frequently than forced-choice questions in findings on message conveyance."[25]

Verbatim reports, where there is no manipulation of independent variables (e.g., surveys), require respondents to engage in introspection, identifying the causes of cognitive effects. Nisbett and Wilson argued that people are unable to identify the causes of their cognitive changes, or even the fact that such change has occurred.[26]

Where open-ended questions, eliciting verbatim responses, are not used, closed-ended questions that permit only "yes" or "no" responses are common. The *Thompson Medical* initial decision goes on to state:

> In the final analysis, there is no way to test whether a consumer does or does not take a certain meaning from an ad other than putting that direct question to the consumer and asking the consumer to affirm or deny that the claim was made.[27]

This, too, is subject to problems. When asked to respond to a yes–no question there is a natural tendency to answer "yes." This is known as a "yeasaying" bias.[28]

Another serious problem with these methods is that the particular context (surrounding articles or programming) of the ad may mask the

---

F.2d 554 (2d Cir. 1984). A similar remark is found in *ITT Continental:*

> [T]hese questions were not designed and would not be likely to elicit consumers' perceptions of the latent or implied message contained in the advertising such as those challenged in the complaint. Rather, the questions asked were designed to and usually only elicited the interviewee's recall of the explicit message projected by the advertisement.

ITT Continental, *supra* note 3, at 977.

[25]Preston, *supra* note 2, at 656. He concluded,

> Why are the standardized methods likely to continue favoring open-end questions? It is because their questions . . . can be used for any and all ads about any and all products. Forced-choice questions, such as "On the basis of this ad, does this product contain aspirin?" are necessarily customized rather than standardized.

Id. at 666.

[26]Nisbett and Wilson, *Telling More Than We Can Know: Verbal Reports on Mental Processes,* 84 PSYCHOL. REV. 231 (1977).

[27]Thompson Medical Co., *supra* note 24, at 697.

[28]*Id.* at 806, 808.

effects, through proactive and retroactive interference.[29] A commercial that is deceptive may not reveal those effects, because the commercials or events occurring before or after may make specific recall of the ad difficult or impossible, even though the effects of the deception remain in consumers' minds.

The long period of time between viewing the ads and responding to the survey in the Burke approach makes this interference a particularly strong possibility. However, in its attempt to emulate a natural contextual environment for ads, ASI also presents several potentially interfering stimuli. These include entertainment segments and other commercials. Although this is an advantage for measuring ad efficacy, it presents potential confounds for measuring deceptiveness. A retroactive or proactive interference from these other stimuli may add or subtract meaning from the ads, defeating our purpose.

Also like Burke, ASI was designed to measure ad recall. The contextual interference was designed to purposely confound recall, simulating a natural context to determine whether an ad will be recalled in a real-world viewing situation. By testing several ads in the same context, it is possible to rank order their memorability and to gauge whether a particular ad will communicate in a complex viewing context. This is inappropriate for testing deceptiveness. Although an ad might not be deceptive when squeezed between a given two messages, it very well could be deceptive between two other messages or when viewed in isolation. It is rare that an ad is seen only once, or in one context. Briefly stated, if this method does detect deceptiveness we cannot be certain whether it was caused by the ad or by an interaction of ad and context.

Although the Burke method has been used in several FTC cases, and acknowledged by the Commission as appropriate evidence of consumer cognitions,[30] it remains significantly less than the ideal. In its attempt to secure external validity by having consumers view the ad in the comfort of their own home and natural viewing environment, it has sacrificed assurance of internal validity.[31] Without doubt it is a useful tool. Between

---

[29]*See*, e.g., Thorson and Reeves, *Effects of Over-Time Measures of Viewer Liking and Activity During Programs and Commercials on Memory for Commercials*, 13 ADVANCES IN CONS. RES. 549 (1985).

[30]Sterling Drug, *supra* note 14, at 462.

[31]"Internal validity" refers to how valid our assumption is that one thing is caused by another. In this instance, we cannot be certain viewers are accurately recalling what they saw the day before, so we can not really assume respondents' impressions were caused only by the ad they saw the night before. There is low internal validity. "External validity" refers to how valid our assumption is that what occurred to this person would occur to many others. If viewers are placed in a small room with no furniture, and bright lights on them, few other viewers would be in similar situations when watching a commercial, so these viewers might act different than most. We could not assume others would react the same

the several problems just mentioned, however, along with the fact it is designed to measure comprehension without concern for belief, a better method is desirable.

Although the ASI method is a substantially better test of deceptiveness than Burke, because of its forced-exposure setting and the shorter time period between viewing the ads and responding to questions about them, it remains subject to many of the same inadequacies. Although it clearly has some value, as seen in cases where it has been used, behavioral scientists and regulators should be dissatisfied with this technique for testing deceptiveness.

Other Methods

There are several other forms of behavioral research used in FTC deception cases. One type is simply a derivation of the forced-exposure situation used in the ASI tests. In these methods participants may be stopped in shopping malls, asked to view print ads or commercials on the spot, and then requested to complete a questionnaire. Three shopping mall intercept tests can be seen in *Thompson Medical*.[32]

Another form apparent in that case is the "focus group,"[33] which involves bringing consumers into a room and having a trained moderator probe the group for answers to research questions. This is a common procedure in marketing research, but its effectiveness for determining the meaning conveyed by an ad more closely resembles individual consumer testimony in an FTC case than it does survey research.[34]

Finally, there are consumer satisfaction surveys, which typically are mailed to purchasers by a manufacturer for comments and problems regarding the purchased product,[35] and image or penetration studies, which measure the perception of a specific brand as compared to its competitors.[36] Certain inferences can be made from these studies as to the effectiveness of an ad or campaign, and may even reflect the impact

---

way. *See discussion* in Cook and Campbell, *supra* note 3, at 37. Burke tried to ensure a natural viewing situation, so they can more validly assume others would react similarly.

[32]These included the Video Storyboard Test, the FRC Test, and the Lieberman Test. *Id.* at 698 and 804.

[33]Two of these appear in the record: (a) the Schneider Focus Groups, and (b) Nicholas Research Focus Groups. *Id.* at 698–99. *See also,* Chrysler Corp., 87 F.T.C. 719, 748 (1976), *modified,* Chrysler v. FTC, 561 F.2d 357 (D.C. Cir. 1977), *modified order,* 90 F.T.C. 606 (1977).

[34]"[G]roup discussions may not be the best way to survey the impressions conveyed by an advertisement." Chrysler Corp., *supra* note 33, at 748.

[35]*See, e.g.,* Sears, Roebuck and Co., 95 F.T.C. 406, 449 (1980).

[36]*See, e.g.,* Sterling Drug, Inc., *supra* note 14, at 696.

of a continuing deceptive claim, but they are of little use in measuring the perception of a specific claim in a specific ad. Causal inference is virtually impossible. These measures are simply too "coarse" to assess the effects of a single claim, and have been specifically rejected by the FTC.[37]

It is readily seen that none of these methods is specifically tailored to detect deceptiveness in ads. The consequence is that several of the methods mentioned here are useful, and have been adopted by the regulators, but they all represent a poor fit when viewed in light of the theory presented in chapter 5. The measurement instrument may be insufficiently sensitive to detect all deceptiveness. It also may be unnecessarily cumbersome. Although these methods need not be truly generalizable,[38] shopping mall intercept studies and focus groups take this to an extreme. Also, most of these measures are too "coarse" to accurately judge the meaning of a single claim, as can be seen in the consumer satisfaction and the image/penetration studies. Finally, the typical dependent variable in each method is comprehension, rather than belief. This is not to suggest that those methods are *worthless*. Some are useful, in lieu of a better method, but there is substantial room for improvement. Although none of these methods are especially sensitive to detecting deceptiveness, this means that where they uncover deceptiveness it probably affects *many* consumers. A more sensitive measure, however, might detect more subtle violations.

METHODS USED IN ACADEMIC RESEARCH

Methods for measuring deceptiveness have been a concern outside regulatory proceedings, as well. Scholarly researchers hoping to criticize or improve the regulatory process frequently measure deceptiveness of certain claim types, to test FTC assumptions about deceptiveness or nondeceptiveness. The methods used in these studies, however, vary widely. The sensitivity of each measure differs, the method used in one instance may not be applicable to other deceptiveness questions, and the lack of equivalence of method makes it nearly impossible to know whether "deceptiveness" in one study is functionally equivalent to "deceptiveness" in another.

Shimp, for example, explored the potentially deceptive consequences

---

[37]Preston, *supra* note 2, at 676.

[38]National probability samples are not required for a method to be acceptable for FTC regulation. Preston, *supra* note 2. However, methods, like focus groups, that base their findings on very small samples, purposively chosen, are unlikely to be acceptable evidence in FTC cases.

of incomplete comparative statements in ads, using an experimental technique devised for that purpose.[39] He measured the meanings comprehended (rather than believed) by subjects through both a Likert scale and a constant-sum scaling technique of agreement responses to three alternative closure statements for each incomplete comparative. The second approach was expressly used to discover whether the results of the first were artifacts of the method.[40] Shimp interpreted his results to suggest that "receivers of an ad comprehend . . . more than what is actually contained,"[41] and that incomplete comparisons are therefore misleading.[42] Ironically, his methods are something of an incomplete comparison.

Shimp presupposed that if subjects derive different referents for the incomplete comparatives, they are being misled.[43] Unfortunately, he did not compare those comprehended meanings to objective truth. He expressly *assumed* that because there are multiple meanings they can not all be true. Without this comparison it is impossible to assess deceptiveness. It may be, in fact, that each of the perceived meanings of the incomplete comparisons was *true,* or so close to truth that no regulator would challenge them. Without making this comparison it is impossible to conclude there has been deceptiveness. A second problem, one inherent in his method, is that his method contained no experimental controls, thereby handicapping any attempt at causal inference. Finally, he offers no test of materiality with his method. Although Shimp's research is extremely valuable for the study of comprehension, his methods are inadequate for deceptiveness research.

In a study of the deceptiveness of "puffery," Rotfeld and Rotzoll, unlike Shimp, tested *belief* of product attributes in an experimental setting.[44] The methods used by these researchers involved asking subjects to separately list literal and implied claims they perceived in each ad, and to classify the claims by whether they felt the claims to be true. The claims had been pre-coded as "fact claims" or "puffery claims." The percentage of subjects believing the fact claims versus puffery claims was then compared.[45] These researchers concluded, "Generally, respondents did not

---

[39]Shimp, *Do Incomplete Comparisons Mislead?* 18 J. ADV. RES. 21 (Dec. 1978).

[40]There were actually *four* phases to Shimp's experiment. Only the two primary methods are discussed here. *Id.* at 23.

[41]*Id.* at 24.

[42]*Id.* at 27.

[43]Shimp remarked, "Since it is unlikely that all interpretations are correct, some consumers must inevitably be misled." *Id.* at 22.

[44]Rotfeld and Rotzoll, *Puffery vs. Fact Claims—Really Different?*, 1981 CURRENT ISSUES & RES. IN ADV. 85.

[45]*Id.* at 88–91.

perceive fact and fact-implied claims as possessing greater credibility than puffs and the claims they implied."[46]

Although this study used the more appropriate dependent variable, belief, it suffers from the same basic maladies in Shimp's study: no control group, and no factual referent. The lack of control group is especially valuable to note, because causal inference from belief is impossible without controlling for prior-held beliefs. Also, its open-ended question, asking subjects to list claims they perceived in the ads, leaves the possibility that there may be some more subtle claim that the regulators may suspect the ad to make, but that the experimental subjects fail to mention: the verbatim problem. Finally, the forced choice of "belief" or "nonbelief" of each claim makes this measure less sensitive than need be. A better technique would use a scale permitting subjects to indicate *degree* of belief. Even if subjects believe one claim *less* than another, they may respond that they believe both claims, because they are forced to choose all or nothing. But, the greater the belief, the greater the deceptiveness. Degree of belief is valuable information, lost with this method.

Even in lieu of the deficiencies in these two studies, it can readily be seen that their differences make it difficult to equate their results.[47] If Shimp's method was to find certain claims deceptive, and Rotfeld and Rotzoll found others nondeceptive, it would be unclear whether the difference was attributable to the claims or to the methods used to assess them. A standardized procedure capable of testing deceptiveness from a variety of claim types, including incomplete comparisons and puffery, could permit both better knowledge of what claims are likely to deceive and a relative indicator of which claims are *most* deceptive.

GENERAL DESIGNS FOR DECEPTIVENESS MEASUREMENT

It should be clear by now that neither the methods typically used in FTC proceedings, nor those found in scholarly research are very satisfying. Although no method is ever perfect, it appears there is significant margin for improvement. There is a need for a method tailored to the measure of deceptiveness, to maximize sensitivity and internal validity, which is both legally cognizable and applicable to a wide range of claims. Where the prior section considered some of the methods created and used for specific scholarly studies, to test specific types of claims, this section looks

---

[46]*Id.* at 102.

[47]Another example of these varied approaches can be found in Barbour and Gardner, *Deceptive Advertising: A Practical Approach to Measurement,* 11 J. ADV. 21 (1982).

at methods designed for more general application to test deceptiveness of a broad variety of claims.

Only a few efforts have been made to develop methods optimized to measure deceptiveness of a broad selection of claims. Gardner offered three alternative methods for measuring deceptiveness.[48] The first he called the Normative Belief Technique (NBT).[49] This method starts from "the assumption that there is some 'optimal' set of functional product attributes for each product class."[50] In other words, each product class has a set of attributes that are important (i.e., material) to adequately informed consumers.

The first step of this technique, therefore, requires that these salient attributes be identified for the product class under study. The second step is to sort out which of these attributes are functional and which are nonfunctional. Both of these steps are accomplished by consumer surveys or experiments, along with input by product experts. The third step is to "establish acceptable ranges of probabilities" that each attribute is associated with the product (i.e., the probability of association between attribute and product that adequately informed consumers would name, if asked). What this does is to establish "norms" of how *adequately informed* consumers perceive a product class, against which consumers exposed to ads can be compared. Gardner explained:

> Then, after advertisements for specific brands of hair shampoo have been shown to a wide range of consumers, the analysis would consist of looking for those specific brands within the product class (i.e., hair shampoo) that exceeded the internal estimate. Those brands that had estimates that fell within or below the previously determined range . . . would be deemed nondeceptive.[51]

Gardner's second method is called the Consumer Impression Technique (CIT).[52] According to Gardner, "This is not a sophisticated technique. . . ."[53] Here, consumers are exposed to ads, then asked to state what the ad was telling them. These responses would then be compared to actual facts. He did not discuss specific measurement instruments or conditions, but suggested they should be properly designed and controlled.

The final method he offered is the Expectation Screening Procedure

---

[48]Gardner, *Deception in Advertising: A Conceptual Approach*, 39 J. MKTG. 40 (Jan. 1975).
[49]*Id.* at 44.
[50]*Id.*
[51]*Id.*
[52]*Id.* at 45.
[53]*Id.*

(ESP).[54] In this situation consumers would be polled to find norms of what consumers expect to see in a given product class when evaluating a product in that class. If, upon comparison to those norms, responses to a given ad significantly deviate from that norm, that ad would be singled out by the FTC for a more thorough investigation.

It should be immediately apparent that the ESP approach is not directly applicable for testing deceptiveness. In that regard, its acronym is apt, for it would require insight comparable to extra sensory perception to find an ad deceptive using this criterion. However, it is intended not as an accurate test of deceptiveness, but as a "screening" device for finding ads that deserve greater regulatory attention. It is proffered only as a tool, to aid the FTC in marshalling its resources. Even for that limited purpose, however, it appears too gross a measure, and probably less effective than the present FTC approach. Like the methods of Shimp and of Rotfeld and Rotzoll, discussed earlier, it provides no references to the true product attributes.

The CIT approach should look familiar to the reader. This technique is essentially one used in FTC regulatory proceedings. Its description is not very specific, here, but it reflects most of the methods (Burke, ASI, Focus Groups) used in those regulatory hearings. Consequently, this adds nothing to our search for a better measure.

By far the most intriguing of the three methods is the NBT. The problems with this technique, however, are numerous. The most troublesome is that it, like the ESP, is only a screening device. Gardner, in a later article, suggested that all three of these techniques are "designed as screening devices, i.e., they should not be used at this time to definitely prove or disprove deception in advertising."[55] Like the ESP, this method has no factual referent. Also like the ESP, the NBT focuses on an entire product class, rather than a product within that class. Another problem is its limitation to "functional" attributes. This rather arbitrary limitation would prohibit deceptiveness claims based on evaluative product claims, which may, in fact, be deceptive.[56] The NBT also predetermines which attributes are material, within a whole class of products, leaving no room for the possibility that through the claims in an ad the materiality of that claim might be manipulated. It is unlikely that "blue crystals" in a laundry detergent would normally be a salient product attribute, but it is possible that an ad could cause consumers to overestimate the value of that

---

[54]*Id.*

[55]Gardner, *Deception in Advertising: A Receiver Oriented Approach to Understanding*, 5 J. ADV. 5, 10 (1976).

[56]Shimp and Preston, *Deceptive and Nondeceptive Consequences of Evaluative Advertising*, 45 J. MKTG. 22 (Winter 1981).

attribute, effectively adjusting its materiality level. One final problem is that Gardner does not specify the means by which the product class norms are determined.

Although the NBT has several crippling weaknesses, the notion of comparing the effects of an ad to normative beliefs is a creative and valuable concept. This is a form of experimental control that has merit. If the beliefs of adequately informed consumers do not accurately reflect the true product attributes, advertisers should not be held accountable for those inaccurate beliefs. This assumes that even those persons with adequate information may not have perfect knowledge or beliefs, because each consumer processes that information with a different set of expectations and prior-held beliefs. It would be unfair to compare beliefs derived from an ad to actual attributes, given this limitation of human information processing abilities. Rather than compare beliefs to fact, the better approach is to compare beliefs to beliefs derived from sufficient information. This recognizes that ineradicable miscomprehension is inherent in the communication process, as depicted in Fig. 6.1.

At about the same time as Gardner's proposal, Armstrong and Russ suggested a Salient Belief Technique (SBT) for testing deceptiveness.[57] In a later article, Armstrong, Gurol, and Russ restated this method:

> Conceptually, the salient belief technique suggests that deception occurs when consumers perceive and believe false claims either made or implied by an ad. To be of any concern, however, these false claims must be relevant to consumers' decisions to purchase a brand in the product category. Falsely held beliefs about an irrelevant attribute are technically a deception, but

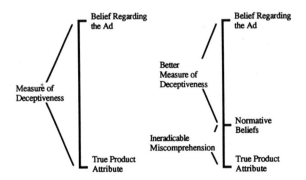

FIG. 6.1.   Application of normative beliefs.

---

[57]Armstrong and Russ, *Detecting Deception in Advertising*, 23 MSU Bus. Topics 21 (Spring 1975). This method was later tested by Armstrong, Kendall, and Russ, *Applications of Consumer Information Processing Research to Public Policy Issues*, 2(3) Comm. Res. 232 (July 1975).

because they are unlikely to affect the decision process it seems useful to distinguish between them and falsely held beliefs that are relevant.[58]

To this point the SBT follows the theory of the deception process presented in the previous chapter, using belief as an operational definition of deceptiveness, and materiality as a weighting factor. From this standpoint it is a legally and behaviorally valid measure.

The procedure involves three steps: (a) identifying claims that relevant consumers perceive from the ad; (b) determining externally which of the claims are false; and (c) measuring perceptions, beliefs, and saliences of a representative sample of consumers exposed to the ad.[59] Subjects are shown the ad, asked what claims the ad is making, and then requested to indicate the importance of the claimed attribute and the degree to which they believed the claim.[60]

Again, there are problems with this method. First, and foremost, is the fact that the "scores" on perception, belief, and salience are multiplied to obtain a final measure of deceptiveness, treating ordinal data as ratio. Second, it relies on the claims consumers report seeing, in the same manner as verbatim responses used in FTC cases, which may not reveal the claims of concern. Third, there are no experimental controls, to ensure that (a) the deceptiveness results from exposure to the ad, or (b) the response is deceptiveness rather than ineradicable miscomprehension. Finally, it requires the FTC to establish a threshold SBT score for each product or product category beyond which an ad would be considered deceptive. These last three deficiencies are acknowledged by its designers.[61] In the final analysis, the SBT approach is not a bad one, but it does little to improve upon those methods presently in use by the regulators, and the multiplication of scores suggested by the authors actually detracts from its usefulness.[62]

More recently, in 1985, another method was offered. Grunert and Dedler devised a Misleading Components Approach (MCA).[63] Regarding those previous methods, they argued:

---

[58]Armstrong, Gurol, and Russ, *Detecting and Correcting Deceptive Advertising*, 6 J. CONS. RES. 237, 238 (Dec. 1979).

[59]*Id.*

[60]Armstrong, Kendall, and Russ, *supra* note 57, at 235.

[61]*Id.* at 237–8.

[62]This method was actually used in at least one other study, where the scores were erroneously multiplied. Mann and Gurol, *An Objective Approach to Detecting and Correcting Deceptive Advertising*, 54 NOTRE DAME LAW. 73 (1978). These researchers, however, modified the technique slightly, to increase its sensitivity. *Id.* at 93. At the time of this study, its authors considered this to be "the only approach devised yet which actually measures advertising deception." *Id.*

[63]Grunert and Dedler, *Misleading Advertising: In Search of a Measurement Methodology*, 4 J. PUB. POL. & MKTG. 153 (1985).

All the procedures presented are concerned with determining *cases* of misleading advertising. This basic concern has also usually caused investigators to use real (or at least realistic) advertisements as stimuli. While this certainly enhances external validity, it also prevents the evolution of a theory of misleading advertising, because we cannot usually specify exactly which elements of the advertising message caused the false beliefs.[64]

This criticism is somewhat overstated, because at least two of Gardner's three techniques were *not* case oriented. Their argument regarding theory development seems not to be a problem of using real ads as much as it highlights the need for good experimental controls, permitting greater causal inference.

As a result of this perceived problem, Grunert and Dedler presented a method that focuses on causes rather than cases. Their goal is to permit researchers to build a typology of misleading components of ads (i.e., a list of ad elements that tend to deceive).[65] This would be a method of creating a typology much like Preston's,[66] presented in chapter 3, except that where Preston's was derived by categorizing claims the FTC has regulated, theirs would derive directly from consumer perceptions. Where Preston's is descriptive of the law, theirs would describe consumer cognitions.

The MCA uses no complete ads as stimuli, to control confounding by other ad elements. Messages prototypic of a particular ad component are drawn from real ads, and are used to compose stimuli for two conditions: (a) the actual text, and (b) a "qualified," or more complete, version. For example, the hauling capacity of an automobile was described in the first condition as "for up to 1,113 liters of load," and in the qualified condition as "for up to 1,113 liters of load when the rear seats are folded down."[67] Belief is then measured with a single question (e.g., "How big do you believe the trunk of this car is in relation to other cars?").

This is an interesting idea, but it, too, is flawed. First, as the authors stated this is only applicable for theoretical study, and is not appropriate for "real-world" case studies. Second, it is useful only for deceptiveness arising from written text, and is not directly adoptable for study of pictorial, auditory, or structural ad features. Third, the FTC is concerned only with deceptiveness as it arises from a reading of the ad as a whole, and the theory presented in the last chapter suggests that deceptiveness may arise from an interaction of ad elements as well as from their main

---

[64]*Id.* at 157.

[65]*Id.* at 158.

[66]Preston, *The Federal Trade Commission's Identification of Implications As Constituting Deceptive Advertising*, 57 CINCINNATI L. REV. 1243 (1989).

[67]*Supra* note 63, at 160.

effect. Consequently, the resulting typology may bear no resemblance to legally cognizable deceptiveness. Fourth, the dependent measure is unipolar. I discuss this at greater length later, but the scale is relative (more or less belief) without definite endpoints against which to compare it, making its interpretation difficult (or impossible). Finally, there is no measure of materiality. Even if we build a typology of deceptive claims, many of them may have no bearing on behavior, making them irrelevant to practical application.

On the positive side, this method picks up Gardner's concept of comparing beliefs that result from a claim to beliefs that are normative. Through their qualified-text condition, these researchers are creating adequately informed subjects to serve as a control group against which to assess the test group.

With this technique it is possible to control for miscomprehension that is unavoidable (ineradicable) in the communication process.[68] Preston and Richards used this same method, measuring comprehension rather than belief as a dependent variable, to demonstrate the difference between miscomprehension that is eradicable and that which is ineradicable.[69] In effect, any miscomprehension that is eradicable is deceptiveness by implication, but the ineradicable variety is "noise" in the communication process *not* attributable to deceptiveness. This aspect of the Grunert and Dedler design, and Gardner's concept of measuring normative beliefs, manages to separate deceptiveness from inherent miscomprehension, subtracting the effect of the latter. This comparison is a more valid one than those used by the FTC. Additionally, if subjects are randomly sampled this approach will also control for prior knowledge of and beliefs about the product or product class, permitting attribution of causation to the experimental stimulus.

Finally, Russo, Metcalf, and Stephens offer one last method.[70] With this technique ads were altered to remove potentially misleading wording or qualities in much the same manner as Grunert and Dedler's qualified text, except that Russo et al. used the entire ad. Experimental subjects were then assigned to three treatment conditions: original ad, corrected ad, and no ad (control). They were instructed to read and evaluate the entire ad, and were then directed to answer questions designed to assess belief in both the claim at issue and a legitimate claim in the ad.

---

[68]Preston and Richards, *Consumer Miscomprehension as a Challenge to FTC Prosecutions of Deceptive Advertising,* 19 J. MARSHALL L. REV. 605 (1986).

[69]Preston and Richards, *Consumer Miscomprehension and Deceptive Advertising: A Response to Professor Craswell,* 68 B. U. L. REV. 431 (1988).

[70]Russo, Metcalf, and Stephens, *Identifying Misleading Advertising,* 8 J. CONS. RES. 119 (1981). A slight variation of this method is found in Burke, DeSarbo, Oliver, and Robertson, *Deception by Implication: An Experimental Investigation,* 14 J. CONS. RES. 438 (1988).

This method is the best one proposed to date. These researchers recognize the need for a control to permit causal inference. Where the original-ad condition did not significantly differ from the control condition, even though differing from the true product attributes, they conclude the ad is not responsible for the misconception. By using a corrected-ad condition, they also acknowledge the Gardner normative belief concept, permitting isolation of ineradicable miscomprehension. Finally, unlike the "screening devices" and Grunert and Dedler's MCA, this method can be applied to real ads in FTC cases.

Although this design represents a quantum improvement over previous methods, it is also subject to additional improvement. First, this method permits comparison of original ad to corrected ad, allowing experimenters to reveal a difference between the two, but it does not permit showing a *meaningful* difference. In other words, if the corrected-ad group believes A (relative true belief), and the FTC charges the advertiser with implying B (false belief), this method can determine that original-ad group beliefs differ from A, but not that they are the same as B. In fact, depending on the scaling of the questions asked of subjects, and the statistical power, a very minute difference can be statistically significant, while being far from what the advertiser is charged with implying.

The second problem, related to the first, is that they provide no guidelines for scaling the questionnaire. It is unclear whether they asked bipolar "yes–no" questions, or used Likert-type or some other response scale. Scaling is particularly important, because it may or may not provide a measure of *relative* deceptiveness and may exaggerate or suppress effects. It is also important for standardization, so deceptive effects in one case can be meaningfully compared to other cases.

Third, their method is limited to "correctable" ads. They stated, "An ad is correctable if the misleading claim can be removed without reducing its legitimate power to persuade."[71] Not all ads challenged by the FTC would meet this criterion. In fact, I suspect that a large number would not, because the deceptive claim goes to the heart of the ad. How, then, can we test those ads? Their criteria and approach to creating these alternative stimuli make this an extraordinarily cumbersome approach, which is quite clearly inapplicable for testing a large number of claims. If alternative "corrected" messages are to be used, the method for creating them should not be sensitive to the persuasibility of the claim tested, otherwise it will not be a broadly applicable technique.

Finally, in a related issue, I suggest the corrected version should not be an ad. Besides the obvious fact that composing realistic corrected ads

---

[71]Russo et al., *supra* note 70, at 122.

would be very difficult or expensive, Preston and Scharbach found that consumers expand the meaning of ads to a greater extent than other forms of message.[72] The "adequately informed" comparison group should receive its information from a nonadvertisement, to ensure that the resulting "ineradicable miscomprehension" is truly ineradicable. That level could very well be higher for an ad than for other messages, so a regulation based upon a corrected *ad* would effectively permit a higher level of deceptiveness. If a product cannot be promoted in an ad with the same level of ineradicable miscomprehension as a non-ad, public policy would suggest that it is a product not capable of being advertised. To find otherwise would indicate that the ad must survive at whatever the cost.[73]

This is clearly the best method available, but it still leaves much to be desired. The method that follows attempts to correct some inadequacies of the Russo et al. method.

THE RELATIVE PROXIMITY INDEX (RPI)

Scaling

Connotative Relativity Problem. In the design that follows I attempt to correct or improve on the several problems highlighted in the foregoing methods. The Russo et al. technique accomplishes much of this, but its deficiencies, including failure to provide a false-belief reference point and guidance for scaling, center on the need to account for connotative relativity.

Many implied claims may be relative, for example, a claim like "Brand X gets clothes clean" may mean many things to many people. To some, "clean" may mean dirt is removed, to others it may mean stains are

---

[72]Preston and Scharbach, *Advertising: More Than Meets the Eye?*, 11 J. ADV. RES. 19 (June 1971).

[73]The decision in FTC v. Colgate-Palmolive Co., 380 U.S. 374 (1965), considering the potential deceptiveness of a "mock-up" demonstration on television used by an advertiser to overcome the technical limitations of the television medium, echoes this sentiment:

Respondents claim that it will be impractical to inform the viewing public that it is not seeing an actual test, experiment or demonstration, but we think it inconceivable that the ingenious advertising world will be unable, if it so desires, to conform to the Commission's insistence that the public not be misinformed. If, however, it becomes impossible or impractical to show simulated demonstrations on television in a truthful manner, this indicates that television is not a medium that lends itself to this type of commercial, not that the commercial must survive at all costs.

Id.

removed, and yet others may expect clothes to look like new. Therefore, the claim is connotatively relative, but relative to what? Consumers' responses may be difficult to interpret, because each consumer's inferred meaning may differ, and there are no "markers" or "end-points" against which these statements can be compared. If we were to charge that the claim deceptively implies Brand X will remove 100% of dirt, when in fact it will only remove 75%, this deceptiveness is difficult to test without meaningful endpoints. Where consumers indicate they believe Brand X will make clothes "clean," we have no way of knowing whether that is 75% or 100%. If we ask them, more directly, whether it gets clothes 100% clean, and they say "no," it could mean they believe it will get clothes anywhere from 0%–99% clean. Clearly, endpoints are needed to control for this relativily effect.

To establish anchor points of meaning for relative comparison, it is necessary to create a semantic continuum along which to place an evaluation. Perhaps one of the best and most popular mechanisms for scaling connotative meaning is the "semantic differential," developed by Charles E. Osgood.[74] Osgood's formulation of this measurement incorporated a 7-step continuum between bipolar adjectives, for each of several dimensions, with the purpose of triangulating the meaning of a given word between those dimensions. For example, the word "ice" might be rated along dimensions which include those shown in Fig. 6.2. The results of testing this word might reveal the relative meaning to be "hard" and "cold." The distance from center on each scale represents the "intensity" of impression, or relative position between each descriptor.[75] To test the meaning of "clean," just given, we might present consumers with three bipolar scales, about dirt, stains, and newness, to discover the meaning consumers attach to that word. It is interesting to note that Osgood anticipated application of this method to mass communication research, and particularly advertising,[76] although little has been done in this context.[77]

The present method adopts some of the general concepts of the semantic differential, but there are significant differences between the

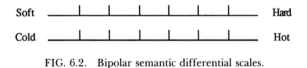

FIG. 6.2.   Bipolar semantic differential scales.

---

[74]Osgood, *The nature and measurement of meaning,* 49 Psych. Bull. 222 (1952).
[75]*Id.* at 226.
[76]C. Osgood, G. Suci, and P. Tannenbaum, The Measurement of Meaning 331 (1975).
[77]Finstuen, *Use of Osgood's Semantic Differential,* 41 Psychol. Reports 1219, 1221 (1977).

purposes of Osgood's test and the assessment of deceptiveness. The semantic differential attempts to locate an unknown meaning in the universe of possible connotations, although regulatory determination of deceptiveness starts with an accusation of meaning with no concern for other connotations. From a practical standpoint this means that there is no need for a triangulation process, because the staff of the FTC, through its charges, establishes the dimensions of legal relevance. Only one scale will be needed for most charges made by the agency.

In *Coca-Cola Co.*,[78] advertisements for the company's Hi-C fruit drink fell under attack. The drink was advertised in one commercial depicting a man loudly munching an apple during a dramatic moment of a television program, disturbing the others in his family, and then voluntarily exchanging the apple for a glass of Hi-C. The message that follows includes, "Hi-C is the easy way to enjoy the good taste of fruit, and it's quiet . . . . Made from fresh fruit and naturally sweetened . . . . Lots of Vitamin C, too . . . . It's the Sensible Drink."[79] As the consequence of this and other ads, the Commission staff claimed:

> . . . respondents have represented and are now representing, directly and by implication, that:
> a) Said drink is the beverage that is uniquely suitable for use by children with regular meals, light meals and food eaten between meals.
> b) Nutritionally unbalanced meals that are consumed with said drink constitute healthy dietary practices for children and families.
> c) Said drink is the beverage that is "The Sensible Drink," nutritionally and economically, as a source of vitamin C.
> d) Said drink is made with fresh fruit and has a high fruit content comparable to fresh fruits and fruit juices.
> e) Said drink is unqualifiedly good for children and children can drink as much of it as they like without adverse health or nutritional implications.
> f) Said drink is particularly high in vitamin C content even as compared to other beverages widely known as high in vitamin C content, specifically citrus fruit juices.[80]

By these charges, the legally salient components of meaning in these ads are defined. These specific FTC charges can help us to derive appropriate scales, with meaningful endpoints, to test beliefs based upon specifically defined meanings. For example, in (c), in the previous FTC quote, we can see the charged claim that the drink is sensible "nutritionally" and "economically." In (d) respondent is charged with claiming the

---

[78]83 F.T.C. 746 (1973).
[79]*Id.* at 750.
[80]*Id.* at 751.

drink has "high fruit content" comparable to fruit juices. In (e) we see the charged claim that the drink is "good for children." In (f) they are charged with representing that the drink is "high in vitamin C content even as compared to other beverages." This is not an exhaustive list of the claims involved in those charges, but they are adequate for purposes of illustration. On dichotomous continua, like those of the semantic differential, these components could be expressed, in part, as shown in Fig. 6.3. Rather than test the multidimensional connotations of a claim about the product's nutritional characteristics, as with the true semantic differential method, we are interested only in whether the product is nutritious or non-nutritious, so we use only one scale for that claim.

This approach to scaling the salient dimension in the *Coca-Cola Co.* case offers particular promise for empirically testing deceptiveness, because it not only permits subjects to make a "yes" or "no" response to FTC charges, but also to indicate an intensity of belief in either direction. The natural consequence of this quasicontinuum on each dimension is to lend greater resolution to the exploration into consumer cognitions. In a statistical sense, it poses the null hypothesis (nondeceptiveness) at one end of the spectrum and the alternative hypothesis (deceptiveness) at the other end, allowing subjects to place their data point between the two.

If properly structured, forced-choice questions like this may be preferred by the FTC as a more valid measure than the frequently used open-end questions with verbatim responses.[81] I go farther than the FTC, to suggest this is a *substantial* improvement over verbatims. Whether verbatim answers are through aided or unaided recall methods, they are

Indicate on the scales, below, what you believe to be the true features of Hi-C:

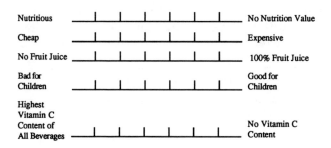

FIG. 6.3.   Dichotomous breakdown of FTC charges.

---

[81]Preston stated, "[W]here the levels [of consumers seeing a claim as being made when measured by] forced-choice are significantly high and the levels for open-ended are not, as can often happen, the forced-choice is likely to be called more valid than the open-ended." Preston, *supra* note 2, at 667.

difficult to code and analyze, they can seldom be used as more than a binary "yes" or "no" measure of FTC allegations, they are very sensitive to the manner in which the questions and probes are worded, and each subject may differ in his or her perceived alternatives.

Most closed-ended questions are equally inferior. Responses to these methods are also normally binary in nature, or they offer a scaling procedure like the Likert scale. An example that may typify this approach is shown in Fig. 6.4.

This is unsatisfactory, because disagreement with the statement has no meaning. Perhaps disagreement suggests it is not "good" for children but rather "great" for them. More than one question would be required to coax more information from subjects, which is both inefficient and makes analysis more complex. Only a bipolar scale like the one proposed enables a parsimonious measure of each charge, indicating connotation *relative* to preselected endpoints.

Consistency Problem. Another problem with these other measures is that the wording or scaling from case to case, or even from charge to charge within a single case, may vary. Inconsistencies may cause great variation in how each charge is measured, and in alternative hypotheses to which they are compared.

This can be illustrated by the example just given. Although "good for children" might be viewed as an alternative hypothesis, what is the null? Is it "great for children," "bad for children," "offers no particular benefit for children," or any number of other comparators? The concept of "good" is multidimensional, and experimenters might choose many different endpoints for a single scale. Each case or charge, therefore, might be measured with null hypotheses having different distances from the proffered alternative. The number "91" would fall at one end of a scale with 90 and 100 as endpoints, but at the other end of a scale using the endpoints 1 and 100. A more distant null in one instance may make the selection of the alternative more likely in that case than in others.[82]

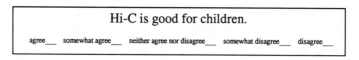

FIG. 6.4.   Likert-type scale.

---

[82]This may tend to misrepresent the interpretability of the results to the fact-finder. There has long been an evidenced reluctance, or mere failure, to implement the use of behavioral evidence in FTC cases. Richards and Preston, *Quantitative Research: A Dispute Resolution Process for FTC Advertising Regulation,* 40 OKLA. L. REV. 593 (1987). Inconsistent results might serve to further exacerbate inadequate receptions and application of behavioral data. Legally, this would reflect on its likely probative value.

A further refinement of the bipolar scaling is in order to satisfy this "consistency" criterion. The endpoints of the scales must be both meaningful and repeatable, so that each advertiser and each claim is subject to an equitably similar scrutiny. If one advertiser might be subject to a much less stringent scale, making nondeceptiveness more probable, it would be both unfair and legally untenable. This seems a near impossibility, because legal charges are so heterogeneous. "Good for children" can be opposed by "bad for children" or "not good for children." In this example, "bad" implies a negative, whereas "not good" may imply either a negative or a null effect. In some cases it may be necessary to detect a negative and in others a negative may make no sense. The alternative of "100% Fruit Juice" might be "no fruit juice" or it might be "not 100% Fruit Juice," which suggests a completely different scale. The former would be biased in favor of the advertiser, and the later in favor of regulation.

An alternative to manufacturing an elaborate set of rules for scaling, to ensure consistency, is to depend on "truth" and "falsity" as endpoints (see Fig. 6.5). The procedure described here explains how these ends can be located empirically, to guarantee both legal relevance and replicability from case to case.

Creating the Scales. The first step to evaluating an ad for potential deceptiveness is to define the salient dimensions to be measured. As previously shown, this is simply a matter of looking to the FTC complaint. Those dimensions have been predetermined by the regulatory agency, and enumerated as alleged direct or implied misrepresentations.

The next step requires assignment of endpoints to a bipolar scale for each dimension. The procedure that follows does not require the exactitude just suggested, because, as I show later, the endpoints delineated at this stage are not used as true comparators for the claim at issue. This procedure, however, results in consistent approximations of appropriate endpoints. Again we can look to the FTC complaint, along with its evidence, to assign those endpoints.

The charges dictate one end, by stating, presumably, a legally sufficient falsity to incur regulatory wrath. The resultant "false" end of the scale should mirror that charge, in substance. The fourth stated representation from *Coca-Cola Co.,* for example, is "said drink is made with fresh fruit and has a high fruit content comparable to fresh fruits and fruit juices."[83]

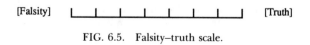

FIG. 6.5.   Falsity–truth scale.

---

[83]*Supra* note 78, at 751.

On this single dimension, one end of the scale should be stated as, "High fruit content comparable to fresh fruits and fruit juices," or its substantive equivalent.

The opposing pole of the scale, then, should be an approximation of "truth." Typically this truth is objectively determinable. Through the administrative "discovery" process the FTC can determine the actual fruit content of Hi-C.[84] Of course, until the matter is proved in an administrative hearing it remains only the "alleged" truth. It is this alleged truth that should serve as the endpoint. If the drink has very little fruit in its formula (e.g., 5%), the other endpoint might state, "Contains 5% fruit or fruit juice." Because only an approximation is necessary, and this figure is so low, it would be equally acceptable to state, "Contains no fruit or fruit juice." So long as this is very close to the truth it will not render the facts indeterminable[85] (see Fig. 6.6).

In other instances the objective truth may be more difficult to find. It is necessary, however, for the Commission staff to have its legal case fully prepared by the time its complaint is filed, and a part of that case must include a showing of evidence to prove the "truth." At the time that case is complete, except for the empirical test discussed here, the alleged (provable) truth should be known. It is this "truth" that should be used as the "true" endpoint.[86]

If that "truth" can be proved by the FTC, it is an appropriate concept to use for the remaining scale endpoint. If, on the other hand, the FTC is unable to prove it, the case will probably be lost, anyway. At the very least, failure to prove that truth will render this experimental data of little probative value, so an endpoint should not be chosen that is too ambitious and cannot be proved to be true. To prove that people perceive Hi-C as having fruit content closer to 100% than 5% does little to advance the FTC's case if it can only establish the truth to be something less than 60% fruit juice.

Contains No Fruit or Fruit Juice — High Fruit Content Comparable to Fresh Fruits and Fruit Juices

FIG. 6.6.   Approximation of scale endpoints.

---

[84]The FTC can demand documentation, test results, and can conduct its own laboratory tests to evaluate the "truth" about product attributes.

[85]As a rule of thumb, such approximations should be used only where the truth is unquantifiable or where the quantifiable percentage is less than the percentage represented by a single step on the scale. In this instance there are seven steps, making each worth about 14.3% of the total scale, so "No fruit juice" should only be used where the actual percentage is less than 14.3.

[86]This suggests, of course, that the empirical measure should not be undertaken until all evidence regarding the "truth" has been collected.

Stimuli

The Role of Ineradicable Miscomprehension. Once the scales are created, the next step involves preparation for empirical evaluation of those endpoints. It is this step that permits this method to be extremely repeatable and meaningful.

The particular choice of phrasing used for each end of the scale may continue to be subject to multiple interpretations. It might be that even a blatant lie, an explicit factual misrepresentation, would not fall at the "false" extreme of this belief scale. It might also be that although the product has little nutritional value, *if given the facts* consumers would nonetheless consider it more nutritional than some alternatives, thereby rating it higher on the nutrition scale than the "truth" endpoint.

Rating an ad on the bipolar truth–falsity RPI scale *presumes* a painfully honest ad would be evaluated to fall at the extreme "truth" end of the scale, and that a blatant lie would fall at the other extremity, with assessment of the actual ad buried somewhere between the two. These hypothetical frequency distributions are shown in Fig. 6.7. Unfortunately, this assumes no error at the ends of the scale. This is contrary to the proposition that there is some level of error inherent in all mediated communications (i.e., ineradicable miscomprehension). It also presumes there are no pre-existing beliefs to affect that evaluation.

A more satisfying approach would entail empirical measurement not only of the advertisement, but of the endpoints. Any differences, therefore, between the truth end of the scale and consumer evaluation of a carefully constructed true message should be attributable to ineradicable miscomprehension (and prior-held beliefs), as would any resultant gap between the falsity end and evaluations of a blatantly false message. Figure 6.8 depicts a frequency distribution much like Fig. 6.7, except that it reveals how the evaluation of an ad falling at the center of the scale can actually be closer to falsity than truth (or vice versa). Neither the true nor the false conditions fall at the ends of the scale in Fig. 6.8, representing ineradicable miscomprehension (and prior beliefs) on both ends.

In addition, false messages may be subject to different inherent levels

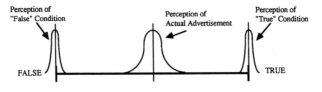

FIG. 6.7.   Assumption of bipolar scale.

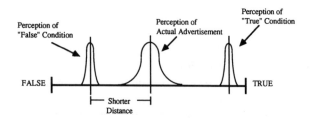

FIG. 6.8. Possible results violating assumption of bipolar scale.

of miscomprehension than do true messages. Consumers may be more or less willing to perceive some claims than others, even if the claims are clear and explicit, particularly if they are impressive. It requires no extraordinary intuition to guess that such impressive claims might be more frequent in instances of false claims than true ones. Although this is mere conjecture, if it bears any truth an assessment of an ad that falls in the middle of the RPI scale would actually be closer to one end than the other after ineradicable miscomprehension is subtracted from each end. A solution to the problem of ineradicable miscomprehension is to create and empirically measure true and false messages at the same time we are testing the challenged ad.

Creating Alternative Stimuli. Creation of the false message, like its counterpart endpoint of the scale, should be derived in part from the FTC complaint. The message should take the form of a memorandum or factsheet, with the actual claims from the original ad being modified to eliminate alleged implications and supplant them with explicit falsities that mirror each FTC allegation. For example, if the original included a disclaimer, alleged by the FTC to be overlooked by many consumers, it should be removed altogether. A single false memorandum can be used to represent the falsity endpoint of all concerned dimensions. The true message should also take the form of a memorandum or factsheet, listing only the true attributes of the product.

To illustrate this, suppose we wish to test one of the charges in *Figgie International.*[87] This case involved the sale of home heat detectors for residential fire protection. One of the charges in that case alleged that the company's promotional material represented that "Respondent's fire alarm systems combining heat detectors and smoke detectors provide significantly greater fire warning protection for occupants than smoke detectors alone.[88] The truth of the matter, alleged by the FTC staff,

[87] 107 F.T.C. 313 (1986).
[88] *Id.* at 314.

was that "Respondent's fire alarm systems combining heat detectors and smoke detectors do not provide significantly greater fire warning protection for occupants than smoke detectors alone."[89] The statement in the promotional material that was subject of the challenge, along with the statements derived for the true and false messages follow:

1. *Ad Statement:* "Mechanical heat detectors are essential to provide the reliability that smoke detectors lack and to guard against the many types of fires where smoke detectors may be ineffective."
2. *True Statement:* "Using heat detectors and smoke detectors together will not provide significantly greater fire protection than using smoke detectors alone."
3. *False Statement:* "Using heat detectors and smoke detectors together will provide significantly greater fire protection than using smoke detectors alone."

The factsheet format of these messages will give them the appearance of unbiased truth, so language of a persuasive nature should be avoided. This differentiates these alternative messages from the "corrected" ads used by Russo et al.[90] described earlier. The true message, just presented, might be incredible in a persuasive ad. Subjects might completely disbelieve the entire ad. Advertisers simply do not make such statements. However, placing this statement in the context of a company's internal memorandum should give it substantial credibility.

Modifications, of course, may be necessary under some circumstances. For example, if pictorial deception is alleged, or where words are inadequate to convey the truth and the attribute is visually observable, it may be necessary to include true/false illustrations in these memoranda. Where the charge suggests consumers may make a comparison (e.g., "as much vitamin C as orange juice"), comparative data should be given in the memoranda. The greatest problem here is helping consumers to comprehend the data (e.g., 20 mg. vitamin C). The language must be simplified to ensure subjects will make an informed decision. Of course, if a fact cannot be adequately simplified, the advertiser should not be held responsible to accomplish this same impossibility in its advertising.

There is little threat that, in creating the memoranda, the FTC will "load" the outcome by biasing the wording of the memorandum. If it states a falsity more egregious than the one in the complaint, the results will be biased against the Commission. If the wording is less "false" than stated in the complaint, the probative value of the results will be

---

[89]*Id.*
[90]*Supra* note 70.

vulnerable to attack and the stated falsity in the memorandum runs greater risk of being found insufficient to support legal action. If respondents, rather than the FTC, conduct the experiment, similar evidentiary realities will help to contain the threat of bias.

Sampling

Randomized sampling is essential for optimal use of this method, not just for external validity but for internal validity as well. Recall that to use belief rather than comprehension as a dependent variable, we must be able to infer causation regarding beliefs about the product/service. This is accomplished through experimental manipulation of different levels of the independent variable: message truth. The inference that belief will vary for these levels, however, relies on the assumption that subjects were randomly sampled, such that each of the three groups came to the experiment with approximately the same basal beliefs. If this assumption is unjustified, the "relatively false" belief may reflect differences in prior knowledge and prior-held beliefs of subjects in those groups. Randomization, therefore, helps us control for those prior-held beliefs and knowledge.

Although there are frequently economic realities that hinder true randomization in academic research, I propose for purposes of FTC application that stratified multistage cluster sampling be implemented. This would require, first, that the agency identify the population of relevant consumers, looking primarily to the target market and target audience. Second, the geographic area of the market would be divided into several segments (usually states), which would serve as the primary sampling units (PSU). A small group of those PSUs would be sampled (e.g., three to four states). Third, those PSUs would be broken into secondary sampling units (SSU; e.g., counties) which would then be sampled.

The experiment would then be conducted in a centrally located town or city in each selected SSU, and consumers would be sampled through random-digit dialing (if the product is a mass-distributed consumer item) or a systematic sampling of consumers from a relevant association directory or mailing list. With this method, the experiment could be conducted once in each of the few selected SSUs, making this a relatively economical procedure. If several ads appropriate to the same market are to be tested, all of them could then be tested at the same time, making this even more economical.

Procedure

Exposure Conditions.   After subjects have been sampled, they should be invited to a central location for the experiment. Several subjects can be run at the same time, so long as they are in the same exposure condition and the experimenter can ensure that each is following the specific directions.

Stimuli should be prepared, as previously described, for the three exposure conditions: true message, original ad, and false message. In addition, I recommend a fourth condition be added for diagnostic purposes: a no-message condition. The no-message condition would consist of a stimulus presenting only the product/service name, a generic descripter (e.g., "laundry detergent," or "automobile"), and the manufacturer's name. This condition will help to identify prior-held belief, without the influences that may occur in the other three conditions.[91]

The nature of the four conditions, being variations of the same ad, makes it necessary that this be a between-subjects design. Consequently, subjects must be randomly assigned to one of four different groups, so that each subject sees only one condition for each tested ad.

Presentation.   Subjects should be exposed to the stimulus, whether print or television, without editorial or programming context. Although this may inhibit ecological validity, it ensures that any resulting deception is not because of context and should help to alleviate the handicap created by using only a single exposure. Ads are normally designed for a greater exposure frequency, with each exposure often in a different context, so the addition of context to a single-exposure experiment does not fully approximate realistic viewing, but it may significantly diminish the measure's sensitivity. In fact, ads are often seen out of context, such as on a billboard, or walking into a room when a commercial is on the television. Exposure to the stimulus, isolated from context, appears both justifiable and superior to exposure in context.

After showing the stimulus, it should be removed from view. It is seldom that consumers have the ad in hand when making a purchase. Many alleged deceptive claims would be nondeceptive if a close reading was attainable at the time of purchase. It is the representation of the ad as it appears in memory that is important. Specific questions about the product/service should not be asked until the stimulus is out of view.

Subjects should next be given a questionnaire asking the appropriate

---

[91]This addition is similar to the no-ad control used by Russo, Metcalf, and Stephens, *supra* note 70.

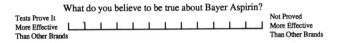

FIG. 6.9.   Belief-based question about product attribute.

questions about their specific beliefs regarding the product attributes (e.g., see, Fig. 6.9).

The scale for response should provide at least seven divisions. Although the exact number of divisions is fairly unimportant, except that it should be an odd number so that subjects can choose the centerpoint, I suggest a 13-point scale. This larger number of divisions will give subjects the illusion of greater precision.

Subjects should also be asked to rank the subject attribute on a materiality scale. The same basic method of scaling can be used as was used to measure belief (e.g., see Fig. 6.10). In the same way that we offer truth and falsity as endpoints on the belief scale, we offer materiality and immateriality as endpoints on this scale. Therefore, only two questions need be asked of subjects regarding each claimed product attribute: one for belief and one for materiality.[92]

Finally, some additional diagnostic questions can be asked to evaluate the success of randomization. Those questions include how familiar the subjects are with the product, how much experience they have with it, and whether they have seen it advertised before.

Would this feature be a factor in your decision whether or not to buy this product?

Would Be A
Primary Factor └─┴─┴─┴─┴─┴─┴─┴─┴─┴─┴─┴─┘ Would Not Affect
My Decision

FIG. 6.10.   Materiality question about product attribute.

---

[92]Although psychometric studies typically ask multiple questions to assess a single construct, the criteria presented above significantly limit the latitude for creating more than one question to test Belief or Materiality of a claimed product attribute. Additional questions could only be slight variations, otherwise they would invalidate the study-to-study consistency intended by this method, and they could also risk threatening the legal validity of the study. This does not seem a serious concern, however. Multiple questions are normally used because the constructs being measured are abstract, with each subject having a different meaning (e.g., "clean"), and multiple indicators are required to triangulate that meaning and to be certain that the construct is being accurately measured. In the present instance we are not concerned with the specific meanings attached to the construct, but only with relative proximity of those constructs to two dichotomous endpoints with definite legal meaning. Consequently, the use of multiple questions is probably unwise and unnecessary.

Analysis and Interpretation

Analysis is straightforward. The intent is to discover whether belief of the ad condition is closer to the "truth" condition or the "falsity" condition.

There are four possible ways to interpret the results of this experiment. First, we could look at the differences between "truth" and the ad (see comparison type 1 in Fig. 6.11). If evaluation of the ad is significantly different from evaluation of the true memorandum, we could conclude the ad is deceptive. However, as with the Russo et al. method, we have no way to know whether that significant difference is a meaningful one. I think it is also reasonable to expect beliefs formed by exposure to an ad to be different from those formed by a memo. This would set the standard so high almost any ad would be found deceptive.

Second, we could look at the difference between the ad and "falsity" (see comparison Type 2 in Fig. 6.11). If the ad is significantly different from falsity, we could consider the ad nondeceptive. This, however, suffers from the same shortcomings as the truth versus ad comparison. We have no way of knowing the difference is meaningful, and it would set the standard so low that many deceptive ads would not be detected. This would not be an improvement over conventional methods.

Third, we might assess whether the ad condition is significantly different from the control condition in the direction of falsity (see comparison Type 3 in Fig. 6.11). This would indicate that, no matter what the prior-held beliefs, the ad contributed to some false conceptions. However, we still cannot determine whether that difference is meaningful. If the control group and the "truth" group held the same beliefs, this would give us the same results as the first approach. Subjects could have substantially true beliefs, but because they differ from the control they would be deemed deceptive. This would effectively negate the use of persuasive language in ads.

The best approach is to determine whether the ad goes beyond mere

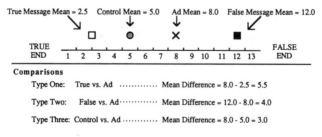

FIG. 6.11 Example results of three different comparisons.

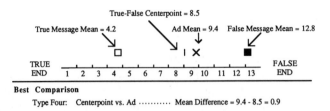

FIG. 6.12.   Example result of best comparison.

persuasion, and into deceptiveness, by discovering whether evaluations of the ad are *closer* to evaluations of "truth" or those of "falsity" (i.e., their relative proximity to the two dichotomous evaluations). If the ad fell closer to falsity than truth, then we know that the difference between ad and truth is meaningful (see Fig. 6.12).

This can be accomplished by finding the centerpoint between truth and falsity, as measured, observing to which side of that point the mean evaluation of the ad falls, and testing whether the difference between the two is statistically significant. The centerpoint is easily found by averaging the mean evaluations the true and false memoranda. On a 13-point scale (steps coded 1–13), if the mean "true" evaluation is 2.0, and the mean "false" evaluation is 11.0, the new center would be 6.5 rather than the original 7.0. This effectively creates a new scale, replacing the absolute endpoints with measured ones.

Statistical analysis is then possible using either a t test or a one-group analysis of variance. If the mean evaluation of the ad falls on the "false" side of center, and significantly differs from center, it should be deemed deceptive. Therefore, if significantly closer to true it would be nondeceptive. However, if the ad does not deviate significantly from center, I suggest that the alleged deceptiveness has not been substantiated, and so should also be considered nondeceptive.

It may appear to some readers that, conceptually, a scale centerpoint has no meaning under the law, and therefore is an improper point of comparison. I will concede that point, in the abstract, but the truth and falsity endpoints, being derived directly from the FTC charges, do have conceptual justification, and this formula is simply a means of measuring the relative proximity to those endpoints. Although I continue in the following chapter to make reference to the centerpoint (conceptually, the formula presented above is Ad−Centerpoint=Deceptiveness), an alternative formula that yields the same results without reference to a centerpoint is

$$\frac{(\text{Ad} - \text{Truth Endpoint}) + (\text{Ad} - \text{Falsity Endpoint})}{2} = \text{Deceptiveness}$$

This formula requires calculation of the ad's deviation from the means of both endpoints, however, which is somewhat more cumbersome. Again, the resulting numbers will be identical, so I prefer the simpler formulation, using a centerpoint.

The materiality measure would be handled in a similar manner, except that it is unnecessary to calculate a centerpoint. Because we cannot effectively manipulate materiality in the way that we manipulate falsity for the deceptiveness measure, we must assume that the original scale endpoints for materiality are accurate. Consequently, we need only find whether the evaluation of a claim's materiality falls on the material side ("would be a primary factor"), significantly differing from the actual scale center. If the claim is determined to be both material and deceptive, we could then conclude it regulable.

SUMMARY

The method presented here is specifically tailored to measure deceptiveness, and no other aspect, of advertisements. It is a sensitive, robust, and legally valid method, arguably superior to its predecessors.

Directions are provided for consistent derivation of scales in actual FTC cases. Although the discussion does not address scaling for purely academic research, the same approach is easily adapted to the purposes of individual researchers without significant loss of consistency.

The next chapter uses this method to test claims formerly declared by the FTC, through traditional fact-finding methods, to be deceptive. This serves as a rough estimate of the method's convergent validity vis-à-vis the regulatory norm.

Pilot Study

Chapter 6 proposed a method for measuring deceptiveness, and explained the logic by which the method was derived. The most basic, and essential, question regarding that method was not answered, however. We must yet determine whether the method will detect deceptiveness. This chapter attempts to provide an answer by testing this method and comparing its results to those of the FTC.

It is advisable to empirically assess the internal validity of a new method. This typically requires a test of "convergent" validity, comparing the results of the new measure to a previously accepted method, to discover whether both assessments of a construct converge (e.g., both find the same claims to be deceptive).[1] In this instance the best comparator for the proposed method is the traditional FTC fact-finding process. If the results of this technique, when testing ads previously confronted by the Commission, substantially agree with the determinations of the regulators, it seems safe to assume some degree of validity.

This process is not without problems. The first, and most severe, problem derives from the fact that I am suggesting an *improvement* over present FTC methods. Any discrepancy between my results and those of the FTC may be explainable either as a failure of my method to properly

---

[1]Fiske, *Convergent-Discriminant Validation in Measurements and Research Strategies,* in D. Brinberg and L. Kidder, New Directions for Methodology of Social and Behavioral Science: Forms of Validity in Research No. 12 77 (1982); T. D. Cook and D. T. Campbell, Quasi-Experimentation: Design and Analysis Issues for Field Settings 61 (1979).

measure deceptiveness, or as evidence of the inadequacies of the FTC methods. This issue is incapable of empirical resolution.

A second major problem arises from the fact that the findings of the FTC in no way rank order the deceptiveness of claims, saying claim A is more deceptive than claim B, making correlational analysis of the new versus traditional methods impossible.[2] In fact, the FTC does not even find claims to be either deceptive or nondeceptive. Its decisions normally declare only that a claim is deceptive, or that there is *insufficient evidence* to conclude that it is deceptive. Therefore, even where the Commission does not find a claim deceptive, it may still be deceptive but the evidence presented in the hearing was too meager to prove that point. This fact prohibits any true finding of convergent validity.

Given these limitations, any hope of assessing convergence of the two methods is hopelessly confounded. I would argue that my method is presumptively superior because, unlike traditional FTC methods, it is derived from theory, and this technique is specifically designed to circumvent the weaknesses of its predecessors. The validity of this argument must ultimately be determined by the reader. Consequently, the experiment that follows uses the proposed method to test claims previously encountered by the FTC, and the results of the two methods are compared for both similarities and dissimilarities, but no attempt is made to fully validate the method.

METHOD

The method used here conforms generally to the design presented in chapter 6. The subject pool, however, is restricted to a convenience sampling of university students.

Subjects

Recruited as subjects were 150 undergraduate students. These subjects were taken on a volunteer basis from two Principles of Advertising classes in the School of Journalism and Mass Communication at the University of Wisconsin—Madison. As an incentive for participation, subjects were given extra credit points in their respective classes. All students in those classes were offered an opportunity to participate. Prior to participation in the experiment, subjects were screened to ensure that they had normal

---

[2]Churchill referred to validation by correlating two measures as "Pragmatic Validity." G. CHURCHILL, MARKETING RESEARCH: METHODOLOGICAL FOUNDATIONS 2D 256 (1979).

or corrected-to-normal vision at typical reading distances. No uncorrected vision problems were encountered.

Materials

Stimuli. The intent of this experiment was to apply the proposed method to test advertisements, and their associated claims, that were previously found deceptive by the FTC. However, given the fact that more recent cases tend to incorporate greater use of external evidence, such as consumer surveys, than did older cases,[3] along with the threat that older ads might be inherently less believable because of their dated content or style, the sampling of FTC cases was restricted to the recent 10-year period from 1977 through mid-1986.

During that time period the Commission considered 179 advertising cases. Of those, 156 (87.2%) ended with consent orders, where advertisers simply agreed to cease certain challenged practices without litigating the issues involved. Because these cases were not decided on their merits there was no finding of deceptiveness, so they were deemed inappropriate for this study.[4] Of the remaining 23 cases (12.8%), many of them were parallel cases, involving either the same product and different defendants or similar claims for similar products. Duplications were not considered acceptable, because greater variety would permit a better estimate of the method's validity. Others were advertising cases that involved some issue other than deceptiveness. These clearly did not apply. Finally, a few cases could not be used because insufficient information was supplied in the published decisions to locate or reconstruct the challenged advertisements, and the Commission files for these cases were inaccessible, making it impossible to test them. After elimination of these unusable cases, only six remained: *Sterling Drug*[5] (Bayer Aspirin), *Sears*[6] (Lady Kenmore dishwashers), *Kroger*[7] (Price Patrol Survey), *Thompson Medical*[8] (Aspercreme analgesic rub), *Litton*[9] (Litton microwaves), and *Cliffdale*[10] (Ball-Matic automotive device). In addition to the ads drawn

---

[3]Preston, *Data-Free at the FTC? How the Federal Trade Commission Decides Whether Extrinsic Evidence of Deceptiveness is Required,* 24 AMER. BUS. L. J. 359, 361 (1986).

[4]This search was conducted in FTC DECISIONS, Volumes 89–107 (1977–86). Volume 107 was the latest available compilation of cases at the time selection was made.

[5]102 F.T.C. 395 (1983).

[6]95 F.T.C. 406 (1980).

[7]98 F.T.C. 639 (1981).

[8]104 F.T.C. 648 (1984).

[9]97 F.T.C. 1 (1981).

[10]103 F.T.C. 110 (1984).

from those six cases, two recent ads for other products, not challenged by the FTC, were also added to this pool of test stimuli.

Ideally, the actual ads challenged in the six cases should be used, but reliance on FTC cases makes this a virtual impossibility in most instances. The original ads are frequently chosen from obscure publications, and the publications in which they appeared are almost never disclosed in the decisions. At best, a published decision may reprint a poor, and frequently illegible, xerographic copy of the ad. As a consequence, actual ads were located and used in this experiment for only two of the cases involved, but mock versions were composed for the remaining four from the published information in those decisions. The reconstructed ads were made as true to the original as possible, incorporating the general layout, design, and illustrations (where replicable). The ads were composed on an Apple Macintosh computer and printed on an Apple LaserWriter printer, resulting in a relatively authentic appearance. These ads appear in Appendix A.

"True" and "false" memoranda were also constructed to correspond to each ad, based on the FTC complaint in the applicable case. These stimuli were made to appear like typewritten interoffice memoranda listing numerous product/service attributes, all derived from the FTC complaint. The "true" memos can be seen in Appendix B, and the "false" memos in Appendix C.

Finally, stimuli presenting only the product name, product type, and manufacturer or seller name were prepared. These stimuli were designed as controls, for diagnostic purposes, presenting no attribute information. These no-attribute-information stimuli can be seen in Appendix D.

Questionnaires. A one- or two-page questionnaire was prepared for each ad. The questions assessed several product attributes, some of which were experimentally manipulated in the true and false memoranda, and some that were not manipulated but were used to mask the purpose of the experiment.

Each attribute was assessed on three separate 13-point scales: (a) belief that the attribute is associated with the product/service, (b) confidence in that belief, and (c) materiality. The first and third of these were derived in accordance with the procedure outlined in chapter 6. Belief scale polarities (i.e., whether the "true" statement appeared at the left or right end) were randomized to avoid reactivity[11] in the measure. The "confidence" scale was included only for diagnostic and exploratory pur-

---

[11]Cook and Campbell referred to reactive measures as "Hypothesis-Guessing Within Experimental Conditions," in Cook and Campbell, *supra* note 1, at 66.

poses. Additionally, each ad was assessed for product name familiarity, experience with the product, and prior exposure to advertising for the product. These scales were also included merely for diagnostic reasons. Finally, each subject was asked four demographic questions to determine the following characteristics about the participants: (a) age, (b) sex, (c) university classification, and (d) family income.

A parallel questionnaire set was constructed to assess comprehension, rather than belief. Instead of asking subjects to rate what they believed about the product/service, they were asked to rate what they thought the ad to be claiming. Aside from this re-wording, the questionnaires were identical to those used to measure Belief. Questionnaires appear in Appendix E.

Design

The experimental design consisted of five treatments for each advertisement. One treatment was the "true" memorandum, another was the "false" memorandum, a third was the no-attribute-information control, a fourth was the original ad (measured for belief), and the last was the original ad (measured for comprehension). This was a between-subjects design, so each subject viewed only one treatment for each of the eight products/services. To permit them to see more than one treatment for a product would have substantially increased the probability of subjects anticipating the purpose of the experiment, and modifying their responses in reaction to that perceived purpose.

Five exposure conditions were formed from these treatments. Four of the conditions included two each of the first four treatments just listed, so that each subject evaluated all eight products/services, seeing two true memos, two false memos, two controls, and two original ads. Subjects in the fifth condition saw only original ads and rated only their comprehension of the ads. This condition included only the one treatment, to avoid subjects mistakenly rating belief when presented with the comprehension questionnaire, or visa versa, because the questionnaires were so similar in appearance. Presentation order in each condition was randomized, to control for order effects.

Procedure

Subjects participated in small groups, up to 12 in each. Each group was assigned to a single condition, so that all subjects in a group viewed the same stimuli. The experimental setting was a classroom or meeting room. Subjects were assigned to conditions according to the time at which they participated. Conditions were rotated from session to session so that no condition was the same in two consecutive sessions, and experimental sessions were offered at a wide variety of times and days. Because subjects chose their own time of participation, according to the time at which they were available, and because there is no theoretical basis for expecting a confound to result from this self-assignment (e.g., there is no reason to expect that gullible subjects are more likely to select one particular time or day in a manner different from nongullible subjects) this was expected to approximate randomization. Practical limitations imposed by using student subjects with widely varying schedules necessitated this restriction.

Subjects were each given a questionnaire booklet, specific to their exposure condition, consisting of a cover sheet with instructions (see Appendix E), followed by 10 stimulus and questionnaire pairs, and ending with the demographic questionnaire. The first two stimulus-questionnaire pairs in each booklet were used simply for warm-up purposes, and were not included in later analysis.

Subjects were instructed to turn each page of the booklet only upon direction of the experimenter. Subjects would view a stimulus on one page, and only after they all indicated they had completed reading the material they would be permitted to turn the page and answer the appropriate questionnaire, so that the stimulus would be out of view. The time of exposure to the stimulus, therefore, was self-governed, and varied from stimulus to stimulus. Times varied from a few seconds, for the control stimuli, to about three minutes for the most complex stimulus (the Ball-Matic ad). This process was repeated until all stimuli had been viewed and evaluated, and ended with completion of the demographic questionnaire.

THESES

In each FTC case multiple charges are made. It is not unusual for an advertiser to be alleged to have made five or six distinct deceptive claims. It is likewise typical that a whole group of advertisements, rather than a single ad, is involved in the action. However, any one of those ads may make only one or a few of the challenged claims. The ads chosen for this experiment varied in the number of challenged claims they represented, each reflecting two to four of those claims. Consequently, the number of manipulated claims for each product/service in the experiment also varied.

The first hypothesis is that where the FTC staff has charged deceptive claims to have been made, and found by the Commission to have been made, subjects' beliefs will fall significantly closer to their beliefs of the "false" message than to their beliefs of the "true" message, as measured from the centerpoint between the two. Because I argued in chapter 6 that my method should be an improvement over the FTC's practices, agreement is not expected on every claim. However, collapsing across all of the claims should reveal a significant difference from center in the "false" direction.

The charges included in this group follow. Shown in brackets, at the beginning of each claim, is a signifier (e.g., C2) used as an abbreviation for that claim later in this chapter. The letter signifies the product/service, and the number corresponds to its position on the questionnaire. For example, C2 represents Cliffdale (C) and the second attribute (2) appearing on its questionnaire:

1. *Cliffdale (Ball-Matic)*[12]
   Respondents represented and now represent, directly or by implication, that:

   a. [C2] The Ball-Matic is an important, significant, and unique new invention;[13]

   b. [C5] The Ball-Matic when installed in a typical automobile and used under normal driving conditions will significantly improve fuel economy;[14]

   c. [C3] Under normal driving conditions, a typical driver can usually obtain a fuel economy improvement of 20% (or more) or an improvement that will approximate or equal four miles per gallon when the Ball-Matic is installed in his/her automobile;[15]

   d. [C4] Results of consumer usage, as evidenced by consumer endorsements, prove that the Ball-Matic significantly improves fuel economy.[16]

2. *Litton*[17]
   Litton has represented, directly or by implication, that:

   a. [L1] A survey proves Litton microwaves are recommended,

---

[12]Charges appear *supra* note 10, at 111–12.
[13]*See* findings, *id.* at 166.
[14]*Id.* at 167.
[15]*Id.*
[16]*Id.* at 170–71.
[17]Charges appear *supra* note 9, at 2–4.

used, chosen, or otherwise preferred by independent microwave oven service technicians;[18]

b. [L3] A survey proves that Litton microwaves are superior to
competitors' products.[19]

3. *Kroger*[20]
Respondent has represented, directly or by implication, that:

a. [K1] The results of the Price Patrol Survey prove that shopping
at Kroger, rather than at competitors' stores, will result in lower
overall expenditures;[21]

b. [K3] The Price Patrol Survey is a methodologically sound
survey.[22]

4. *Sears*[23]
Respondents represented . . . that:

a. [S2] The Lady Kenmore dishwasher would completely remove,
without prior rinsing or scraping, all residue and film from
dishes, pots, and pans in cooking and baking according to
normal consumer recipes and under other circumstances normally and expectably encountered by consumers;[24]

b. [S4] Dishes in the top rack of the Lady Kenmore dishwashers
would get as clean as those in the bottom rack without prior
rinsing or scraping.[25]

5. *Bayer*[26]
It was represented directly or by implication:

a. [B2] That Bayer Aspirin has been tested against 200 other
brands of aspirin for quality, purity, freshness, stability, and
speed of disintegration, and that the results of the tests demon-

---

[18]*See* findings, *id.* at 71–72. Several separate charges were made by the FTC, but they
involved use of the survey in a large number of ads. Because it was unclear which ad
contributed to the conveyance of each charge, the test allegation used here combines them
into one statement.

[19]*Id.* at 71–72.

[20]Charges appear *supra* note 7, at 641.

[21]*See* findings, *id.* at 731.

[22]*Id.* at 731–32. Because it was feared that subjects might not understand the term
methodologically sound, the phrase *scientifically based* was substituted in the experiment.

[23]Charges appear *supra* note 6, at 406–7.

[24]*See* findings, *id.* at 512.

[25]*Id.*

[26]Charges appear *supra* note 5, at 403.

strated that Bayer Aspirin is qualitatively superior to all other brands tested in all respects, and therapeutically superior to all of the other brands tested.[27]

6. *Aspercreme*[28]

Respondents represented and now represent, directly or by implication, that:

a. [A1] Aspercreme contains aspirin;[29]
b. [A4] Aspercreme is a recently discovered or developed drug product;[30]
c. [A5] Valid studies have scientifically proven that Aspercreme is more effective than orally ingested aspirin for the relief of arthritis, rheumatic conditions, and their symptoms.[31]

It should be noted, as well, that the Commission often finds insufficient evidentiary support for some of the charges. Although this is not necessarily the same as finding the claim *non*deceptive, it is the best indication available that a claim is not deceptive. Three of the claims in the ads selected for this experiment were charged to be deceptive, but not found deceptive by the Commission.

The second hypothesis, therefore, is that where the FTC has charged deceptive claims to have been made, but *not* found by the Commission to have been made, subjects' beliefs will not fall significantly closer to their beliefs of the "false" message than to their beliefs of the "true" message. The null hypothesis in this instance includes *either* a finding of no significance or of significance in the "true" direction. Again, this will be tested by collapsing across all involved claims. The charges included in this group follow:

1. *Kroger*[32]

a. [K4] The results of the Price Patrol Survey prove that most items in respondent's stores are priced lower than in competitors' stores (i.e., that the survey sampled all products sold by Kroger).[33]

---

[27]*See* findings, *id.* at 755.
[28]Charges appear *supra* note 8, at 650.
[29]*See* findings, *id.* at 808–10.
[30]*Id.* at 810–11.
[31]*Id.* at 811.
[32]*Supra* note 7, at 641.
[33]This claim was not found to have been made. *Id.* at 729.

2. *Sears*[34]

   a. [S5] The Lady Kenmore "Semi-Wash" cycle, by giving dishes an "extra-hot 155° final rinse," destroyed all harmful and other bacteria and microorganisms on the dishes and pots and pans (i.e., dishes would be sterilized).[35]

3. *Bayer*[36]

   a. [B3] That a recommended dose of Bayer Aspirin relieves nervous tension, anxiety and irritability and improves user's mood.[37]

The third hypothesis concerns the two advertisements included in the experiment that were not subject to FTC actions. The outcome here is inherently less predictable, making an hypothesis difficult to formulate. The two ads were chosen from Sunday newspaper inserts, because it appeared they *might* be making deceptive implications, just as the FTC might suspect an ad to be deceptive. They were included primarily as an illustration of how researchers can create scale endpoints and memoranda statements for scholarly inquiry. Based on the advertisements, alone, the following deceptive implications were suspected:

1. *American Eagle Belt Buckle*

   a. [E3] That the buckle's serial number and purchaser are registered with the U.S. Government rather than the seller's company.
   b. [E4] That the diamond mounted on the buckle is 1/4 carat rather than 1/4 point.
   c. [E5] That the buckle is made substantially of precious metals rather than inexpensive metals lightly covered with gold and silver platings.

2. *35mm Camera*

   a. [T2] That the camera is a single lens reflex design rather than a simple viewfinder design.
   b. [T3] That an electronic flash unit is included with the camera at no extra cost.

---

[34]*Supra* note 6, at 406–7.
[35]*Id.* at 512.
[36]*Supra* note 5, at 403.
[37]*Id.* at 755.

    c. [T4] That the lens of the camera is removable and interchange-
able with other lenses.

    d. [T5] That the camera is made of metal rather than plastic.

    e. [T7] That the camera is made by a known major manufacturer
rather than an "off-brand."

Each of these claims is assumed false. By purchasing the products it
would have been possible to substantiate their falsity, but that was unnecessary for present purposes. For most of the claims the "truth" of the
product was discoverable by close examination of the ad. Personal knowledge of the product type was sufficient to establish the truth regarding
the other claims involved. This third hypothesis is that the ads will be
evaluated to fall closer to the false message than to the true message.

The fourth hypothesis is that all of the claims just stated will be rated
by subjects on the materiality scale significantly closer to the "material"
end of the scale ("would be a primary factor" in my purchase decision),
than to the "immaterial" end ("would not affect my decision") as measured from the centerpoint. Recall that the Commission normally presumes materiality when a claim is found deceptive, so by empirically
testing materiality, this, too, should represent an improvement over current FTC practice. However, because this is intended as an improvement,
it is not safe to assume that every claim will be found material. Consequently, this hypothesis will also be tested by collapsing across all FTC
challenged claims. Claims from the unchallenged ads in Hypothesis 3 will
be analyzed separately under this hypothesis, but in the same manner.
The analyses are separated to permit comparison of this method directly
to that of the FTC without interference from the unchallenged claims
not considered by the FTC.

Hypothesis 5 compares comprehension and belief. In chapter 5 it
was argued that there may be a difference between what consumers
understand an ad to claim and what they believe to be true. It was on
this theoretical premise that the present method is based. Although
not every claim can be expected to render a difference, I predict that
collapsing across all of the challenged claims listed above should reveal
a significant difference between comprehension and belief. Because it is
unlikely that consumers will believe a product to have more impressive
attributes than its promotions claim, any difference should place comprehension in closer proximity, than belief, to the "false" end of the scale.

RESULTS

Several of the questions asked of subjects were exploratory or diagnostic,
and are not reflected in the analysis that follows. Although there are
instances of missing data in the overall data set, no missing data occurred

in the analyses included here, so there was no need to artificially code any data points.

Demographics and Limitations

Table 7.1 depicts the breakdown of subjects by age. Although the range extends from 18 to 42, 46% of subjects were 20 years old. It is doubtful that this population is representative of target audiences for all of the products represented in this experiment, if any. Their experience or "product involvement" with, for example, the purchase of a dishwasher is probably not substantial. As a result, their ability to evaluate these products may not accurately reflect that of the ad's intended audience. This is an unfortunate limitation, but one that is not inherent in the method. It is probably more likely to bias belief than comprehension, because these are not very technically oriented ads. An older or more

TABLE 7.1
Age of Subjects

Age	Count	Percent
18	2	1.33
19	23	15.33
20	69	46.00
21	32	21.33
22	8	5.33
23	5	3.33
24	3	2.00
25	2	1.33
26	1	0.67
27	–	–
28	–	–
29	2	1.33
30	–	–
31	–	–
32	–	–
33	–	–
34	–	–
35	1	0.67
36	–	–
37	–	–
38	–	–
39	–	–
40	1	0.67
41	–	–
42	1	0.67
	150	100.00

TABLE 7.2
Sex of Subjects

Sex	Count	Percent
Female	114	76.0
Male	36	24.0
	150	100.0

experienced group of consumers may have used similar products and be less inclined to *believe* certain claims, but even an inexperienced purchaser is likely to understand the claim. The FTC has consistently held that national probability sampling is unnecessary for testing deceptiveness,[38] but that ruling is predicated on measuring Comprehension. Because beliefs are likely to vary more significantly from consumer to consumer, it is questionable whether the FTC would be so lenient with this method.

One effect that might reasonably be expected to result from this potentially naive population, given its inexperience in knowing what claims to believe, is that the difference between comprehension and belief (Hypothesis 5) will be more suppressed than it would otherwise. Consequently, this does not seem to be a crippling limitation of the study.

Table 7.2 reveals a heavy bias in favor of female subjects. Ideally, the test population should reflect the target audience balance, but that will vary from product to product. Because we are simultaneously testing several different products, presumably with several different audiences, it is impossible to accurately reflect them all in a single test, so some degree of unbalance was inevitable.

In Tables 7.3 and 7.4 we can see that the typical subject was a college junior from a middle-income family. This is a well-educated group, that

TABLE 7.3
University Standing of Students

Year	Count	Percent
Freshman	0	0
Sophomore	37	24.67
Junior	90	60.00
Senior	20	13.33
Graduate	3	2.00
	150	100.00

[38]*See, e.g., supra* note 5, at 459 and 467 n.5; Bristol-Myers, 102 F.T.C. 21, 326 n.30 (1983); California Milk Producers Advisory Bd., 94 F.T.C. 429, 463 (1979); Sun Oil Co., 84 F.T.C. 247, 271 (1974).

TABLE 7.4
Family Income of Subjects

Income	Count	Percent
Low	10	6.67
Middle	103	68.67
High	37	24.67
	150	100.00

may be less susceptible to deception than the average purchaser. If such a bias exists, it could act to diminish the predicted effects under Hypothesis 1, while exaggerating the effects of Hypothesis 5. However, this high level of formal education may be more than offset by the subjects' lack of product education or experience in the marketplace. Income level is somewhat high, but is fairly representative of the general population.

Because subjects were not truly randomly sampled some assurance was needed that the biases revealed above were evenly distributed across conditions. An analysis of variance (ANOVA) was done for each of these four demographic factors, comparing all five conditions, to locate any significant differences. As can be seen in Table 7.5, no differences were discovered.

Deceptiveness Measure of Claims Found Deceptive by the FTC

As outlined at the end of chapter 6, our aim is to compare evaluations of the ad, the true message, and the false message, to determine the relative proximity of the ad to the other two messages. Assuming the null

TABLE 7.5
Demographic Means of Subjects

	Condition					F-value	Probability
	1	2	3	4	5		
Age	20.43	20.27	21.33	21.00	21.60	1.03	0.39
Sex	1.23	1.23	1.33	1.23	1.17	0.57	0.68
Income	3.03	2.83	3.07	3.00	2.70	1.61	0.18
Year	1.90	1.83	1.90	1.73	1.73	0.74	0.57

Sex: 1 = Female, 2 = Male
Year: 1 = Freshman, 2 = Sophomore, 3 = Junior, 4 = Senior, 5 = Graduate
Income: 1 = High, 2 = Middle, 3 = Low

hypothesis to be no deceptiveness, if we can conclude with statistical certainty that the ad is evaluated significantly closer to the false message than the true, the ad should be deemed deceptive. A 13-point scale was used for evaluations, with its steps coded from 1 to 13, making the scale centerpoint = 7.

To find the relative proximity of the ad to the other evaluations, it was necessary to establish the true and false evaluations as new endpoints, comparing the ad evaluation to *their* centerpoint. To accomplish this task the mean of the true evaluations for a given ad was used as one end and the mean of the false as the other, then the mean of those two points served as the center. Analysis involved merely comparing two means, the centerpoint and the mean evaluation of the original ad, using a one-group ANOVA technique (a t test could have been used with equal results). The results of this claim by claim analysis for Hypothesis 1 are shown in Table 7.6 and are depicted in Fig. 7.1 Because the hypothesis predicts an overall effect, the evaluations for all of the included claims were compared to the mean centerpoint using the same one-group ANOVA technique. The composite mean belief of the claims was 9.262, as compared to a mean centerpoint of 6.540 for a significant difference of 2.722 $[F (1,419) = 167.989, p < 0.01]$ in the "false" direction.

Although the hypothesis predicted an overall composite effect, it also seems useful to look at separate analyses of each claim, as depicted in

TABLE 7.6
Mean Belief Evaluations of Challenged Claims Previously Found Deceptive

		True	Center	Ad	False	F-value
Cliffdale	C2	2.767	7.167	11.200	11.567	64.674**
	C3	1.500	6.750	9.233	12.000	11.287**
	C4	2.733	6.550	9.933	10.367	13.178**
	C5	1.867	6.767	9.200	11.667	8.572**
Litton	L1	1.667	6.717	10.133	11.767	27.937**
	L3	1.733	3.433	7.667	5.133	30.899**
Kroger	K1	3.767	7.883	10.500	12.000	14.069**
	K3	1.667	6.117	5.433	10.567	0.751
Sears	S2	1.367	6.167	11.067	12.967	34.647**
	S4	1.367	7.017	12.167	12.667	459.899**
Bayer	B2	2.267	6.950	9.900	11.633	14.003**
Aspercreme	A1	2.200	6.334	6.833	10.467	0.332
	A4	1.500	6.016	5.800	10.533	0.085
	A5	4.067	6.684	10.600	9.300	32.926**
	Overall	2.176	6.540	9.262	10.903	167.989**

$n = 30$
* = Significant at 0.05
** = Significant at 0.01

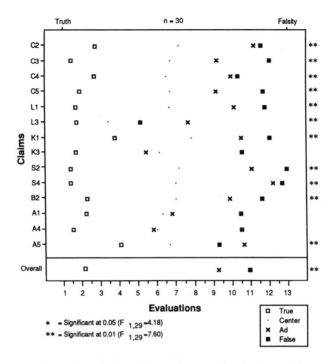

FIG. 7.1. Plot of mean belief evaluations for challenged claims previously found deceptive.

Table 7.6 and Fig. 7.1. Of the 14 claims tested there is strong significance in the direction of deceptiveness for 11 (78.6%) when tested individually. An interesting, and unexpected, result occurred in two of those instances (L3 and A5): the ads were rated more "false" than the false memoranda. The remaining three claims can not be concluded to be deceptive.

Deceptiveness Measure of Claims Not Found Deceptive by the FTC

The three claims meeting the criteria of the second hypothesis were analyzed in the same manner as those just given. The mean belief of these claims was 5.878, with a mean centerpoint of 7.244, yielding a significant difference of 1.368 [$F (1,89) = 7.266, p < 0.01$]. However, the difference was in the "true" direction, and so did not indicate deceptiveness. Recall that this is intended to be a one-tail test for significance only in the "false" direction. Again, it is useful to view individual analyses of the claims, although the hypothesis concerned only the composite effect. The results of a claim by claim analysis appears in Table 7.7 and Fig. 7.2.

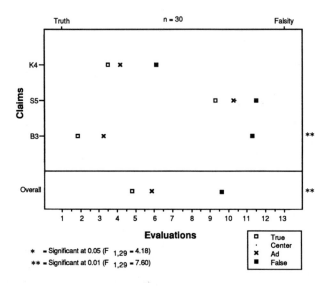

FIG. 7.2.   Plot of mean belief evaluations of challenged claims not
previously found deceptive.

None of the three claims here can be concluded to be deceptive, when tested individually. Only one of the claims significantly differs from the centerpoint, and it falls closer to its true counterpart. In fact, all three of the ads have means closer to true than to false, although two insignificantly differ from center.

Evaluation of Ads Not Addressed by the FTC

The two advertisements addressed by the third hypothesis were tested for both deceptiveness and materiality, using the same procedures as those used for the FTC-addressed claims just given. Overall mean belief

TABLE 7.7
Mean Belief Evaluations of Challenged Claims
Not Previously Found Deceptive

		True	Center	Ad	False	F-value
Kroger	K4	3.500	4.783	4.167	6.067	0.671
Sears	S5	9.300	10.400	10.267	11.500	0.035
Bayer	B3	1.833	6.550	3.200	11.267	39.561**
	Overall	4.878	7.244	5.878	9.611	7.266**

$n = 30$
* = Significant at 0.05
** = Significant at 0.01

TABLE 7.8
Mean Belief Evaluations of Unchallenged Claims

		True	Center	Ad	False	F-value
Amer. Eagle	E3	2.733	7.467	5.300	12.200	5.953*
	E4	1.533	7.083	6.233	12.633	0.871
	E5	3.200	7.800	6.833	12.400	1.003
35mm Camera	T2	3.100	7.833	8.167	12.567	0.260
	T3	3.400	7.534	4.067	11.667	6.761*
	T4	4.833	7.900	7.133	10.967	0.944
	T5	2.400	7.400	5.567	12.400	5.832*
	T7	1.733	7.133	9.167	12.533	4.733*
	Overall	2.867	7.519	6.558	12.171	9.361**

$n = 30$
* = Significant at 0.05
** = Significant at 0.01

of the claims was 6.558, and the mean centerpoint was 7.519, for a significant difference of 0.961 [$F(1,239) = 9.361, p < 0.01$] in the "true" direction, evidencing no deceptiveness. The individual claim results can be seen in Table 7.8 and Fig. 7.3.

Of the eight claims tested, only one of them (12.5%) was found deceptive. Six means of the nondeceptive claims fell on the side of center

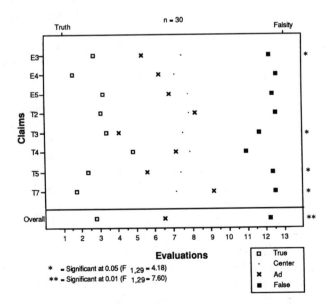

FIG. 7.3. Plot of mean belief evaluations of unchallenged claims.

toward the "true" evaluation, and three of those were significantly toward truth.

Materiality

Materiality is incapable of being confidently manipulated in a manner similar to comprehension or belief. This means that we cannot compare the ad claims to alternative "true" and "false" evaluations. Consequently, the actual centerpoint of the scale must be used for reference, in the same way that we used a calculated centerpoint in the preceding analyses.

Because there were five treatments, with each measuring materiality, there were five times as many evaluations for materiality as for deceptiveness. The question then arises whether the evaluations from all treatments should be used, or should we use only part of the data. The comprehension treatment was summarily excluded because it was added only for purposes of this experiment, and would not normally be included in this method as proposed. Any bias that might be introduced by this difference in dependent measure, therefore, was removed. Although there was no basis for expecting product Materiality to differ from treatment to treatment, a one-way ANOVA was conducted to discover whether any difference existed between evaluations under the four remaining conditions, revealing a significant difference [F (3,2996) = 20.58, $p < 0.01$]. Although the mean evaluations for three of the treatments were very close, claim evaluations from the false memoranda appear to result in greater materiality (mean for True = 4.935, Control = 5.020, Ad = 4.913, False = 3.732). Consequently, to avoid unintended effects on materiality assessments caused by the experimental manipulations, it was decided that only those evaluations made in the original-ad treatment should be used for analyses.

Using the data from the ad treatment, the overall mean for materiality for the 17 FTC challenged claims was 4.680, which significantly differs from center (7.0) in the "Material" direction [F (1,509) = 210.578, $p < 0.01$]. The mean for the eight claims from the two non-challenged ads was 5.408, which was also a significant difference [F (1,239) = 29.656, $p < 0.01$]. The results of each of the 17 claims can be seen in Fig. 7.4, and the eight nonchallenged claims in Fig. 7.5

It can be seen that 13 of the 17 challenged claims (76.5%) were found to significantly differ from the center of the scale in the direction of materiality. Only 4 of the 8 unchallenged claims (50.0%) fell significantly toward materiality.

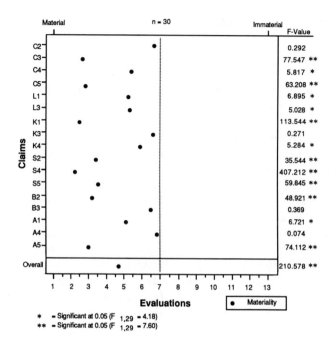

FIG. 7.4.   Plot of mean materiality evaluations of the 17 challenged claims.

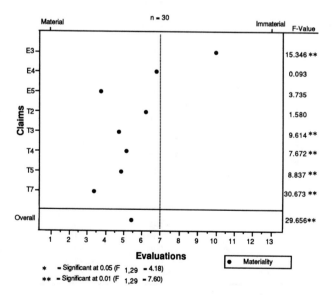

FIG. 7.5.   Plot of mean materiality evaluations of unchallenged claims.

Belief Versus Comprehension

From the theory presented in chapter 5 it was predicted that in some instances comprehension would be a poor estimator of belief, because a claim may be understood but not believed, for a variety of reasons. This, however, was not anticipated to occur in every instance. In fact in many claims the substance of the claim may be taken at face value. Across the claims assessed here it was possible, if not likely, that there would be no difference between Comprehension and belief for a large percentage of them. Again, a composite analysis is necessary. Belief and comprehension measures of the original ads were collapsed across all 17 claims and tested by a simple one-way ANOVA. Belief yielded a mean of 8.665 and comprehension a mean of 9.686, with a significant difference of 1.022 $[F\ (1,1018) = 13.122, p < 0.01]$. It is important to note that comprehension of the ad claims was rated more false than belief of those claims. More evidence of this difference can be seen in the claim by claim analysis in Table 7.9 and Fig. 7.6. For all but two of the claims comprehension fell farther right, indicating greater falsity, than belief. Although most of those differences are insignificant, the general pattern is apparent. In

TABLE 7.9
Mean Belief and Comprehension Evaluations of the 17 Challenged Claims

		Belief	*Comp.*	*F-value*
Cliffdale	C2	11.200	11.567	0.354
	C3	9.233	10.700	2.477
	C4	9.933	12.133	7.370**
	C5	9.200	11.833	7.278**
Litton	L1	10.133	10.233	0.010
	L3	7.667	9.600	2.843
Kroger	K1	10.500	12.500	7.088**
	K3	5.433	5.700	0.066
	K4	4.167	4.400	0.049
Sears	S2	11.067	12.367	2.823
	S4	12.167	12.333	0.141
	S5	10.267	11.867	3.131
Bayer	B2	9.900	12.133	5.649*
	B3	3.200	4.200	1.517
Aspercreme	A1	6.833	7.433	0.249
	A4	5.800	5.133	0.418
	A5	10.600	10.533	0.004
	Overall	8.665	9.686	13.122**

$n = 30$
* = Significant at 0.05
** = Significant at 0.01

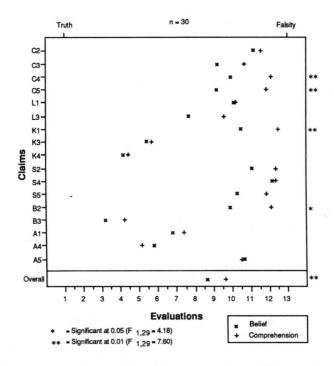

FIG. 7.6.   Plot of mean belief and comprehension evaluations of the
17 challenged claims.

most cases it appears comprehension may be evaluated at least slightly
more false than belief.

FINDINGS BY THREE DIFFERENT METHODS

The FTC approach to testing comprehension differs somewhat from the
comprehension test used here. No specific hypothesis was offered to
predict the similarities or dissimilarities of outcomes of the RPI deceptiveness measure vis-à-vis an FTC type of comprehension measure, but this
seems a useful analysis to augment a true comparison of the RPI method
of the traditional empirical method. It is inadequate to compare the
actual FTC findings to the RPI results, because FTC findings for only
one of the challenged claims (A1) were made on the basis of empirical
data. Consequently, the RPI results will be compared to both the actual
FTC decisions and to the comprehension-only results, just presented,
after conversion to an FTC-type comprehension measure.

Although the prior comparison depicts the juxtaposition of comprehension vis-à-vis belief as measured on these bipolar scales, they are treated here as continuous variables with multiple degrees of accuracy. They are intervally scaled. The FTC, however, does not classify claims by *degree* of deceptiveness; a claim is either deceptive or it is not. This is because a claim is either deceptive enough to cross some threshold of legal impropriety, or it is not. The method proposed in this book, and used here, sets that threshold at a calculated centerpoint and bases the dichotomous deceptive–nondeceptive classification upon statistical deviation of the *mean* evaluation from that threshold.

The FTC's typical approach, by using such measures as verbatims, does not lend itself to using a continuous scale. Instead, respondents' statements are directly classified as either deceptive or nondeceptive, depending upon the words used in their verbatims. Because this is a nominal scaling method (with only two categories), it is not capable of the same statistical evaluation. Consequently, the Commission findings of deceptiveness are not normally based on deviation of the mean, but on the *percentage* of respondents falling into the "deceptive" category.[39] The FTC's general rule of thumb appears to be that at least 20%–25% of respondents must be deceived before the agency will regulate a claim.[40]

For purposes of comparison, a rough translation of the present method to that used by the FTC is possible, using frequency distributions of the comprehension data. The problem in making this conversion is knowing where to draw the line between evaluations that should be classified "deceptive" and those that should be "nondeceptive." Taking the position that ambiguous evaluations, those near the center of the scale, should not be held against the advertiser, subjects rating a claim on the scale anywhere from 9 to 13 were classified as deceptive. The results of this nominal scaling can be found in Table 7.10. Using the FTC 20%–25% guideline, claims B3 and A4 would be clearly nondeceptive, and claims K3 and K4 would be marginal. All other claims are clearly deceptive.

The results of this comprehension-only assessment can now be compared to the FTC decisions and to the outcome of the RPI belief-based measure. This comparison can be seen in Table 7.11. It can be seen that there is substantial agreement between the three methods, but some disagreement. There is an 82.4% agreement between the FTC decisions and the FTC-type Comprehension measure, an 82.4% agreement between the FTC decisions and the RPI method, and a 76.5% agreement between the FTC-type comprehension measure and the RPI method.

---

[39]Jacoby and Small refer to this as the N% criterion. Jacoby and Small, *The FDA Approach to Defining Misleading Advertising*, 39 J. MKTG. 65, 66 (1975).

[40]Preston and Richards, *Consumer Miscomprehension as a Challenge to FTC Prosecutions of Deceptive Advertising*, 19 J. MARSHALL L. REV. 605, 613–14 (1986).

TABLE 7.10
Percent of Subjects Comprehending a False Message

	Percentages	
Claim	Nondeceptive	Deceptive
C2	10.00	90.00
C3	23.33	76.67
C4	3.33	96.67
C5	6.67	93.33
L1	26.67	73.33
L3	30.00	70.00
K1	3.33	96.67
K3	76.67	23.33
K4	80.00	20.00
S2	6.67	93.33
S4	6.67	93.33
S5	6.67	93.33
B2	6.67	93.33
B3	93.33	6.67
A1	56.67	43.33
A4	83.33	16.67
A5	20.00	80.00

TABLE 7.11
Comparison of Three Methods

	FTC	Comp.	RPI
C2	D	D	D
C3	D	D	D
C4	D	D	D
C5	D	D	D
L1	D	D	D
L3	D	D	D
K1	D	D	D
K3	D	D*	N
K4	N	D*	N
S2	D	D	D
S4	D	D	D
S5	N	D	N
B2	D	D	D
B3	N	N	N
A1	D	D	N
A4	D	N	N
A5	D	D	D

D = Deceptive
N = Nondeceptive
* = Marginal Results

DISCUSSION

The purpose of this experiment was to discover whether, and to what extent, the results of this RPI method would coincide with traditional FTC fact-finding regarding deceptiveness. Because the Commission's determinations are not restricted to empirical testing, and frequently rely upon multiple indications of deceptiveness (more than one survey or survey method, expert testimony, consumer testimony, and Commission expertise may be used in decisions), the likelihood that a single method will fully concur with those findings is probably very low. This is especially so given that the FTC dispositions of 16 of the 17 challenged claims were determined without reliance on empirical data. In spite of these inherent pitfalls, the legal reality remains that deceptiveness is what the FTC says it is,[41] making FTC decisions the only wholly valid method against which to compare any new technique. Although the Relative Proximity Index (RPI) method was designed in the previous chapter as an improvement upon alternative methods, its validity under the law can not be substantiated until it is shown capable of distinguishing deceptive from nondeceptive claims, as seen from the viewpoint of those who determine what is or is not deceptive. This experiment, therefore, has attempted a rough form of validation.

Challenged Claims Previously Found Deceptive

Resulting from this validation goal, it was predicted that claims previously found deceptive by the Commission would, on average, likewise be found deceptive under the parameters defined for deceptiveness under this method. Hypothesis 1, tested by collapsing across the 14 challenged claims determined deceptive by the FTC, was supported. Looking at an individual analysis of the claims revealed a less than perfect correlation between the results of this method and the FTC's findings, which was expected, but indicated a 78.6% agreement between the two. Although not perfect, this is a high correlation.

Although it is possible to conclude this method to be less than 100% efficient, this variation *may* be explained by the inadequacies in sampling for the present study, acknowledged earlier. This would place the fault for not detecting deceptiveness, in three instances, not on the method

---

[41]As Preston correctly pointed out, "An ad is legally deceptive when a majority of the five commissioners votes its opinion that the ad has that capacity." Preston, *The Difference Between Deceptiveness and Deception, and Why It Should Matter to Lawyers, Researchers, and Advertisers,* 1982 PROC. OF THE AMER. ACADEMY OF ADV. 81, 81 (1982).

but on the limitations in its application, thereby containing those deficiencies to the present experiment.

Of course, the explanation for disagreement on these three may not stem from the method or its application. It was explained in chapter 3 that the Commission need not, and does not always, seek empirical consumer evidence of deceptiveness,[42] and in chapter 6 that where such evidence is sought the methods typically used are subject to some notable failings. The present method was specifically crafted to be superior to those common fact-finding processes, so differences were expected and it should be no surprise that some differences were discovered. If there is any surprise, here, it should be the fact that the outcome of this experiment, given the expected differences along with the sampling limitations, agreed so closely with FTC findings. Therefore, I would argue that the extent of disagreement in the results, here, primarily reflects the needed improvements in the regulatory process, argued in chapter 6.

It is interesting to note that for two of the claims (L3 and A5) there was a crossover, where the ad was evaluated more deceptive than its corresponding false memorandum. Although this result is troublesome, it should be noted that the results in both instances agree with the FTC findings. This phenomenon may result from poor drafting of the false memoranda, or it may be that some claims are less believable when *expressly* stated (as in the memoranda) than when merely *implied* (as in the ads). The latter is an interesting proposition, deserving further attention.

One other possibility is that subjects tended not to read or fully process the "false" claims involved. In both cases the subject claim was the longest sentence in the false memo, so subjects may not have taken the time to read that sentence. I suspect that this is closer to the truth. If so, experimenters should take pains to simplify statements in the constructed memoranda, if it can be done without sacrificing the substance of the claim, to ensure each claim will be read.

Challenged Claims Not Previously Found Deceptive

The method, of course, must not only be capable of detecting deceptiveness, it must be able to distinguish those claims that are not deceptive. If nondeceptive claims are found deceptive by this technique, it is of little use. This is difficult to test, because the Commission's practice is not to

---

[42] *See also* Brandt and Preston, *The Federal Trade Commission's Use of Evidence to Determine Deception*, 41 J. MKTG. 54 (1977); Preston, *supra* note 3.

find claims nondeceptive, but rather to state only that they have not been *proved* deceptive.

The number of claims usable to test Hypothesis 2 was smaller than for the former hypothesis, making the results of this test less conclusive. However, collapsing across the claims revealed no deceptiveness. The hypothesis was, therefore, fully supported. In fact, all of the three claims tested, individually, were found nondeceptive. Not only did the mean scores not fall *significantly* to the deceptiveness side of the centerpoint, each of the means fell on the nondeceptive side, although only one was significantly far to that side. Consequently, it appears this method does, indeed, distinguish between deceptive and nondeceptive claims.

Deceptiveness of Unchallenged Claims

Two ads not involved in any published FTC actions were tested, predicting that the claims involved, overall, would be deceptive. This was a speculative venture, with a primary purpose of illustrating the use of this method to test ads outside the FTC arena. Clearly, the hypothesis was not supported. In fact, of eight claims only one was found deceptive.

Although these two ads were chosen because I honestly suspected they might include several deceptive claims, the results indicate that my own ability to identify deceptiveness is unequivocally poor. Although the FTC certainly did a better job of spotting deceptiveness, that is probably because the charges in those cases were instigated as the result of consumer complaints, rather than being attributable to their experience and expertise. This shows, at least, that it can be difficult to judge deceptiveness without reliance on empirical tests. This tends to lend some support to arguments for more extensive use of empirical consumer research in FTC advertising cases,[43] to help in that identification. It also supports arguments in favor of a theoretical dialogue to advance predictive abilities for identifying deceptiveness, as suggested in chapter 5.

Materiality

Analysis of a claim's regulability is not complete unless we can also show whether or not that claim is material. Materiality was analyzed here for all 17 of the FTC-challenged claims previously discussed, even though materiality of the nondeceptive claims is a legally moot point, and was likewise analyzed for the eight unchallenged claims.

---

[43]*See, e.g.,* Richards and Preston, *Quantitative Research: A Dispute Resolution Process for FTC Advertising Research,* 40 OKLA. L. REV. 593 (1987).

It was separately predicted in Hypothesis 4 that Materiality would be found (a) across all of the FTC-challenged claims, and (b) across all of the unchallenged claims. This hypothesis was supported in both instances. However, as with the deceptiveness measure, when claims were separately analyzed the FTC was substantially more successful at identifying material claims than was this author.

In spite of the Commission's relative success at identifying materiality, three of the four FTC-challenged claims found immaterial were claims determined regulable by the Commission. In fact, two of those claims (K3 and A4) were found neither deceptive *nor* material in this experiment, where the FTC found them *both* deceptive and material, although the other claim (C2) was quite clearly deceptive under this method. One of the claims determined nondeceptive (A1) was nonetheless found material.

At the very least this suggests that deceptiveness or nondeceptiveness of a claim is not determinative of a claim's materiality, and that it should be separately measured. It also suggests the FTC may have been in error in finding K3, A4, and C2 material, keeping in mind the limitations of this experiment. It appears that presumptions of materiality by the Commission may occasionally be disprovable by an advertiser.

Although the materiality measure is even less subject to validation than the deceptiveness measure, these results do raise questions about the adequacy of current FTC practices. However, for each of the tested ads at least *one* of the claims found deceptive and material by the FTC was also found both deceptive and material in this experiment, confirming the regulability of these ads, if not the Commission's findings regarding every claim involved. So, in fairness, it should be recognized that, even if weaknesses exist, it appears the Commission is doing an effective job of regulating *only* ads that have deceptive and material claims.

Belief Versus Comprehension

There also was predicted an overall difference between belief and comprehension evaluations.[44] This prediction goes to the heart of the theory presented in chapter 5, and it is on this assumption of a difference that

---

[44]Upon reviewing this analysis, one researcher questioned this comparison. He suggested that it was inappropriate because, in his words, this is like comparing apples and oranges. By asking two completely different questions of subjects, he felt it impossible to make sense of the difference. I contend, however, that such a comparison is wholly appropriate. The conceptual basis for experimentation posits that as a stimulus is varied (treatment levels of an independent variable) changes in the subject's response (dependent variable) can be measured to learn about the cognitive processes of the subject. This can be depicted as follows:

the method suggested in chapter 6, and used here, was premised. That prediction was supported. Although only 4 of the 17 claims rendered a significant difference, the overall discrepancy was significant.

Perhaps more important than the statistical significance, in this analysis, is the general pattern of the data. For 15 of the claims the mean comprehension was rated more toward the false end of the scale than mean belief. This result was apparent even though the subjects used in this experiment were relatively young and inexperienced consumers. It is foreseeable that older subjects, with greater experience-based skepticism, might well reveal an even greater discrepancy, tending to believe these claims even less.

Two possible consequences of this difference are readily apparent. First, "false" comprehension may be more easily detectable than "false" belief when using a less sensitive measure, because it is more extreme. If, as I suggested in chapter 6, methods like the Burke and ASI surveys are less capable of detecting deception, the fact that they have traditionally measured comprehension rather than belief may have helped to compensate for their deficiencies. Second, this difference suggests, as I do in chapter 5, that consumers may comprehend more falsity than they believe, and that a test of comprehension may overestimate the deceptiveness of a claim. In some instances this could result in regulation of a claim where regulation is not justifiable. The fact that four of the differences were significant suggests this should be an important consideration for future regulatory practice. The greater the difference between comprehension and belief of a given claim, the more important the belief-based RPI method becomes. A comprehension-based measure in those instances would inequitably prejudice the results against the free-speech rights of the advertiser.

That representation, however, is an oversimplified one. Rather than three variables, as shown here, there are really four:

The typical psychometric study holds the question constant and varies only the stimulus, permitting the researcher to infer that differences in response are caused by differences in stimulus. In the present study, however, the stimulus (original ad) has been held constant while only the question (Belief or Comprehension) has been varied, permitting a similar causal inference. The dependent variable in both instances is Deceptiveness, as rated on the same 13-point scale, since my basic premise is that Belief and Comprehension can be interchangeable indicators of Deceptiveness under the law.

Comparison of All Three Methods

In order to better equate these results to FTC methods, the comprehension evaluations were parsed into two nominal categories, deceptive and nondeceptive, to discover what percentage of subjects were deceived by each claim. Because this was a comprehension-only measure, with no experimental manipulations like used for the belief evaluations, it was quite similar to traditional FTC survey methods involving forced exposure (e.g., the ASI method). Using the FTC 20%–25% criterion, 13 of the 17 claims would be clearly regulable. Two (K3 and K4) would be marginal, and might be found regulable, whereas two (B3 and A4) would very probably be considered nondeceptive in the present regulatory atmosphere.

Three distinct comparisons were made. First, there was 82.4% agreement between the FTC decisions concerning the 17 claims and the FTC-type comprehension measure. Only three discrepancies were found (K4, S5, and A4). The first of these, K4, was only marginally deceptive by the comprehension measure, and rendered the smallest percentage of deceptiveness of the two marginal claims. Consequently, this may be seen as a nondiscrepancy. Regarding the second, it is interesting to note that S5 was very deceptive using the comprehension measure, but the Commission did not regulate it. The reason for the Commission not finding this claim to have been made, however, was a lack of evidence rather than because evidence indicated it was not deceptive,[45] so this was not a case where the FTC had a method better than the comprehension measure used here. Had empirical evidence been used, it very probably would have found this claim deceptive, as the comprehension measure does here.

In a similar manner, A4 was found deceptive by the Commission but nondeceptive by the comprehension measure. However, at 16.67% deceptiveness on the comprehension scale this question fell very close to the 20%–25% criterion used by the FTC. Because it was so close to what the Commission normally deems deceptive, this seems to fall logically within the Commission's margin of error where no empirical evidence is used, as was the case here. The differences between the FTC decisions and the comprehension measure, therefore, are easily explained by the lack of empirical data in the FTC fact-finding process for these claims. It should be noted that in the one instance where empirical research was used by the Commission, A1, there is complete agreement as to its deceptiveness. These discrepancies merely support arguments in favor of more extensive use of empirical research by the FTC.

---

[45]Sears, 95 F.T.C. 406, 511 (1980).

Next we can compare the FTC decisions to the results of the RPI method, between which there was 82.4% agreement. This comparison, however, has already been made, in Hypotheses 1 and 2. Given the error attributable to the Commission's failure to use empirical evidence, an even better point of comparison for the RPI method is to the comprehension measure.

These two methods were in 76.5% agreement; still quite a respectable correlation. Disagreements can be found on only four claims (K3, K4, S5, and A1). The first two were only marginally deceptive by the comprehension method, but were clearly nondeceptive with the RPI method. The explanation for these differences seems to be, first, that the RPI method uses the evaluated "true" and "false" endpoints not used by the comprehension technique. I have already argued, in chapter 6, the superiority of the former. Second, the RPI method uses the mean and variance of the distribution of evaluations, whereas the comprehension method depends only on the tail of the distribution, which includes the outliers. Because use of the mean and variance is a more statistically sound approach, with much greater projectability to a larger population, I would argue that the RPI approach is presumptively more valid. However, the difference is marginal, since the comprehension data could be taken as proof of inadequate deceptiveness under the FTC 20%–25% criterion.

The discrepancy of results regarding S5 is directly attributable to addition of the evaluated "true" and "false" endpoints. Regardless of being presented the "truth," subjects evaluating the true memorandum believed the product capable of more impressive feats than it could actually achieve. In this situation, the superiority of a method using evaluated endpoints seems clear.

Finally, although both the FTC (with benefit of empirical data) and the comprehension measure used here determined A1 deceptive, the RPI method found it nondeceptive. Under the RPI measure evaluation of this claim did not significantly differ from the centerpoint, although it fell on the "false" side of center. The comprehension evaluation, however, fell closer to the "false" end of the scale. The different outcomes can be explained by the difference between belief and comprehension, along with the reliance of the comprehension measure upon the tail of the distribution rather than the mean and variance. Both of these explanations suggest an overestimation of deceptiveness by the comprehension technique, further supporting use of the RPI approach.

These analyses indicate a high degree of agreement between the proposed method and the FTC decisions or an FTC-type measurement, on the order of 75%–85%. There are, as expected, a few instances of disagreement. Although the present operationalization of the RPI method is subject to some admitted deficiencies, these disagreements are all explainable by the intended improvements incorporated in this new method. Although there is no way to definitively prove the validity or superiority of this method, these results establish at least a presumption of validity, and point to some significant weaknesses in the typical FTC approach.

Perhaps as important as validation of the method, is the fact that belief was shown to differ from comprehension across these FTC-challenged claims. As a result of this confirmed difference the validity of FTC comprehension-based measurements must be questioned, and the theoretical arguments presented in chapter 5, regarding belief versus comprehension, have been supported.

CHAPTER 8

Summary

This book is intended to serve as a reference for behavioral scientists interested in studying issues related to deception in advertising. There is a need for research in this area, to help regulators more fully understand the mechanism of consumers' minds as it affects their inaccurate beliefs about product attributes. The relative lack of study in this area is suggested here to be, at least in part, the consequence of a lack of knowledge by consumer researchers regarding the legal parameters impinging on this subject matter, along with a concomitant failure of the few researchers involved in this area to take a more methodical approach to its study. In short, there was an inadequate foundation upon which to build a program of research into deceptiveness. To solve the problem a three-part foundation is offered, consisting of (a) a review of how deception is viewed and regulated, (b) a theory of how consumers process deceptive information, and (c) a sensitive and consistent means of measuring deceptiveness.

The second and third chapters described the legal situs of deception, first as a legal construct and then as a behavioral one. That was a strictly normative discussion, explaining how deception is presently regulated and highlighting some common errors made by behavioral researchers. Moving into the behavioral situs of deception, the fourth chapter looked at how behavioral scientists have contributed to deceptiveness research and how deceptiveness fits within a broader social context concerned with injustices. All of the material in those three chapters was directed toward enhancing researchers' understanding of deception and its regulation: the first leg of the tripartite foundation.

The fifth chapter considered how behavioral scientists can improve their contributions to the study and regulation of deceptiveness. It was alleged, there, that progress in this area necessitates a theoretical dialogue, which has been overlooked to date. To begin that dialogue, a theoretical information-processing model of the deceptiveness process is proposed. Unlike its few predecessors, this model suggests several antecedents to the formation of a deceptive inference. Unlike the FTC approach, the model suggests that belief is a better measure of deceptiveness than comprehension, provided beliefs derived from other sources can be experimentally controlled. This provided the second part of the three-part foundation.

Building upon the premise of belief as a superior dependent variable, a method for testing deceptiveness is offered in the sixth chapter to provide the third leg of the foundation. Previous methods used by the FTC and in academic research are reviewed, their weaknesses are considered, and their strengths are used to derive the new method. Finally, that method is tested in the seventh chapter, and concluded to be at least presumptively valid.

Although this book was organized to give some semblance of a progression, like a staircase with each step built upon the last and leading toward a summit (i.e., the experiment) it is better viewed as these three distinct constituents. Using another analogy, it is more like a tripod, with each of the three legs separate but all of them necessary to support future systematic research. This is important because the second section, the theory, built upon only a part of the first; and the third, the method, used only a portion of the second. What this means is that there are many other hypotheses to be derived from each section than the ones ultimately explored in chapter 7. I have attempted to use only enough of this material to illustrate that behavioral scientists have much more to contribute to our knowledge of deceptiveness than has already been offered by them.

Because chapters 2 through 4 are normative descriptions, most of the implications of this book, aside from an improvement in normative understanding, grow out of the theory and method developed here. Those implications fall into three categories.

First, several legal principles have been clarified, and their relationships to behavioral concepts described, so that future researchers can avoid the errors to which their predecessors have succumbed. With this "primer" to deceptiveness research, it is hoped that fewer mistakes will arise in subsequent work.

Second, some improvements have been recommended for adoption in FTC practice. These improvements include the desirability of separating deceptiveness from ineradicable miscomprehension when assessing the effects of an ad claim, as suggested earlier by Preston and Richards.[1] This recommendation was reflected in the definition of deceptiveness proposed in chapter 5. The resulting evaluations of the "true" and "false" memoranda in chapter 7 appear to support suppositions that either ineradicable miscomprehension or prior beliefs tend to mediate those evaluations, because the evaluations did not fall at the extreme ends of the scales, although no attempt was made to separate these effects. Although it is unclear that discounting levels of deceptiveness by this inherent level of miscomprehension would have much effect on the outcome of FTC regulatory efforts, this is a more equitable approach because it does not hold advertisers accountable for unavoidable errors in consumer information processing.

An even more important improvement suggested here is the use of belief rather than comprehension as a dependent variable. Through the experiment in chapter 7 it was found that there is, indeed, a difference between comprehension and belief of claims challenged by the FTC, and that in some instances that difference is significant. By relying upon comprehension the Commission is in jeopardy of regulating nondeceptive claims, because the comprehension measure tends to inflate the deceptiveness rating of a claim. Although the Commission was previously bound to comprehension measures by the survey methods used, the experimental procedure presented here would allow measurement of belief while controlling for prior-held beliefs. This improvement, like the one just mentioned, would be a more equitable treatment for advertisers.

The third group of implications concern how behavioral researchers can improve their contributions to our knowledge of deceptiveness: the primary focus of this book. The proposed method is designed to be usable in FTC proceedings, but it is likewise applicable to academic study. I propose its use for future research, where applicable, as a standard method, to permit the results of each study to be equated to the results of another. In this way if the results of two studies differ, we can have some degree of assurance that the difference is a real one, and not attributable to the measurement method. If this method was also adopted for use by the FTC, we could then have the additional assurance that our results would likewise equate to regulatory practice and be applicable to that practice.

Certainly the method could also be used by advertisers, to help them

---

[1]Preston and Richards, *Consumer Miscomprehension as a Challenge to FTC Prosecution of Deceptive Advertising*, 19 J. MARSHALL L. REV. 605 (1986).

avoid the fist of the regulator before-the-fact or to disprove the regulator's allegations, but there is danger in that course of action. Because tests conducted by an advertiser can be acquired and used by the FTC, even where the advertiser is unhappy with the results and does not wish introduce those tests into evidence, advertisers may be reluctant to conduct such research.[2] Adoption of this method by the advertising community, consequently, is probably not likely in the immediate future.

Future research might begin by extracting other ideas from the theoretical model, exploring further the roles of perception, attention, comprehension, and prior knowledge in the deceptiveness process. Several ideas for additional research are suggested in the discussion of that model, but are yet untested. Although the model may seem quite detailed, the most salient portion, from perception to belief, should be scrutinized and refined. Other ideas may also be extracted and tested, including the proposition that some claims may alter affect without substantially modifying belief, thereby accomplishing the advertisers' goals of invoking a purchase intent without creating deceptiveness.

An area of particular need for more study is the relationship of materiality, as measured through self-report at belief, to actual purchase behavior. This seems to be the weakest link in our ability to predict behavioral effect of a single claim on a consumer. Although relatively little research has been conducted into the chain of behavioral events involved in deceptiveness, virtually none has been dedicated to the study of materiality.

Throughout this book I attempted to unearth issues in need of additional discussion and study. Because the substance of this work is primarily conceptual, more questions are raised than are answered. The implications and future research possibilities uncovered are too numerous to exhaust in this summary, but I have highlighted some important ones. With the background, theory, and method presented in the foregoing pages a tentative foundation is established for a more organized and coherent program of research into what types of claim deceive consumers and why those consumers are deceived. In the area of deceptive advertising it is this knowledge of the workings of consumer minds that falls most squarely within the expertise of the behavioral researcher, and it is in this area that behavioral scientists can make their greatest contribution to the regulation of advertising.

---

[2]Rosch, *Marketing Research and the Legal Requirements of Advertising*, 39 J. MKTG. 69 (1975).

Original Advertisements

185

Quality is No.1 at Litton!

76% of the independent microwave oven service technicians surveyed recommend Litton.

Litton leads all brands.

PREFERENCE FOR SPECIFIC BRANDS AMONG TECHNICIANS SERVICING THOSE BRANDS				AVERAGE PREFERENCE FOR LITTON vs. ALL
Brand to Brand	Litton vs. G.E.	Litton vs. Amana	Litton vs. Magic Chef	COMPETION (weighted ave.)
Which Microwave Oven Brand would recommend to a friend?	59% vs 23%	56% vs 18%	81% vs 1%	76% vs 8%
Which Microwave Oven Brand is easiest to repair?	68% vs 5%	65% vs 8%	71% vs 0%	72% vs 4%
Which Microwave Oven Brand is the best quality?	48% vs 16%	50% vs 26%	69% vs 1%	63% vs 9%
Which Microwave Oven Brand requires fewest repairs?	38% vs 22%	42% vs 24%	59% vs 3%	53% vs 12%
Which Microwave Oven Brand do you have in your home?	48% vs 19%	50% vs 18%	70% vs 5%	67% vs 10%

Among independent technicians servicing Litton and competitive microwave ovens, an average of 76% of those surveyed said they would recommend Litton to a friend. And an average of 63% identified Litton brand ovens as having the best quality.

You'll find it in our full line of advanced countertop microwave ovens, double ovens, and combin- ation microwave ranges. And in such Litton features as Vari- Cook™ oven control, Vari-Temp™ automatic temperature control, and Memorymatic™ microwave prog- ram cooking. Innovative ways to microwave more foods better.

Need any more reasons to buy Litton? Ask your Litton dealer for a microwave cooking demon- stration. For his name and address, call us right now, toll free 800-328-7777.

Respondents represent independent micro-wave oven service agencies who service at least two brands of microwave ovens (one of them Litton) and do not represent a factory named service agency. Percentages ad to less than 100% due to other responses and no preferences.

LITTON
Microwave Cooking

Litton...changing the way America Cooks.

KROGER IS THE LOW PRICE LEADER IN ATLANTA

FOR THE 38 TH STRAIGHT WEEK

Never in the past 38 weeks has our pledge to you meant so much. It merits repeating: "Kroger is dedicated to the principle of pricing products so that we will be lower priced on more items more often than other stores." We have lived up to that pledge, as proved by the Kroger Price Patrol.

The consumer price index published by the federal government, as released through the news media in the last several weeks, explains that for the first time in fifteen years the American family will spend a higher proportionate share of their incomes for food.

Periodically an independent agency checks each major food store to reflect costs of a "typical" week's groceries. The most recent check determined Kroger to be from 2.5 to 8% below other food stores.

We maintain that pledge, which means that even though prices will increase, shopping Kroger will enable you to spend less for your food than at any other store.

STORE	A	B	C	D	E	F	G
KROGER WAS LOWER ON THIS MANY ITEMS CHECKED	73	96	100	76	98	129	118
KROGER WAS HIGHER ON THIS MANY ITEMS CHECKED	20	9	22	27	20	4	7
KROGER WAS THE SAME ON THIS MANY ITEMS CHECKED	54	10	21	47	22	8	8

ACTUAL CHECK LIST FOR WEEK ENDING AUGUST 18, 1973 AVAILABLE AT ALL KROGER STORES FOR YOUR INSPECTION.

Each week our group of Atlant housewives visits leading food retail and so called discount stores. They check prices on over 150 items. Not the kind of items you buy once a year, but basics, staples every housewife needs in her kitchen everyday ....

Sears Lady Kenmore.
The do-it-itself dishwasher.

No scraping. No pre-rinsing. Lady Kenmore has 6 powerful hot water jets for the bottom rack, surging hot water with enough force to scrub every dish, pot and pan *really* clean. Even baked-on food comes off.

And the dishes on top get as clean as those on the bottom. Because every cup and glass is scoured inside and out by a field of eight upper jets.

Then there's Lady Kenmore's protected pulverizer for leftovers. It's kind of a mini-grinder with 12 stainless steel teeth that grind soft foods into tiny particles that wash right down the drain. (Of course, water is always fresh and clean—the water that rinses your dishes hasn't washed them.)

And our 8 *different* cycles include Sani-wash, which gives your dishes an extra-hot 155° final rinse. So everything is hygienically clean.

What's more, Sears Lady Kenmore is built to perform. But if you ever do have a problem, you can rely on Sears service.

Sears Lady Kenmore does just about everything, itself. So you really do have freedom from scraping and pre-rinsing. That's why we call it The Freedom Maker. The

Sears Freedom Maker, both built-in and portable, is available at Sears, Roebuck and Co. stores and through the catalog.

The *Freedom Maker*™

188

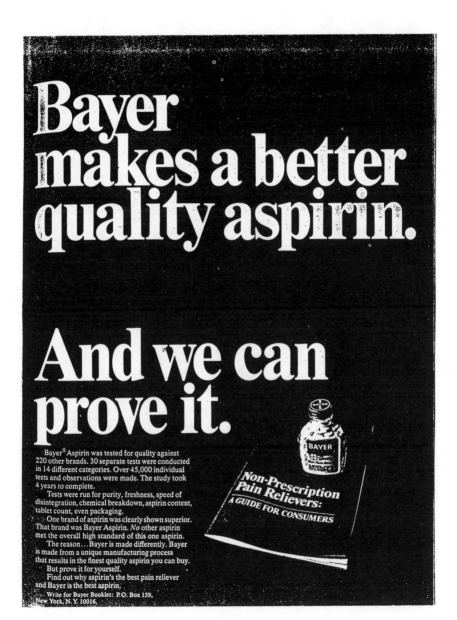

Bayer makes a better quality aspirin.

And we can prove it.

Bayer® Aspirin was tested for quality against 220 other brands. 30 separate tests were conducted in 14 different categories. Over 45,000 individual tests and observations were made. The study took 4 years to complete.

Tests were run for purity, freshness, speed of disintegration, chemical breakdown, aspirin content, tablet count, even packaging.

One brand of aspirin was clearly shown superior. That brand was Bayer Aspirin. *No* other aspirin met the overall high standard of this one aspirin.

The reason...Bayer is made differently. Bayer is made from a unique manufacturing process that results in the finest quality aspirin you can buy.

But prove it for yourself.

Find out why aspirin's the best pain reliever and Bayer is the best aspirin.

Write for Bayer Booklet: P.O. Box 159, New York, N.Y. 10016.

Non-Prescription Pain Relievers: A GUIDE FOR CONSUMERS

At last! A remarkable breakthrough for arthritis pain: Aspercreme.

Aspercreme is an effective arthritis medicine which concentrates all the strong relief of aspirin directly at the point of pain.

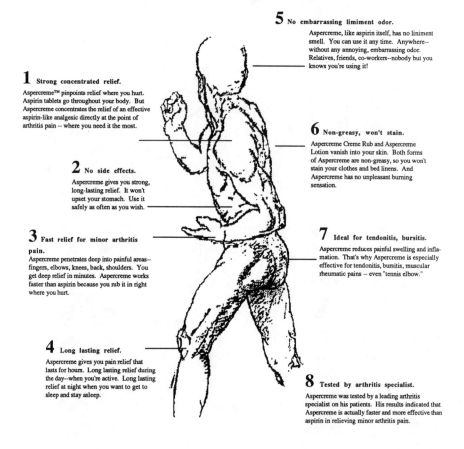

5 No embarrassing limiment odor.

Aspercreme, like aspirin itself, has no liniment smell. You can use it any time. Anywhere-- without any annoying, embarrassing odor. Relatives, friends, co-workers--nobody but you knows you're using it!

1 Strong concentrated relief.

Aspercreme™ pinpoints relief where you hurt. Aspirin tablets go throughout your body. But Aspercreme concentrates the relief of an effective aspirin-like analgesic directly at the point of arthritis pain -- where you need it the most.

6 Non-greasy, won't stain.

Aspercreme Creme Rub and Aspercreme Lotion vanish into your skin. Both forms of Aspercreme are non-greasy, so you won't stain your clothes and bed linens. And Aspercreme has no unpleasant burning sensation.

2 No side effects.

Aspercreme gives you strong, long-lasting relief. It won't upset your stomach. Use it safely as often as you wish.

3 Fast relief for minor arthritis pain.

Aspercreme penetrates deep into painful areas-- fingers, elbows, knees, back, shoulders. You get deep relief in minutes. Aspercreme works faster than aspirin because you rub it in right where you hurt.

7 Ideal for tendonitis, bursitis.

Aspercreme reduces painful swelling and infla- mation. That's why Aspercreme is especially effective for tendonitis, bursitis, muscular rheumatic pains -- even "tennis elbow."

4 Long lasting relief.

Aspercreme gives you pain relief that lasts for hours. Long lasting relief during the day--when you're active. Long lasting relief at night when you want to get to sleep and stay asleep.

8 Tested by arthritis specialist.

Aspercreme was tested by a leading arthritis specialist on his patients. His results indicated that Aspercreme is actually faster and more effective than aspirin in relieving minor arthritis pain.

"True" Memoranda

M E M O R A N D U M

From: Product Management Division

Product Characteristics

Product Name: Ball-Matic
Product Type: Air-Bleeder Valve for Automobiles
Seller: Cliffdale Associates
Attributes:

- Permits additional air to enter combustion chamber of engine, with the intent of increasing fuel economy.

- No scientific tests have been conducted to prove the Ball-Matic will increase fuel economy.

- Air-bleed devices similar to Ball-Matic have been sold for many years.

- Ball-Matic may somewhat increase fuel economy for automobiles with rich air/fuel mixtures.

- Ball-Matic will not significantly increase fuel economy when installed in a typical car, under normal driving conditions.

- The highest fuel savings to be expected are approximately 5%, and a _loss_ may be expected on 1974 and newer cars.

- Product testimonials are available, but many of them are from business associates of the seller, and others are from several years ago.

- Priced at $12.95.

M E M O R A N D U M

From: Product Management Division

Product Characteristics

Product Name: Litton Microwave Cooking Products
Product Type: Microwave Ovens
Seller: Litton Systems, Inc.
Attributes:

- A range of ovens offered, varying in price and features.

- Major competitors include Amana, Magic Chef, and Sharp microwaves.

- Some features include VariCook oven control, VariTemp automatic temperature control, and Memorymatic program cooking.

- There is no evidence that Litton microwaves are recommended, used, chosen, or otherwise preferred in any respect more often than competitors' products.

- There is no evidence that Litton microwaves are superior to competitors' products in any respect.

- 115-120 factory service locations, and many independent service agencies outside those locations are authorized to provide service for Litton microwaves.

M E M O R A N D U M

From: Merchandise Management Division

Research Characteristics

Product Name: Price Patrol Survey
Product Type: Price Comparison
Seller: The Kroger Company
Attributes:

- Survey compares Kroger prices to major competitors.

- Survey is not scientifically-based.

- Survey does not include meat or produce in its sample, and compares only high-volume commodities that are not private labels.

- Used by 1,250 retail food stores operated by Kroger.

- Survey does not prove that shopping at Kroger, rather than at competitors' stores, will result in lower overall expenditures.

- Survey is conducted by independent shoppers, not under the direct control of Kroger.

- Survey does show that Kroger's prices are lower than some competitors on some items.

M E M O R A N D U M

From: Product Management Division

Product Characteristics

Product Name: Lady Kenmore
Product Type: Dishwasher
Seller: Sears, Roebuck & Co.
Attributes:

- Most expensive dishwasher sold by Sears.

- Upper rack is circular, and revolves during agitation cycles.

- Lower rack is square.

- Prior scrubbing, scraping or rinsing is necessary to clean heavily soiled dishes.

- Heavily soiled dishes may not clean as efficiently in the top rack as they will in the bottom rack.

- Includes 8 different wash and rinse cycles.

- Includes 14 water jets.

- Sani-Wash cycle provides 155 degree final finse, to hygenically clean dishes.

MEMORANDUM

From: Product Management Division

Product Characteristics

Product Name: Bayer Aspirin
Product Type: Oral Analgesic
Seller: Sterling Drug
Attributes:

- Relieves minor pain.

- No evidence exists to suggest that a recommended
  dose of Bayer Aspirin will relieve nervous
  tension, anxiety, and irritability, or that it
  will improve user's mood.

- For many years Bayer was the nation's leading
  over-the-counter analgesic.

- Although Bayer has been tested against 200 other
  brands of aspirin for quality, purity, freshness,
  stability, and speed of disintegration, there is
  a substantial question, recognized by experts,
  concerning the quality and interpretation of
  these tests. Consequently, Bayer cannot claim to
  be therapeutically superior to all other brands.

- Bayer brand aspirin has been sold for nearly a
  century.

MEMORANDUM

From: Product Management Division

Product Characteristics

Product Name: Aspercreme Creme Rub & Lotion Rub
Product Type: Analgesic
Seller: Thompson Medical Company
Attributes:

- Not for oral ingestion.

- Does not contain aspirin.

- Is applied by rubbing onto painful areas of the
  body.

- Is based upon an ingredient used for many years.

- Involves no new technology.

- Has not been proven more effective than orally-
  ingested aspirin for relief of arthritis,
  rheumatism, and their symptoms.

- Causes no side effects.

- Has no liniment smell.

- Non-greasy and will not stain clothes.

MEMORANDUM

From: Product Management Division

Product Characteristics

Product Name: American Eagle Belt Buckle
Product Type: Belt Buckle
Seller: International Mint
Attributes:

- Individually numbered.

- Number is registered with the seller's company.

- Buckle is made of inexpensive metals and is thinly plated with silver, decorated with very thin gold plating.

- Buckle is set with one very tiny diamond (0.0025 Carat).

- Comes with Certificate of Authenticity.

- Comes with Presentation Case.

- Money-back guarantee.

MEMORANDUM

From: Product Management Division

Product Characteristics

Product Name: 35mm Camera
Product Type: Camera
Seller: Direct Connection
Attributes:

- 50mm lens permanently attached, with 4 exposure settings and non-adjustable focus.

- Solid plastic construction.

- Uses separate window for aiming: not a single lens reflex design.

- Flash is not included.

- Uses 35mm color or black & white film.

- Comes with plastic carrying case, lens cover, and shoulder strap.

- "Hot Shoe" flash holder attached.

- One-year warranty.

- Not made by a major camera manufacturer.

"False" Memoranda

M E M O R A N D U M

From: Product Management Division

Product Characteristics

Product Name: Ball-Matic
Product Type: Air-Bleeder Valve for Automobiles
Seller: Cliffdale Associates
Attributes:

- Permits additional air to enter combustion chamber of engine, with the intent of increasing fuel economy.

- Scientific tests prove the Ball-Matic will significantly increase fuel economy.

- Ball-Matic is an important, significant, and unique new invention.

- Ball-Matic will significantly increase fuel economy for most automobiles, except Volkswagons.

- Ball-Matic, when installed in a typical car under normal driving conditions, will significantly improve fuel economy.

- Under normal driving conditions, a typical driver can usually obtain a fuel economy of 20% (or more) or an improvement that will approximate or equal four miles per gallon.

- Consumer endorsements prove that consumers experience significant improvement in fuel economy.

- Priced at $12.95.

M E M O R A N D U M

From: Product Management Division

Product Characteristics

Product Name: Litton Microwave Cooking Products
Product Type: Microwave Ovens
Seller: Litton Systems, Inc.
Attributes:

- A range of ovens offered, varying in price and features.

- Major competitors include Amana, Magic Chef, and Sharp microwaves.

- Some features include VariCook oven control, VariTemp automatic temperature control, and Memorymatic program cooking.

- A scientific survey of microwave service technicians proves that the majority of independent microwave oven service technicians have Litton microwave ovens in their homes.

- A scientific survey of microwave service technicians proves that the majority of independent microwave oven service technicians are of the opinion that Litton microwave ovens are superior to all other microwave oven brands.

- 115-120 factory service locations, and many independent service agencies outside those locations are authorized to provide service for Litton microwaves.

M E M O R A N D U M

From: Merchandise Management Division

Research Characteristics

Product Name: Price Patrol Survey
Product Type: Price Comparison
Seller: The Kroger Company
Attributes:

- Survey compares Kroger prices to major competitors.

- Survey is scientifically-based.

- Survey represents a random sample of products carried by Kroger stores.

- Used by 1,250 retail food stores operated by Kroger.

- Survey proves that shopping at Kroger, rather than at competitors' stores, will result in lower overall expenditures.

- Survey is conducted by independent shoppers, not under the direct control of Kroger.

- Survey shows that Kroger's prices are lower than those of its competitors.

M E M O R A N D U M

From: Product Management Division

Product Characteristics

Product Name: Lady Kenmore
Product Type: Dishwasher
Seller: Sears, Roebuck & Co.
Attributes:

- Most expensive dishwasher sold by Sears.

- Upper rack is circular, and revolves during agitation cycles.

- Lower rack is square.

- No Prior scrubbing, scraping or rinsing is necessary to clean dishes, including heavily soiled dishes.

- Dishes, whether lightly or heavily soiled, will clean as efficiently in the top rack as they will in the bottom rack.

- Includes 8 different wash and rinse cycles.

- Includes 14 water jets.

- Sani-Wash cycle provides 155 degree final finse, to sterilize dishes.

From: Product Management Division

Product Characteristics

Product Name: Bayer Aspirin
Product Type: Oral Analgesic
Seller: Sterling Drug
Attributes:

- Relieves minor pain.

- Tests prove that a recommended dose of Bayer
  Aspirin will relieve nervous tension, anxiety,
  and irritability, and improve user's mood.

- For many years Bayer was the nation's leading
  over-the-counter analgesic.

- Bayer has been tested against 200 other brands of
  aspirin for quality, purity, freshness,
  stability, and speed of disintegration, and the
  results of the tests demonstrate that Bayer
  Aspirin is therapeutically superior to all of the
  other brands tested.

- Bayer brand aspirin has been sold for nearly a
  century.

M E M O R A N D U M

From: Product Management Division

Product Characteristics

Product Name: Aspercreme Creme Rub & Lotion Rub
Product Type: Analgesic
Seller: Thompson Medical Company
Attributes:

- Not for oral ingestion.

- Contains aspirin.

- Is applied by rubbing onto painful areas of the
  body.

- Is based upon a newly-developed ingredient.

- Involves a new scientific principle.

- Proved more effective than orally-ingested
  aspirin for relief of arthritis, rheumatism, and
  their symptoms.

- Causes no side effects.

- Has no liniment smell.

- Non-greasy and will not stain clothes.

MEMORANDUM

From: Product Management Division

Product Characteristics

Product Name: American Eagle Belt Buckle
Product Type: Belt Buckle
Seller: International Mint
Attributes:

- Individually numbered.

- Number is registered with the United States Government.

- Buckle is made of silver, decorated with gold.

- Buckle is set with one 0.25 Carat diamond.

- Comes with Certificate of Authenticity.

- Comes with Presentation Case.

- Money-back guarantee.

MEMORANDUM

From: Product Management Division

Product Characteristics

Product Name: 35mm Camera
Product Type: Camera
Seller: Direct Connection
Attributes:

- Interchangeable 50mm lens, with variable exposure settings and variable focus.

- Solid metal construction.

- Single lens reflex, with through-the-lens viewing.

- Flash is included.

- Uses 35mm color or black & white film.

- No case, lens cover, and shoulder strap included.

- "Hot Shoe" flash holder attached.

- One-year warranty.

- Made by a major camera manufacturer.

No-Attribute-Information
Control Stimuli

Ball-Matic

Automotive air-bleeder valve, by Cliffdale

Litton Microwave Ovens

Microwave Oven, by Litton Systems, Inc.

Price Patrol Survey

Price comparison, by The Kroger Company

Lady Kenmore

Dishwasher, by Sears, Roebuck & Co.

Bayer Aspirin

Analgesic, by Sterling Drug

Aspercreme

Analgesic Rub, by Thompson Medical Co.

American Eagle Belt Buckle

Belt Buckle, by International Mint

35mm Camera

Camera, by Direct Connection

Instructions and Questionnaires

Read Carefully!
Do Not Turn the Page Until Instructed

Instructions for Participants

You are participating in a study of consumer values and knowledge. On the attached pages you will see advertisements, memos, and other product or service information. Each of those pages will be followed with a page or two of questions for you to answer. Your task is to review the information about each product, and then to answer the questions as accurately as you can.

When you are done with a page, put your pencil or pen down and look up, to let the experimenter know you are ready to go to the next page. Never turn a page until you are told to do so, and never look back to a previous page.

Many of the questions, here, will ask you to mark your answer on a scale, with several spaces, like this example:

Do you believe you can accurately complete this questionnaire?

I Believe   I Believe
I Can Do   I Will Find
An Excellent   This Questionnaire
Job |___|___|___|___|___|___|___|___|___|___|___|___|___| Impossible to Complete

---

To answer a question like the one above, you should place an X in one of the spaces (**not** on a line between the spaces) that represents what you actually believe. If, for example, you believe that you can do a very good job, you would answer this question by putting an X at or near the leftmost space:

| X |___|___|___|___|___|___|___|___|___|___|___|___|___|

If, however, you believe that you could do an adequate, but less than excellent, job, you might put your X closer to the center:

|___|___|___|___| X |___|___|___|___|___|___|___|___|

You will also be asked to rate, in a similar manner, how confident you are of those beliefs:

How Confident Are You?

Very   Very
Unconfident |___|___|___|___|___|___|___|___|___|___|___|___|___| Confident

---

Again, you should place an X on this scale. If, in this example, you marked "excellent" above and you are very confident that your belief is accurate, you should place an X to the far right on this scale. If you believe that you will do an excellent job, but you are not totally confident that your belief will prove accurate, your X would not be all the way to the right.

Please answer every question, and do it as accurately as you can. Your help with this test is greatly appreciated. If you have any questions, please ask now.

Look Up, and Do Not Turn the Page Until Instructed!

Ball-Matic

1. a) What do you believe to be true about this product?

    Costs Over $20 |___|___|___|___|___|___|___|___|___|___|___|___|___|___|___| Costs Under $20

    b) How Confident Are You?

    Very Unconfident |___|___|___|___|___|___|___|___|___|___|___|___|___|___|___| Very Confident

    c) Would this feature be a factor in your decision whether or not to buy this product?

    Would Be A
    Primary Factor |___|___|___|___|___|___|___|___|___|___|___|___|___|___|___| Would Not Affect
    My Decision

2. a) What do you believe to be true about this product?

    Is a New Invention |___|___|___|___|___|___|___|___|___|___|___|___|___|___|___| Is Not a New Invention

    b) How Confident Are You?

    Very Unconfident |___|___|___|___|___|___|___|___|___|___|___|___|___|___|___| Very Confident

    c) Would this feature be a factor in your decision whether or not to buy this product?

    Would Be A
    Primary Factor |___|___|___|___|___|___|___|___|___|___|___|___|___|___|___| Would Not Affect
    My Decision

3. a) What do you believe to be true about this product?

    Will Increase Gas Mileage
    20% or More for a Typical
    Driver in Normal
    Conditions |___|___|___|___|___|___|___|___|___|___|___|___|___|___|___| Will Increase Gas
    Mileage 5% or Less
    for a Typical Driver
    In Normal Conditions

    b) How Confident Are You?

    Very Unconfident |___|___|___|___|___|___|___|___|___|___|___|___|___|___|___| Very Confident

    c) Would this feature be a factor in your decision whether or not to buy this product?

    Would Be A
    Primary Factor |___|___|___|___|___|___|___|___|___|___|___|___|___|___|___| Would Not Affect
    My Decision

4. a) What do you believe to be true about this product?

    Endorsements
    Prove That Consumers
    Experience Significant
    Fuel Savings |___|___|___|___|___|___|___|___|___|___|___|___|___|___|___| Endorsements Do Not
    Prove That Consumers
    Experience Significant
    Fuel Savings

    b) How Confident Are You?

    Very Unconfident |___|___|___|___|___|___|___|___|___|___|___|___|___|___|___| Very Confident

    c) Would this feature be a factor in your decision whether or not to buy this product?

    Would Be A
    Primary Factor |___|___|___|___|___|___|___|___|___|___|___|___|___|___|___| Would Not Affect
    My Decision

5. a) What do you believe to be true about this product?

    Will Not Significantly
    Increase Fuel Economy
    In a Typical Car Under
    Normal Conditions |___|___|___|___|___|___|___|___|___|___|___|___|___|___|___| Will Significantly
    Increase Fuel Economy
    In a Typical Car Under
    Normal Conditions

    b) How Confident Are You?

    Very Unconfident |___|___|___|___|___|___|___|___|___|___|___|___|___|___|___| Very Confident

    c) Would this feature be a factor in your decision whether or not to buy this product?

    Would Be A
    Primary Factor |___|___|___|___|___|___|___|___|___|___|___|___|___|___|___| Would Not Affect
    My Decision

6. How familiar are you with this product name?

    Never Heard of It |___|___|___|___|___|___|___|___|___|___|___|___|___|___|___| Very Familiar

7. Do you have any experience with this product?

    Have Used It
    Frequently |___|___|___|___|___|___|___|___|___|___|___|___|___|___|___| Have Never
    Used It

8. Have you seen ads for this product before?

    Seen Frequently |___|___|___|___|___|___|___|___|___|___|___|___|___|___|___| Never Seen

Put Down Your Pencil, Look Up, and Do Not Turn the Page Until Instructed!

Litton Microwave

1. a) What do you believe to be true about this product?

    Proof Exists That Litton
    Microwaves Are
    Preferred By
    Independent
    Microwave Oven
    Service Technicians |___|___|___|___|___|___|___|___|___|___|___|___|___|___| There is No Proof That Litton Microwaves Are Preferred By Independent Microwave Oven Service Technicians

    b) How Confident Are You?

    Very Unconfident |___|___|___|___|___|___|___|___|___|___|___|___|___|___| Very Confident

    c) Would this feature be a factor in your decision whether or not to buy this product?

    Would Be A
    Primary Factor |___|___|___|___|___|___|___|___|___|___|___|___|___|___| Would Not Affect My Decision

2. a) What do you believe to be true about this product?

    Available With
    Automatic Temperature
    Control |___|___|___|___|___|___|___|___|___|___|___|___|___|___| No Automatic Temperature Control Available

    b) How Confident Are You?

    Very Unconfident |___|___|___|___|___|___|___|___|___|___|___|___|___|___| Very Confident

    c) Would this feature be a factor in your decision whether or not to buy this product?

    Would Be A
    Primary Factor |___|___|___|___|___|___|___|___|___|___|___|___|___|___| Would Not Affect My Decision

3. a) What do you believe to be true about this product?

    There is No Proof
    Litton Microwaves
    Are Superior To
    Competitors'
    Products |___|___|___|___|___|___|___|___|___|___|___|___|___|___| Proof Exists That Litton Microwaves Are Superior To Competitors' Products

    b) How Confident Are You?

    Very Unconfident |___|___|___|___|___|___|___|___|___|___|___|___|___|___| Very Confident

    c) Would this feature be a factor in your decision whether or not to buy this product?

    Would Be A
    Primary Factor |___|___|___|___|___|___|___|___|___|___|___|___|___|___| Would Not Affect My Decision

4. How familiar are you with this product name?

    Never Heard of It |___|___|___|___|___|___|___|___|___|___|___|___|___|___| Very Familiar

5. Do you have any experience with this product?

    Have Used It
    Frequently |___|___|___|___|___|___|___|___|___|___|___|___|___|___| Have Never Used It

6. Have you seen ads for this product before?

    Seen Frequently |___|___|___|___|___|___|___|___|___|___|___|___|___|___| Never Seen

Put Down Your Pencil, Look Up, and Do Not Turn the Page Until Instructed!

Kroger Price Patrol Survey

1. a) What do you believe to be true about this Survey?

| Survey Proves Shopping at Kroger, Rather Than Competitors' Stores, Will Result in Lower Overall Expenditures | |_|_|_|_|_|_|_|_|_|_|_|_|_|_|_| | Survey Does Not Prove Shopping at Kroger, Rather Than Competitors' Stores, Will Result in Lower Overall Expenditures |

   b) How Confident Are You?

| Very Unconfident | |_|_|_|_|_|_|_|_|_|_|_|_|_|_|_| | Very Confident |

   c) Would this feature be a factor in your decision whether or not to buy from this store?

| Would Be A Primary Factor | |_|_|_|_|_|_|_|_|_|_|_|_|_|_|_| | Would Not Affect My Decision |

2. a) What do you believe to be true about this Survey?

| Conducted By Kroger Employees | |_|_|_|_|_|_|_|_|_|_|_|_|_|_|_| | Conducted by Independent Shoppers |

   b) How Confident Are You?

| Very Unconfident | |_|_|_|_|_|_|_|_|_|_|_|_|_|_|_| | Very Confident |

   c) Would this feature be a factor in your decision whether or not to buy from this store?

| Would Be A Primary Factor | |_|_|_|_|_|_|_|_|_|_|_|_|_|_|_| | Would Not Affect My Decision |

3. a) What do you believe to be true about this Survey?

| Not Scientifically Based | |_|_|_|_|_|_|_|_|_|_|_|_|_|_|_| | Scientifically Based |

   b) How Confident Are You?

| Very Unconfident | |_|_|_|_|_|_|_|_|_|_|_|_|_|_|_| | Very Confident |

   c) Would this feature be a factor in your decision whether or not to buy from this store?

| Would Be A Primary Factor | |_|_|_|_|_|_|_|_|_|_|_|_|_|_|_| | Would Not Affect My Decision |

4. a) What do you believe to be true about this Survey?

| Includes Sample of All Products Sold By Kroger | |_|_|_|_|_|_|_|_|_|_|_|_|_|_|_| | Does Not Sample Certain Products Sold By Kroger |

   b) How Confident Are You?

| Very Unconfident | |_|_|_|_|_|_|_|_|_|_|_|_|_|_|_| | Very Confident |

   c) Would this feature be a factor in your decision whether or not to buy from this store?

| Would Be A Primary Factor | |_|_|_|_|_|_|_|_|_|_|_|_|_|_|_| | Would Not Affect My Decision |

6. How familiar are you with this store name?

| Never Heard of It | |_|_|_|_|_|_|_|_|_|_|_|_|_|_|_| | Very Familiar |

7. Do you have any experience with this store?

| Have Used It Frequently | |_|_|_|_|_|_|_|_|_|_|_|_|_|_|_| | Have Never Used It |

8. Have you seen ads for this Price Patrol Survey before?

| Seen Frequently | |_|_|_|_|_|_|_|_|_|_|_|_|_|_|_| | Never Seen |

Put Down Your Pencil, Look Up, and Do Not Turn the Page Until Instructed!

Lady Kenmore Dishwasher

1. a) What do you believe to be true about this product?

   Includes 6
   Waterjets |___|___|___|___|___|___|___|___|___|___|___|___|___|___| Includes 14
   Waterjets

   b) How Confident Are You?

   Very Unconfident |___|___|___|___|___|___|___|___|___|___|___|___|___|___| Very Confident

   c) Would this feature be a factor in your decision whether or not to buy this product?

   Would Be A
   Primary Factor |___|___|___|___|___|___|___|___|___|___|___|___|___|___| Would Not Affect
   My Decision

2. a) What do you believe to be true about this product?

   Prior Scrubbing,
   Scraping or Rinsing
   is Necessary to
   Clean Heavily
   Soiled Dishes |___|___|___|___|___|___|___|___|___|___|___|___|___|___| No Prior Scrubbing,
   Scraping or Rinsing
   is Necessary to
   Clean Heavily
   Soiled Dishes

   b) How Confident Are You?

   Very Unconfident |___|___|___|___|___|___|___|___|___|___|___|___|___|___| Very Confident

   c) Would this feature be a factor in your decision whether or not to buy this product?

   Would Be A
   Primary Factor |___|___|___|___|___|___|___|___|___|___|___|___|___|___| Would Not Affect
   My Decision

3. a) What do you believe to be true about this product?

   Includes 8 Different
   Wash/Rinse Cycles |___|___|___|___|___|___|___|___|___|___|___|___|___|___| Includes 4 Different
   Wash/Rinse Cycles

   b) How Confident Are You?

   Very Unconfident |___|___|___|___|___|___|___|___|___|___|___|___|___|___| Very Confident

   c) Would this feature be a factor in your decision whether or not to buy this product?

   Would Be A
   Primary Factor |___|___|___|___|___|___|___|___|___|___|___|___|___|___| Would Not Affect
   My Decision

4. a) What do you believe to be true about this product?

   All Dishes Will Clean
   As Efficiently in Top
   Rack As In Bottom |___|___|___|___|___|___|___|___|___|___|___|___|___|___| Heavily Soiled Dishes
   May Not Clean As
   Efficiently in Top
   Rack As In Bottom

   b) How Confident Are You?

   Very Unconfident |___|___|___|___|___|___|___|___|___|___|___|___|___|___| Very Confident

   c) Would this feature be a factor in your decision whether or not to buy this product?

   Would Be A
   Primary Factor |___|___|___|___|___|___|___|___|___|___|___|___|___|___| Would Not Affect
   My Decision

5. a) What do you believe to be true about this product?

   Sani-Wash Cycle Will
   Sterilize Dishes |___|___|___|___|___|___|___|___|___|___|___|___|___|___| Sani-Wash Cycle Will
   Not Sterilize Dishes

   b) How Confident Are You?

   Very Unconfident |___|___|___|___|___|___|___|___|___|___|___|___|___|___| Very Confident

   c) Would this feature be a factor in your decision whether or not to buy this product?

   Would Be A
   Primary Factor |___|___|___|___|___|___|___|___|___|___|___|___|___|___| Would Not Affect
   My Decision

6. How familiar are you with this product name?

   Never Heard of It |___|___|___|___|___|___|___|___|___|___|___|___|___|___| Very Familiar

7. Do you have any experience with this product?

   Have Used It
   Frequently |___|___|___|___|___|___|___|___|___|___|___|___|___|___| Have Never
   Used It

8. Have you seen ads for this product before?

   Seen Frequently |___|___|___|___|___|___|___|___|___|___|___|___|___|___| Never Seen

Put Down Your Pencil, Look Up, and Do Not Turn the Page Until Instructed!

Bayer Aspirin

1. a) What do you believe to be true about this product?

   Relieves No Pain |___|___|___|___|___|___|___|___|___|___|___|___|___|___| Relieves Minor Pain

   b) How Confident Are You?

   Very Unconfident |___|___|___|___|___|___|___|___|___|___|___|___|___|___| Very Confident

   c) Would this feature be a factor in your decision whether or not to buy this product?

   Would Be A
   Primary Factor |___|___|___|___|___|___|___|___|___|___|___|___|___|___| Would Not Affect My Decision

2. a) What do you believe to be true about this product?

   Tests Prove It
   More Effective
   Than Other Brands |___|___|___|___|___|___|___|___|___|___|___|___|___|___| Not Proved More Effective Than Other Brands

   b) How Confident Are You?

   Very Unconfident |___|___|___|___|___|___|___|___|___|___|___|___|___|___| Very Confident

   c) Would this feature be a factor in your decision whether or not to buy this product?

   Would Be A
   Primary Factor |___|___|___|___|___|___|___|___|___|___|___|___|___|___| Would Not Affect My Decision

3. a) What do you believe to be true about this product?

   Not Proved To
   Relieve Nervous
   Tension, Anxiety,
   Irritability, and
   Improve Your
   Mood |___|___|___|___|___|___|___|___|___|___|___|___|___|___| Proved To Relieve Nervous Tension, Anxiety, Irritability, and Improve Your Mood

   b) How Confident Are You?

   Very Unconfident |___|___|___|___|___|___|___|___|___|___|___|___|___|___| Very Confident

   c) Would this feature be a factor in your decision whether or not to buy this product?

   Would Be A
   Primary Factor |___|___|___|___|___|___|___|___|___|___|___|___|___|___| Would Not Affect My Decision

4. How familiar are you with this product name?

   Never Heard of It |___|___|___|___|___|___|___|___|___|___|___|___|___|___| Very Familiar

5. Do you have any experience with this product?

   Have Used It
   Frequently |___|___|___|___|___|___|___|___|___|___|___|___|___|___| Have Never Used It

6. Have you seen ads for this product before?

   Seen Frequently |___|___|___|___|___|___|___|___|___|___|___|___|___|___| Never Seen

Put Down Your Pencil, Look Up, and Do Not Turn the Page Until Instructed!

Aspercreme

1. a) What do you believe to be true about this product?

   Does Not Contain
   Aspirin |__|__|__|__|__|__|__|__|__|__|__|__|__|__| Contains Aspirin

   b) How Confident Are You?

   Very Unconfident |__|__|__|__|__|__|__|__|__|__|__|__|__|__| Very Confident

   c) Would this feature be a factor in your decision whether or not to buy this product?

   Would Be A
   Primary Factor |__|__|__|__|__|__|__|__|__|__|__|__|__|__| Would Not Affect My Decision

2. a) What do you believe to be true about this product?

   Is Applied By
   Rubbing Onto Painful
   Areas of Body |__|__|__|__|__|__|__|__|__|__|__|__|__|__| Is Taken By Swallowing

   b) How Confident Are You?

   Very Unconfident |__|__|__|__|__|__|__|__|__|__|__|__|__|__| Very Confident

   c) Would this feature be a factor in your decision whether or not to buy this product?

   Would Be A
   Primary Factor |__|__|__|__|__|__|__|__|__|__|__|__|__|__| Would Not Affect My Decision

3. a) What do you believe to be true about this product?

   Causes No Side
   Effects |__|__|__|__|__|__|__|__|__|__|__|__|__|__| May Cause Side Effects

   b) How Confident Are You?

   Very Unconfident |__|__|__|__|__|__|__|__|__|__|__|__|__|__| Very Confident

   c) Would this feature be a factor in your decision whether or not to buy this product?

   Would Be A
   Primary Factor |__|__|__|__|__|__|__|__|__|__|__|__|__|__| Would Not Affect My Decision

4. a) What do you believe to be true about this product?

   Is Based Upon A
   Recently Discovered
   Ingredient |__|__|__|__|__|__|__|__|__|__|__|__|__|__| Is Not Based Upon A Recently Discovered Ingredient

   b) How Confident Are You?

   Very Unconfident |__|__|__|__|__|__|__|__|__|__|__|__|__|__| Very Confident

   c) Would this feature be a factor in your decision whether or not to buy this product?

   Would Be A
   Primary Factor |__|__|__|__|__|__|__|__|__|__|__|__|__|__| Would Not Affect My Decision

5. a) What do you believe to be true about this product?

   Is Not More Effective
   Than Ordinary
   Aspirin For Relief of
   Arthritis, Rheumatism
   and Their Symptoms |__|__|__|__|__|__|__|__|__|__|__|__|__|__| Is More Effective Than Ordinary Aspirin For Relief of Arthritis, Rheumatism and Their Symptoms

   b) How Confident Are You?

   Very Unconfident |__|__|__|__|__|__|__|__|__|__|__|__|__|__| Very Confident

   c) Would this feature be a factor in your decision whether or not to buy this product?

   Would Be A
   Primary Factor |__|__|__|__|__|__|__|__|__|__|__|__|__|__| Would Not Affect My Decision

6. How familiar are you with this product name?

   Never Heard of It |__|__|__|__|__|__|__|__|__|__|__|__|__|__| Very Familiar

7. Do you have any experience with this product?

   Have Used It
   Frequently |__|__|__|__|__|__|__|__|__|__|__|__|__|__| Have Never Used It

8. Have you seen ads for this product before?

   Seen Frequently |__|__|__|__|__|__|__|__|__|__|__|__|__|__| Never Seen

Put Down Your Pencil, Look Up, and Do Not Turn the Page Until Instructed!

American Eagle Belt Buckle

1. a) What do you believe to be true about this product?

   Certificate of Authenticity Included |__|__|__|__|__|__|__|__|__|__|__|__|__|__|__| Certificate of Authenticity Not Included

   b) How Confident Are You?

   Very Unconfident |__|__|__|__|__|__|__|__|__|__|__|__|__|__|__| Very Confident

   c) Would this feature be a factor in your decision whether or not to buy this product?

   Would Be A Primary Factor |__|__|__|__|__|__|__|__|__|__|__|__|__|__|__| Would Not Affect My Decision

2. a) What do you believe to be true about this product?

   Not Individually Numbered |__|__|__|__|__|__|__|__|__|__|__|__|__|__|__| Individually Numbered

   b) How Confident Are You?

   Very Unconfident |__|__|__|__|__|__|__|__|__|__|__|__|__|__|__| Very Confident

   c) Would this feature be a factor in your decision whether or not to buy this product?

   Would Be A Primary Factor |__|__|__|__|__|__|__|__|__|__|__|__|__|__|__| Would Not Affect My Decision

3. a) What do you believe to be true about this product?

   Registered With Seller's Company |__|__|__|__|__|__|__|__|__|__|__|__|__|__|__| Registered With U. S. Government

   b) How Confident Are You?

   Very Unconfident |__|__|__|__|__|__|__|__|__|__|__|__|__|__|__| Very Confident

   c) Would this feature be a factor in your decision whether or not to buy this product?

   Would Be A Primary Factor |__|__|__|__|__|__|__|__|__|__|__|__|__|__|__| Would Not Affect My Decision

4. a) What do you believe to be true about this product?

   Diamond Is 0.0025 Carat |__|__|__|__|__|__|__|__|__|__|__|__|__|__|__| Diamond Is 0.25 Carat

   b) How Confident Are You?

   Very Unconfident |__|__|__|__|__|__|__|__|__|__|__|__|__|__|__| Very Confident

   c) Would this feature be a factor in your decision whether or not to buy this product?

   Would Be A Primary Factor |__|__|__|__|__|__|__|__|__|__|__|__|__|__|__| Would Not Affect My Decision

5. a) What do you believe to be true about this product?

   Made of Inexpensive Metals |__|__|__|__|__|__|__|__|__|__|__|__|__|__|__| Made of Silver and Gold

   b) How Confident Are You?

   Very Unconfident |__|__|__|__|__|__|__|__|__|__|__|__|__|__|__| Very Confident

   c) Would this feature be a factor in your decision whether or not to buy this product?

   Would Be A Primary Factor |__|__|__|__|__|__|__|__|__|__|__|__|__|__|__| Would Not Affect My Decision

6. How familiar are you with this product name?

   Never Heard of It |__|__|__|__|__|__|__|__|__|__|__|__|__|__|__| Very Familiar

7. Do you have any experience with this product?

   Have Used It Frequently |__|__|__|__|__|__|__|__|__|__|__|__|__|__|__| Have Never Used It

8. Have you seen ads for this product before?

   Seen Frequently |__|__|__|__|__|__|__|__|__|__|__|__|__|__|__| Never Seen

Put Down Your Pencil, Look Up, and Do Not Turn the Page Until Instructed!

35mm Camera

1. a) What do you believe to be true about this product?

Includes Plastic
Carrying Case,
Lens Cover &
Shoulder Strap |___|___|___|___|___|___|___|___|___|___|___|___|___|___|___|
Case, Lens
Cover and Strap
Are Not Included

b) How Confident Are You?

Very Unconfident |___|___|___|___|___|___|___|___|___|___|___|___|___|___|___| Very Confident

c) Would this feature be a factor in your decision whether or not to buy this product?

Would Be A
Primary Factor |___|___|___|___|___|___|___|___|___|___|___|___|___|___|___|
Would Not Affect
My Decision

2. a) What do you believe to be true about this product?

Camera Is A Single
Lens Reflex, With
Through-the-Lens
Viewing |___|___|___|___|___|___|___|___|___|___|___|___|___|___|___|
Camera Uses Separate
Window for Viewing,
and is not a Single
Lens Reflex

b) How Confident Are You?

Very Unconfident |___|___|___|___|___|___|___|___|___|___|___|___|___|___|___| Very Confident

c) Would this feature be a factor in your decision whether or not to buy this product?

Would Be A
Primary Factor |___|___|___|___|___|___|___|___|___|___|___|___|___|___|___|
Would Not Affect
My Decision

3. a) What do you believe to be true about this product?

Flash Not Included |___|___|___|___|___|___|___|___|___|___|___|___|___|___|___| Flash Included

b) How Confident Are You?

Very Unconfident |___|___|___|___|___|___|___|___|___|___|___|___|___|___|___| Very Confident

c) Would this feature be a factor in your decision whether or not to buy this product?

Would Be A
Primary Factor |___|___|___|___|___|___|___|___|___|___|___|___|___|___|___|
Would Not Affect
My Decision

4. a) What do you believe to be true about this product?

Lens is
Interchangeable
With Other Lenses |___|___|___|___|___|___|___|___|___|___|___|___|___|___|___|
Lens is
Not
Interchangeable

b) How Confident Are You?

Very Unconfident |___|___|___|___|___|___|___|___|___|___|___|___|___|___|___| Very Confident

c) Would this feature be a factor in your decision whether or not to buy this product?

Would Be A
Primary Factor |___|___|___|___|___|___|___|___|___|___|___|___|___|___|___|
Would Not Affect
My Decision

5. a) What do you believe to be true about this product?

Made of Plastic |___|___|___|___|___|___|___|___|___|___|___|___|___|___|___| Made of Metal

b) How Confident Are You?

Very Unconfident |___|___|___|___|___|___|___|___|___|___|___|___|___|___|___| Very Confident

c) Would this feature be a factor in your decision whether or not to buy this product?

Would Be A
Primary Factor |___|___|___|___|___|___|___|___|___|___|___|___|___|___|___|
Would Not Affect
My Decision

Go to next page, do not wait for instructions to turn page

6. a) What do you believe to be true about this product?

Has No "Hot Shoe"
Flash Holder |__|__|__|__|__|__|__|__|__|__|__|__|__|__|__| Has "Hot Shoe" Flash Holder

b) How Confident Are You?

Very Unconfident |__|__|__|__|__|__|__|__|__|__|__|__|__|__|__| Very Confident

c) Would this feature be a factor in your decision whether or not to buy this product?

Would Be A
Primary Factor |__|__|__|__|__|__|__|__|__|__|__|__|__|__|__| Would Not Affect My Decision

7. a) What do you believe to be true about this product?

Made by Major
Camera
Manufacturer |__|__|__|__|__|__|__|__|__|__|__|__|__|__|__| Not Made by Major Camera Manufacturer

b) How Confident Are You?

Very Unconfident |__|__|__|__|__|__|__|__|__|__|__|__|__|__|__| Very Confident

c) Would this feature be a factor in your decision whether or not to buy this product?

Would Be A
Primary Factor |__|__|__|__|__|__|__|__|__|__|__|__|__|__|__| Would Not Affect My Decision

8. a) What do you believe to be true about this product?

No Warranty |__|__|__|__|__|__|__|__|__|__|__|__|__|__|__| One-Year Warranty

b) How Confident Are You?

Very Unconfident |__|__|__|__|__|__|__|__|__|__|__|__|__|__|__| Very Confident

c) Would this feature be a factor in your decision whether or not to buy this product?

Would Be A
Primary Factor |__|__|__|__|__|__|__|__|__|__|__|__|__|__|__| Would Not Affect My Decision

9. How familiar are you with this product name?

Never Heard of It |__|__|__|__|__|__|__|__|__|__|__|__|__|__|__| Very Familiar

10. Do you have any experience with this product?

Have Used It
Frequently |__|__|__|__|__|__|__|__|__|__|__|__|__|__|__| Have Never Used It

11. Have you seen ads for this product before?

Seen Frequently |__|__|__|__|__|__|__|__|__|__|__|__|__|__|__| Never Seen

Put Down Your Pencil, Look Up, and Do Not Turn the Page Until Instructed!

The following information is necessary to help us interpret the results of this study. The results are confidential, and your name does not appear on this questionnaire.

1. How old are you? _____ [place the appropriate number in the blank]

2. What is your sex? Female____ Male____ [place a checkmark in appropriate blank]

3. What is your year in college? [place a checkmark in appropriate blank]
   Freshman____ Sophomore____ Junior____ Senior____ Graduate Student____

4. Would you consider your family high-income____, middle-income____, or lower-income____.

Comprehension Questionnaires

Ball-Matic

1. a) What does the ad claim about this product?
    Costs Over $20 |__|__|__|__|__|__|__|__|__|__|__|__|__|__|__| Costs Under $20
    b) How Confident Are You?
    Very Unconfident |__|__|__|__|__|__|__|__|__|__|__|__|__|__|__| Very Confident
    c) Would this feature be a factor in your decision whether or not to buy this product?
    Would Be A   Would Not Affect
    Primary Factor |__|__|__|__|__|__|__|__|__|__|__|__|__|__|__| My Decision
2. a) What does the ad claim about this product?
    Is a New Invention |__|__|__|__|__|__|__|__|__|__|__|__|__|__|__| Is Not a New Invention
    b) How Confident Are You?
    Very Unconfident |__|__|__|__|__|__|__|__|__|__|__|__|__|__|__| Very Confident
    c) Would this feature be a factor in your decision whether or not to buy this product?
    Would Be A   Would Not Affect
    Primary Factor |__|__|__|__|__|__|__|__|__|__|__|__|__|__|__| My Decision
3. a) What does the ad claim about this product?
    Will Increase Gas Mileage   Will Increase Gas
    20% or More for a Typical   Mileage 5% or Less
    Driver in Normal   for a Typical Driver
    Conditions |__|__|__|__|__|__|__|__|__|__|__|__|__|__|__| In Normal Conditions
    b) How Confident Are You?
    Very Unconfident |__|__|__|__|__|__|__|__|__|__|__|__|__|__|__| Very Confident
    c) Would this feature be a factor in your decision whether or not to buy this product?
    Would Be A   Would Not Affect
    Primary Factor |__|__|__|__|__|__|__|__|__|__|__|__|__|__|__| My Decision
4. a) What does the ad claim about this product?
    Endorsements   Endorsements Do Not
    Prove That Consumers   Prove That Consumers
    Experience Significant   Experience Significant
    Fuel Savings |__|__|__|__|__|__|__|__|__|__|__|__|__|__|__| Fuel Savings
    b) How Confident Are You?
    Very Unconfident |__|__|__|__|__|__|__|__|__|__|__|__|__|__|__| Very Confident
    c) Would this feature be a factor in your decision whether or not to buy this product?
    Would Be A   Would Not Affect
    Primary Factor |__|__|__|__|__|__|__|__|__|__|__|__|__|__|__| My Decision
5. a) What does the ad claim about this product?
    Will Not Significantly   Will Significantly
    Increase Fuel Economy   Increase Fuel Economy
    In a Typical Car Under   In a Typical Car Under
    Normal Conditions |__|__|__|__|__|__|__|__|__|__|__|__|__|__|__| Normal Conditions
    b) How Confident Are You?
    Very Unconfident |__|__|__|__|__|__|__|__|__|__|__|__|__|__|__| Very Confident
    c) Would this feature be a factor in your decision whether or not to buy this product?
    Would Be A   Would Not Affect
    Primary Factor |__|__|__|__|__|__|__|__|__|__|__|__|__|__|__| My Decision
6. How familiar are you with this product name?
    Never Heard of It |__|__|__|__|__|__|__|__|__|__|__|__|__|__|__| Very Familiar
7. Do you have any experience with this product?
    Have Used It   Have Never
    Frequently |__|__|__|__|__|__|__|__|__|__|__|__|__|__|__| Used It
8. Have you seen ads for this product before?
    Seen Frequently |__|__|__|__|__|__|__|__|__|__|__|__|__|__|__| Never Seen

Put Down Your Pencil, Look Up, and Do Not Turn the Page Until Instructed!

Litton Microwave

1. a) What does the ad claim about this product?

   Survey Proves Litton Microwaves Are Preferred By Independent Microwave Oven Service Technicians |___|___|___|___|___|___|___|___|___|___|___|___|___|___| Survey Does Not Prove Litton Microwaves Are Preferred By Independent Microwave Oven Service Technicians

   b) How Confident Are You?

   Very Unconfident |___|___|___|___|___|___|___|___|___|___|___|___|___|___| Very Confident

   c) Would this feature be a factor in your decision whether or not to buy this product?

   Would Be A Primary Factor |___|___|___|___|___|___|___|___|___|___|___|___|___|___| Would Not Affect My Decision

2. a) What does the ad claim about this product?

   Available With Automatic Temperature Control |___|___|___|___|___|___|___|___|___|___|___|___|___|___| No Automatic Temperature Control Available

   b) How Confident Are You?

   Very Unconfident |___|___|___|___|___|___|___|___|___|___|___|___|___|___| Very Confident

   c) Would this feature be a factor in your decision whether or not to buy this product?

   Would Be A Primary Factor |___|___|___|___|___|___|___|___|___|___|___|___|___|___| Would Not Affect My Decision

3. a) What does the ad claim about this product?

   Survey Does Not Prove Litton Microwaves Are Superior To Competitors' Products |___|___|___|___|___|___|___|___|___|___|___|___|___|___| Survey Proves Litton Microwaves Are Superior To Competitors' Products

   b) How Confident Are You?

   Very Unconfident |___|___|___|___|___|___|___|___|___|___|___|___|___|___| Very Confident

   c) Would this feature be a factor in your decision whether or not to buy this product?

   Would Be A Primary Factor |___|___|___|___|___|___|___|___|___|___|___|___|___|___| Would Not Affect My Decision

4. How familiar are you with this product name?

   Never Heard of It |___|___|___|___|___|___|___|___|___|___|___|___|___|___| Very Familiar

5. Do you have any experience with this product?

   Have Used It Frequently |___|___|___|___|___|___|___|___|___|___|___|___|___|___| Have Never Used It

6. Have you seen ads for this product before?

   Seen Frequently |___|___|___|___|___|___|___|___|___|___|___|___|___|___| Never Seen

Put Down Your Pencil, Look Up, and Do Not Turn the Page Until Instructed!

Kroger Price Patrol Survey

1. a) What does the ad claim about this Survey?

Survey Proves Shopping at Kroger, Rather Than Competitors' Stores, Will Result in Lower Overall Expenditures |___|___|___|___|___|___|___|___|___|___|___|___|___|___|___| Survey Does Not Prove Shopping at Kroger, Rather Than Competitors' Stores, Will Result in Lower Overall Expenditures

   b) How Confident Are You?

Very Unconfident |___|___|___|___|___|___|___|___|___|___|___|___|___|___|___| Very Confident

   c) Would this feature be a factor in your decision whether or not to buy from this store?

Would Be A Primary Factor |___|___|___|___|___|___|___|___|___|___|___|___|___|___|___| Would Not Affect My Decision

2. a) What does the ad claim about this Survey?

Conducted By Kroger Employees |___|___|___|___|___|___|___|___|___|___|___|___|___|___|___| Conducted by Independent Shoppers

   b) How Confident Are You?

Very Unconfident |___|___|___|___|___|___|___|___|___|___|___|___|___|___|___| Very Confident

   c) Would this feature be a factor in your decision whether or not to buy from this store?

Would Be A Primary Factor |___|___|___|___|___|___|___|___|___|___|___|___|___|___|___| Would Not Affect My Decision

3. a) What does the ad claim about this Survey?

Not Scientifically Based |___|___|___|___|___|___|___|___|___|___|___|___|___|___|___| Scientifically Based

   b) How Confident Are You?

Very Unconfident |___|___|___|___|___|___|___|___|___|___|___|___|___|___|___| Very Confident

   c) Would this feature be a factor in your decision whether or not to buy from this store?

Would Be A Primary Factor |___|___|___|___|___|___|___|___|___|___|___|___|___|___|___| Would Not Affect My Decision

4. a) What does the ad claim about this Survey?

Includes Sample of All Products Sold By Kroger |___|___|___|___|___|___|___|___|___|___|___|___|___|___|___| Does Not Sample Certain Products Sold By Kroger

   b) How Confident Are You?

Very Unconfident |___|___|___|___|___|___|___|___|___|___|___|___|___|___|___| Very Confident

   c) Would this feature be a factor in your decision whether or not to buy from this store?

Would Be A Primary Factor |___|___|___|___|___|___|___|___|___|___|___|___|___|___|___| Would Not Affect My Decision

6. How familiar are you with this store name?

Never Heard of It |___|___|___|___|___|___|___|___|___|___|___|___|___|___|___| Very Familiar

7. Do you have any experience with this store?

Have Used It Frequently |___|___|___|___|___|___|___|___|___|___|___|___|___|___|___| Have Never Used It

8. Have you seen ads for this Price Patrol Survey before?

Seen Frequently |___|___|___|___|___|___|___|___|___|___|___|___|___|___|___| Never Seen

Put Down Your Pencil, Look Up, and Do Not Turn the Page Until Instructed!

Lady Kenmore Dishwasher

1. a) What does the ad claim about this product?

    Includes 6
    Waterjets |__|__|__|__|__|__|__|__|__|__|__|__|__|__|__| Includes 14 Waterjets

    b) How Confident Are You?

    Very Unconfident |__|__|__|__|__|__|__|__|__|__|__|__|__|__|__| Very Confident

    c) Would this feature be a factor in your decision whether or not to buy this product?

    Would Be A
    Primary Factor |__|__|__|__|__|__|__|__|__|__|__|__|__|__|__| Would Not Affect My Decision

2. a) What does the ad claim about this product?

    Prior Scrubbing,
    Scraping or Rinsing
    is Necessary to
    Clean Heavily
    Soiled Dishes |__|__|__|__|__|__|__|__|__|__|__|__|__|__|__| No Prior Scrubbing, Scraping or Rinsing is Necessary to Clean Heavily Soiled Dishes

    b) How Confident Are You?

    Very Unconfident |__|__|__|__|__|__|__|__|__|__|__|__|__|__|__| Very Confident

    c) Would this feature be a factor in your decision whether or not to buy this product?

    Would Be A
    Primary Factor |__|__|__|__|__|__|__|__|__|__|__|__|__|__|__| Would Not Affect My Decision

3. a) What does the ad claim about this product?

    Includes 8 Different
    Wash/Rinse Cycles |__|__|__|__|__|__|__|__|__|__|__|__|__|__|__| Includes 4 Different Wash/Rinse Cycles

    b) How Confident Are You?

    Very Unconfident |__|__|__|__|__|__|__|__|__|__|__|__|__|__|__| Very Confident

    c) Would this feature be a factor in your decision whether or not to buy this product?

    Would Be A
    Primary Factor |__|__|__|__|__|__|__|__|__|__|__|__|__|__|__| Would Not Affect My Decision

4. a) What does the ad claim about this product?

    All Dishes Will Clean
    As Efficiently in Top
    Rack As In Bottom |__|__|__|__|__|__|__|__|__|__|__|__|__|__|__| Heavily Soiled Dishes May Not Clean As Efficiently in Top Rack As In Bottom

    b) How Confident Are You?

    Very Unconfident |__|__|__|__|__|__|__|__|__|__|__|__|__|__|__| Very Confident

    c) Would this feature be a factor in your decision whether or not to buy this product?

    Would Be A
    Primary Factor |__|__|__|__|__|__|__|__|__|__|__|__|__|__|__| Would Not Affect My Decision

5. a) What does the ad claim about this product?

    Sani-Wash Cycle Will
    Sterilize Dishes |__|__|__|__|__|__|__|__|__|__|__|__|__|__|__| Sani-Wash Cycle Will Not Sterilize Dishes

    b) How Confident Are You?

    Very Unconfident |__|__|__|__|__|__|__|__|__|__|__|__|__|__|__| Very Confident

    c) Would this feature be a factor in your decision whether or not to buy this product?

    Would Be A
    Primary Factor |__|__|__|__|__|__|__|__|__|__|__|__|__|__|__| Would Not Affect My Decision

6. How familiar are you with this product name?

    Never Heard of It |__|__|__|__|__|__|__|__|__|__|__|__|__|__|__| Very Familiar

7. Do you have any experience with this product?

    Have Used It
    Frequently |__|__|__|__|__|__|__|__|__|__|__|__|__|__|__| Have Never Used It

8. Have you seen ads for this product before?

    Seen Frequently |__|__|__|__|__|__|__|__|__|__|__|__|__|__|__| Never Seen

Put Down Your Pencil, Look Up, and Do Not Turn the Page Until Instructed!

Bayer Aspirin

1. a) What does the ad claim about this product?
    Relieves No Pain |__|__|__|__|__|__|__|__|__|__|__|__|__|__|__| Relieves Minor Pain
    b) How Confident Are You?
    Very Unconfident |__|__|__|__|__|__|__|__|__|__|__|__|__|__|__| Very Confident
    c) Would this feature be a factor in your decision whether or not to buy this product?
    Would Be A   Would Not Affect
    Primary Factor |__|__|__|__|__|__|__|__|__|__|__|__|__|__|__| My Decision

2. a) What does the ad claim about this product?
    Tests Prove It   Not Proved
    More Effective   More Effective
    Than Other Brands |__|__|__|__|__|__|__|__|__|__|__|__|__|__|__| Than Other Brands
    b) How Confident Are You?
    Very Unconfident |__|__|__|__|__|__|__|__|__|__|__|__|__|__|__| Very Confident
    c) Would this feature be a factor in your decision whether or not to buy this product?
    Would Be A   Would Not Affect
    Primary Factor |__|__|__|__|__|__|__|__|__|__|__|__|__|__|__| My Decision

3. a) What does the ad claim about this product?
    Not Proved To   Proved To
    Relieve Nervous   Relieve Nervous
    Tension, Anxiety,   Tension, Anxiety,
    Irritability, and   Irritability, and
    Improve Your   Improve Your
    Mood |__|__|__|__|__|__|__|__|__|__|__|__|__|__|__| Mood
    b) How Confident Are You?
    Very Unconfident |__|__|__|__|__|__|__|__|__|__|__|__|__|__|__| Very Confident
    c) Would this feature be a factor in your decision whether or not to buy this product?
    Would Be A   Would Not Affect
    Primary Factor |__|__|__|__|__|__|__|__|__|__|__|__|__|__|__| My Decision

4. How familiar are you with this product name?
    Never Heard of It |__|__|__|__|__|__|__|__|__|__|__|__|__|__|__| Very Familiar

5. Do you have any experience with this product?
    Have Used It   Have Never
    Frequently |__|__|__|__|__|__|__|__|__|__|__|__|__|__|__| Used It

6. Have you seen ads for this product before?
    Seen Frequently |__|__|__|__|__|__|__|__|__|__|__|__|__|__|__| Never Seen

Put Down Your Pencil, Look Up, and Do Not Turn the Page Until Instructed!

Aspercreme

1. a) What does the ad claim about this product?

   Does Not Contain
   Aspirin |___|___|___|___|___|___|___|___|___|___|___|___|___|___| Contains Aspirin

   b) How Confident Are You?

   Very Unconfident |___|___|___|___|___|___|___|___|___|___|___|___|___|___| Very Confident

   c) Would this feature be a factor in your decision whether or not to buy this product?

   Would Be A
   Primary Factor |___|___|___|___|___|___|___|___|___|___|___|___|___|___| Would Not Affect My Decision

2. a) What does the ad claim about this product?

   Is Applied By
   Rubbing Onto Painful
   Areas of Body |___|___|___|___|___|___|___|___|___|___|___|___|___|___| Is Taken By Swallowing

   b) How Confident Are You?

   Very Unconfident |___|___|___|___|___|___|___|___|___|___|___|___|___|___| Very Confident

   c) Would this feature be a factor in your decision whether or not to buy this product?

   Would Be A
   Primary Factor |___|___|___|___|___|___|___|___|___|___|___|___|___|___| Would Not Affect My Decision

3. a) What does the ad claim about this product?

   Causes No Side
   Effects |___|___|___|___|___|___|___|___|___|___|___|___|___|___| May Cause Side Effects

   b) How Confident Are You?

   Very Unconfident |___|___|___|___|___|___|___|___|___|___|___|___|___|___| Very Confident

   c) Would this feature be a factor in your decision whether or not to buy this product?

   Would Be A
   Primary Factor |___|___|___|___|___|___|___|___|___|___|___|___|___|___| Would Not Affect My Decision

4. a) What does the ad claim about this product?

   Is Based Upon A
   Recently Discovered
   Ingredient |___|___|___|___|___|___|___|___|___|___|___|___|___|___| Is Not Based Upon A Recently Discovered Ingredient

   b) How Confident Are You?

   Very Unconfident |___|___|___|___|___|___|___|___|___|___|___|___|___|___| Very Confident

   c) Would this feature be a factor in your decision whether or not to buy this product?

   Would Be A
   Primary Factor |___|___|___|___|___|___|___|___|___|___|___|___|___|___| Would Not Affect My Decision

5. a) What does the ad claim about this product?

   Is Not More Effective
   Than Ordinary
   Aspirin For Relief of
   Arthritis, Rheumatism
   and Their Symptoms |___|___|___|___|___|___|___|___|___|___|___|___|___|___| Is More Effective Than Ordinary Aspirin For Relief of Arthritis, Rheumatism and Their Symptoms

   b) How Confident Are You?

   Very Unconfident |___|___|___|___|___|___|___|___|___|___|___|___|___|___| Very Confident

   c) Would this feature be a factor in your decision whether or not to buy this product?

   Would Be A
   Primary Factor |___|___|___|___|___|___|___|___|___|___|___|___|___|___| Would Not Affect My Decision

6. How familiar are you with this product name?

   Never Heard of It |___|___|___|___|___|___|___|___|___|___|___|___|___|___| Very Familiar

7. Do you have any experience with this product?

   Have Used It
   Frequently |___|___|___|___|___|___|___|___|___|___|___|___|___|___| Have Never Used It

8. Have you seen ads for this product before?

   Seen Frequently |___|___|___|___|___|___|___|___|___|___|___|___|___|___| Never Seen

Put Down Your Pencil, Look Up, and Do Not Turn the Page Until Instructed!

American Eagle Belt Buckle

1. a) What does the ad claim about this product?

   Certificate of Authenticity Included |__|__|__|__|__|__|__|__|__|__|__|__|__|__| Certificate of Authenticity Not Included

   b) How Confident Are You?

   Very Unconfident |__|__|__|__|__|__|__|__|__|__|__|__|__|__| Very Confident

   c) Would this feature be a factor in your decision whether or not to buy this product?

   Would Be A Primary Factor |__|__|__|__|__|__|__|__|__|__|__|__|__|__| Would Not Affect My Decision

2. a) What does the ad claim about this product?

   Not Individually Numbered |__|__|__|__|__|__|__|__|__|__|__|__|__|__| Individually Numbered

   b) How Confident Are You?

   Very Unconfident |__|__|__|__|__|__|__|__|__|__|__|__|__|__| Very Confident

   c) Would this feature be a factor in your decision whether or not to buy this product?

   Would Be A Primary Factor |__|__|__|__|__|__|__|__|__|__|__|__|__|__| Would Not Affect My Decision

3. a) What does the ad claim about this product?

   Registered With Seller's Company |__|__|__|__|__|__|__|__|__|__|__|__|__|__| Registered With U. S. Government

   b) How Confident Are You?

   Very Unconfident |__|__|__|__|__|__|__|__|__|__|__|__|__|__| Very Confident

   c) Would this feature be a factor in your decision whether or not to buy this product?

   Would Be A Primary Factor |__|__|__|__|__|__|__|__|__|__|__|__|__|__| Would Not Affect My Decision

4. a) What does the ad claim about this product?

   Diamond Is 0.0025 Carat |__|__|__|__|__|__|__|__|__|__|__|__|__|__| Diamond Is 0.25 Carat

   b) How Confident Are You?

   Very Unconfident |__|__|__|__|__|__|__|__|__|__|__|__|__|__| Very Confident

   c) Would this feature be a factor in your decision whether or not to buy this product?

   Would Be A Primary Factor |__|__|__|__|__|__|__|__|__|__|__|__|__|__| Would Not Affect My Decision

5. a) What does the ad claim about this product?

   Made of Inexpensive Metals |__|__|__|__|__|__|__|__|__|__|__|__|__|__| Made of Silver and Gold

   b) How Confident Are You?

   Very Unconfident |__|__|__|__|__|__|__|__|__|__|__|__|__|__| Very Confident

   c) Would this feature be a factor in your decision whether or not to buy this product?

   Would Be A Primary Factor |__|__|__|__|__|__|__|__|__|__|__|__|__|__| Would Not Affect My Decision

6. How familiar are you with this product name?

   Never Heard of It |__|__|__|__|__|__|__|__|__|__|__|__|__|__| Very Familiar

7. Do you have any experience with this product?

   Have Used It Frequently |__|__|__|__|__|__|__|__|__|__|__|__|__|__| Have Never Used It

8. Have you seen ads for this product before?

   Seen Frequently |__|__|__|__|__|__|__|__|__|__|__|__|__|__| Never Seen

Put Down Your Pencil, Look Up, and Do Not Turn the Page Until Instructed!

35mm Camera

1. a) What does the ad claim about this product?

    Includes Plastic
    Carrying Case,   Case, Lens
    Lens Cover &   Cover and Strap
    Shoulder Strap |__|__|__|__|__|__|__|__|__|__|__|__|__|__|__| Are Not Included

    b) How Confident Are You?

    Very Unconfident |__|__|__|__|__|__|__|__|__|__|__|__|__|__|__| Very Confident

    c) Would this feature be a factor in your decision whether or not to buy this product?

    Would Be A   Would Not Affect
    Primary Factor |__|__|__|__|__|__|__|__|__|__|__|__|__|__|__| My Decision

2. a) What does the ad claim about this product?

    Camera Is A Single   Camera Uses Separate
    Lens Reflex, With   Window for Viewing,
    Through-the-Lens   and is not a Single
    Viewing |__|__|__|__|__|__|__|__|__|__|__|__|__|__|__| Lens Reflex

    b) How Confident Are You?

    Very Unconfident |__|__|__|__|__|__|__|__|__|__|__|__|__|__|__| Very Confident

    c) Would this feature be a factor in your decision whether or not to buy this product?

    Would Be A   Would Not Affect
    Primary Factor |__|__|__|__|__|__|__|__|__|__|__|__|__|__|__| My Decision

3. a) What does the ad claim about this product?

    Flash Not Included |__|__|__|__|__|__|__|__|__|__|__|__|__|__|__| Flash Included

    b) How Confident Are You?

    Very Unconfident |__|__|__|__|__|__|__|__|__|__|__|__|__|__|__| Very Confident

    c) Would this feature be a factor in your decision whether or not to buy this product?

    Would Be A   Would Not Affect
    Primary Factor |__|__|__|__|__|__|__|__|__|__|__|__|__|__|__| My Decision

4. a) What does the ad claim about this product?

    Lens is   Lens is
    Interchangeable   Not
    With Other Lenses |__|__|__|__|__|__|__|__|__|__|__|__|__|__|__| Interchangeable

    b) How Confident Are You?

    Very Unconfident |__|__|__|__|__|__|__|__|__|__|__|__|__|__|__| Very Confident

    c) Would this feature be a factor in your decision whether or not to buy this product?

    Would Be A   Would Not Affect
    Primary Factor |__|__|__|__|__|__|__|__|__|__|__|__|__|__|__| My Decision

5. a) What does the ad claim about this product?

    Made of Plastic |__|__|__|__|__|__|__|__|__|__|__|__|__|__|__| Made of Metal

    b) How Confident Are You?

    Very Unconfident |__|__|__|__|__|__|__|__|__|__|__|__|__|__|__| Very Confident

    c) Would this feature be a factor in your decision whether or not to buy this product?

    Would Be A   Would Not Affect
    Primary Factor |__|__|__|__|__|__|__|__|__|__|__|__|__|__|__| My Decision

Go to next page, do not wait for instructions to turn page

35mm Camera (cont'd.)

6. a) What does the ad claim about this product?

Has No "Hot Shoe"
Flash Holder |__|__|__|__|__|__|__|__|__|__|__|__|__|__|__| Has "Hot Shoe" Flash Holder

b) How Confident Are You?

Very Unconfident |__|__|__|__|__|__|__|__|__|__|__|__|__|__|__| Very Confident

c) Would this feature be a factor in your decision whether or not to buy this product?

Would Be A
Primary Factor |__|__|__|__|__|__|__|__|__|__|__|__|__|__|__| Would Not Affect My Decision

7. a) What does the ad claim about this product?

Made by Major
Camera
Manufacturer |__|__|__|__|__|__|__|__|__|__|__|__|__|__|__| Not Made by Major Camera Manufacturer

b) How Confident Are You?

Very Unconfident |__|__|__|__|__|__|__|__|__|__|__|__|__|__|__| Very Confident

c) Would this feature be a factor in your decision whether or not to buy this product?

Would Be A
Primary Factor |__|__|__|__|__|__|__|__|__|__|__|__|__|__|__| Would Not Affect My Decision

8. a) What does the ad claim about this product?

No Warranty |__|__|__|__|__|__|__|__|__|__|__|__|__|__|__| One-Year Warranty

b) How Confident Are You?

Very Unconfident |__|__|__|__|__|__|__|__|__|__|__|__|__|__|__| Very Confident

c) Would this feature be a factor in your decision whether or not to buy this product?

Would Be A
Primary Factor |__|__|__|__|__|__|__|__|__|__|__|__|__|__|__| Would Not Affect My Decision

9. How familiar are you with this product name?

Never Heard of It |__|__|__|__|__|__|__|__|__|__|__|__|__|__|__| Very Familiar

10. Do you have any experience with this product?

Have Used It
Frequently |__|__|__|__|__|__|__|__|__|__|__|__|__|__|__| Have Never Used It

11. Have you seen ads for this product before?

Seen Frequently |__|__|__|__|__|__|__|__|__|__|__|__|__|__|__| Never Seen

Put Down Your Pencil, Look Up, and Do Not Turn the Page Until Instructed!

Case Index

Author Index

Subject Index

A

Affect
attitude as dependent variable, 55–56, 72, 96
equity, 103
role in theory, 55, 76, 95–96, 103
taxonomy, 58, 62

Antitrust, 9–11

Attention
ad complexity, 81
context effects, 81
definition, 80
modality priming, 81, 83
relationship to involvement, 93
role in theory, 74, 76, 80–83
structural interference, 81, 83
surveys, 116
television, 83
theories of, 78–79

B

Behavioral research
FTC use, 6, 27, 32–34, 45, 66–67

Belief
corrective messages, 86

definition, 88
evaluative claims, 51
FTC standard, 22, 24
intensity, 129, 131, 133
manipulation of, 89–90
measurement, 88, 98–103, 119, 120, 122, 125, 128, 129, 140–145
non-advertising messages, 100
normative, 123, 125, 128
posttrial, 89–90
relationship to comprehension, 90–91, 99–100, 156, 166–167, 173–194
relationship to involvement, 93
relationship to puffery, 40–42, 90, 121–122
role in definition, 106
role in theory, 71, 73, 74, 76, 88–91

C

Carry-over effects, 85–86
Causation, 47, 82, 108, 120, 121, 126, 129, 140
Caveat emptor, 14, 15
Claims, *see also* Evaluative claims, Opinion, Puffery, Substantiation, Unfairness